ALTERNATIVE APPROACHES TO
BRITISH DEFENCE POLICY

Also by John Baylis

ANGLO–AMERICAN DEFENCE RELATIONS 1939–1980
CONTEMPORARY STRATEGY: THEORIES AND POLICIES
  (joint author)
NUCLEAR WAR AND NUCLEAR PEACE (joint author)
BRITISH DEFENCE POLICY IN A CHANGING WORLD (editor)
SOVIET STRATEGY (joint editor)

ALTERNATIVE APPROACHES TO BRITISH DEFENCE POLICY

Edited by

John Baylis

MACMILLAN PRESS
LONDON

First published 1983 by
THE MACMILLAN PRESS LTD
London and Basingstoke
Companies and representatives
throughout the world

ISBN 0 333 35113 4 (hardcover)
ISBN 0 333 36393 0 (paperback)

Filmset in Great Britain by
Latimer Trend & Company Ltd, Plymouth

Printed in Great Britain at The Pitman Press, Bath

Contents

Contents

Acknowledgements

The editor wishes to express his sincere thanks to Doreen Hamer and Marian Weston for typing various sections of this book and to Trevor Mepham for his hard work in producing the index.

J.B.

Notes on the Contributors

John Baylis is a Senior Lecturer in the Department of International Politics, University College of Wales, Aberystwyth, and an Academic Adviser at the National Defence college. He is author of *Anglo–American Defence Relations 1939–80*, joint author of *Contemporary Strategy: Theories and Policies* and *Nuclear War and Nuclear Peace*, joint editor of *Soviet Strategy* and the editor of *British Defence Policy in a Changing World*.

Ken Booth is a Senior Lecturer in the Department of International Politics, University College of Wales, Aberystwyth. He is author of *The Military Instrument in Soviet Foreign Policy, 1917–1972*; joint author of *Contemporary Strategy: Theories and Policies*; co-editor of, and contributor to, *Soviet Naval Policy: Objectives and Constraints*; author of *Navies and Foreign Policy*; co-editor of, and contributor to, *American Thinking about Peace and War*; and author of *Strategy and Ethnocentrism*.

Marshal of the Royal Air Force Lord Cameron was involved in fighter and fighter-bomber operations during the Second World War. His post-war appointments have included: Assistant Chief of Defence Staff (Policy), Deputy Commander RAF Germany, Air Member for Personnel Royal Air Force, Chief of the Air Staff, Chief of the Defence Staff. On retirement he became Principal of King's College, London.

Field-Marshal Lord Carver was commissioned into the Royal Tank Corps in 1935 and was continuously on active service in the Second World War from Egypt in 1940 to the end of the North African campaign, in Italy and North West Europe, where he commanded the 4th Armoured Brigade at the age of 29. In the period between then and becoming Chief of the General Staff in 1971, he held important posts on the staff and in command at home, in East Africa, Germany and the Far East. He was Chief of the Defence Staff 1973–6. He is the author of *El*

Alamein and *Tobruk* (in Batsford's Battle series), *Harding of Petherton*, *The Apostles of Mobility*, *War since 1945*, *A Policy of Peace* and is the editor of *The War Lords*.

Michael Chichester retired from the Royal Navy as a Commander in 1961 after thirty years' service. In the Second World War he participated in seven Arctic convoys to North Russia, and in 1944 he was present at the D-Day landings in HMS *Belfast*. In 1955–6 he commanded the destroyer HMS *Contest*. Since then he has been a regular contributor to various international journals, writing on defence, strategic and naval policy issues.

Lawrence Freedman is Professor and Head of the Department of War Studies at King's College London in the University of London. He has held research positions at Nuffield College, Oxford, and at the International Institute for Strategic Studies before becoming Head of Policy Studies at the Royal Institute of International Affairs. He was appointed to the Chair of War Studies in April 1982. In addition to many articles on defence and foreign policy, Professor Freedman is the author of *US Intelligence and the Soviet Strategic Threat*, *Britain and Nuclear Weapons* and *The Evolution of Nuclear Strategy*.

David Greenwood is Director of the Centre for Defence Studies at the University of Aberdeen, Scotland. On leaving the RAF he spent two years as an Economic Adviser at the Ministry of Defence, working in the Programme Evaluation Group. Since moving to Aberdeen in 1967 he has directed several major research projects, published a monograph on *Budgeting for Defence* and written numerous contributions to symposia and journal articles. He has also edited the Aberdeen Centre's series of research papers – *Asides* – and is the author of two of the most recent numbers: *The Polaris Successor System: At What Cost?* and *Reshaping Britain's Defences*. He is a Specialist Adviser to the Defence Sub-Committee of the House of Commons Select Committee on Expenditure and a member of the Foreign and Commonwealth Office's Advisory Panel on Arms Control and Disarmament.

Admiral of the Fleet Lord Hill-Norton's appointments, after specialising in gunnery, periods on the Naval Staff and command of HMS *Ark Royal*, included, latterly, First Sea Lord, Chief of the Defence Staff and Chairman of NATO's Military Committee. He has since published *No Soft Options, the Politico–Military Realities of NATO*, and *Sea Power*.

He writes articles for both professional and topical journals, broadcasts on defence on radio and television and speaks regularly in the House of Lords.

Adam Roberts is Reader in International Relations at Oxford University, and Professorial Fellow of St Antony's College, Oxford. His publications include *The Strategy of Civilian Defence: Non-violent Resistance to Aggression*; *Nations in Arms: The Theory and Practice of Territorial Defence*; and he is co-author of *Czechoslovakia 1968: Reform, Repression and Resistance* and *Documents on the Laws of War*.

Dan Smith is a freelance researcher, author of *The Defence of the Realm in the 1980s*, co-editor of *Protest and Survive* and *Disarming Europe*, and co-author of *The War Atlas*.

John Wilkinson is the Conservative MP for Ruislip, Northwood. An ex-Royal Air Force pilot, he was formerly Personal Assistant to the Chairman of the British Aircraft Corporation. He was Parliamentary Private Secretary to the Secretary of State for Defence, John Nott, during the Falkland Islands War. He is currently a Rapporteur of the Committee on Defence Questions and Armaments of the Western European Union and a Vice-Chairman of the Committee on Science, Technology and Aerospace Questions of the Western European Union.

List of Abbreviations

ABM	Anti-Ballistic Missile
ACA	Agile Combat Aircraft
ADGB	Air Defence of Great Britain
AEW	Airborne Early Warning
ANZUK	Australia, New Zealand, and United Kingdom
ATGW	Anti-Tank Guided Weapons
AWACS	Airborne Warning and Control System
BAOR	British Army of the Rhine
CIDS	Chief of the Imperial Defence Staff
CND	Campaign for Nuclear Disarmament
ECM	Electronic Counter-measures
GCD	General and Comprehensive Disarmament
GDP	Gross Domestic Product
ICBM	Intercontinental Ballistic Missile
INF	Intermediate-range Nuclear Forces
MBFR	Mutual Balanced Force Reductions
MOD	Ministry of Defence
NATO	North Atlantic Treaty Organisation
NIESR	National Institute of Economic and Social Research
OECD	Organisation for Economic Co-operation and Development
PGM	Precision Guided Munitions
RDF	Rapid Deployment Force
SACEUR	Supreme Allied Commander Europe
SALT	Strategic Arms Limitation Talks
SLBM	Submarine-launched Ballistic Missile
SSBN	Ballistic Missile Submarine, Nuclear
SSN	Hunter-killer Submarine, Nuclear
START	Strategic Arms Reduction Talks
VSTOL	Vertical or Short Take-off and Landing

Introduction: Defence Policy for the 1980s and 1990s

JOHN BAYLIS

For the first time in twenty years defence has become a burning issue in British political life. For those in the defence community debates and controversies about military priorities have been a constant feature of the post-Second World War period in the series of defence reviews which have taken place. Apart from Korea in the early 1950s and nuclear weapons in the late 1950s and early 1960s, however, these debates have generally passed the public by. There have been few votes in defence and politicians have had little incentive to immerse themselves in the ongoing strategic debates with their arcane language and complex technological issues.

By the late 1970s this situation had begun to change. A conjunction of domestic and international events stirred the public consciousness and helped to bring defence rather more towards the centre of the political stage. The deterioration of East–West relations; the apparent failure of a decade of multilateral arms control negotiations; technological developments associated with the neutron bomb, Trident, cruise, Pershing II, MX and SS-20 missiles and contemporary decisions to deploy many of these weapons; all helped to create a fear that nuclear war was increasingly possible. This resulted in a rapid growth in peace movements all over Western Europe and to a lesser extent in the USA. In Britain the Campaign for Nuclear Disarmament (CND) has risen, phoenix-like, from the ashes, reflecting a growing questioning both of Britain's independent strategic nuclear deterrent and NATO's nuclear-based strategy of flexible response. This mood among certain sectors of the population has, in turn, given rise to growing attention being given to defence issues by all the political parties in Britain. As a result, the traditional bipartisanship between the front benches of the two major political parties has begun to break down in certain important areas.

1

Indeed the Labour Party in the 1983 Election for the first time in the post-war period not only had a unilateralist mandate from its annual conference but also a leader and shadow Defence Minister who were both convinced unilateralists. As such the nuclear issue has become an important one in contemporary politics.

Important as the nuclear issue is, it is not the only defence question being discussed in recent debates. The decision by the government to alter its priorities somewhat in the 1981 Defence Review also brought a rigorous and public response from the Service most affected by the changes, the Royal Navy. Just as the debate seemed to be settled against the naval lobby, the Falklands crisis broke out in April 1982, with the Navy playing a leading role, reopening once again, even more publicly, discussions about the relative merits of 'continental' and 'maritime' strategies.

The result of all these events is an ongoing debate about British defence policy which is of unprecedented interest and importance. Its importance derives not only from the profound nature of the issues being discussed but also from the fact that major decisions are still to be made. Indeed, as a number of the contributors to this book argue, budgetary and technological pressures will almost certainly create the need for a new defence review in the mid-1980s, with the opportunities that this will bring for modifications and even radical changes in the direction of policy.

It is the purpose of this book to provide an outline of the wide-ranging debate at present underway and a discussion of various alternative approaches to contemporary defence policy that might be followed. It is hoped that this will contribute positively to the debate and perhaps to the decision-making process itself. All of the contributors to this study have had a deep interest in defence for some time and a number of them have had professional experience at the very highest level. They have all contributed in one way or another to the defence debate in recent years and they hold distinctive (and often controversial) views on defence issues. The emphasis therefore is on informed and expert opinion although there has been no attempt to provide an overall consensus on what should be done. The book comes to no conclusions. Indeed, quite the reverse is true. Although there are areas of agreement between some of the authors, wide-ranging disagreements are far more common. What stands out is that there are quite fundamental differences between the experts, even among those who have shared the post of Chief of the Defence Staff. The book has been written in the hope of stimulating further debate. It is up to the reader to make up his or her own mind on the merits of the arguments presented by the various authors.

The choice of contributors and subjects covered in the book was very much in the hands of the editor. And this clearly is a source of some potential criticism. It might be felt by some readers that the range of alternative postures considered, although reasonably wide-ranging, are nevertheless somewhat limited. It could be argued, for example, that existing defence policy should have been dealt with rather more directly than it is. An invitation was in fact sent to the former Secretary of Defence, John Nott, asking him if he (or someone nominated by him) wished to make a contribution to the book. Unfortunately, he declined the invitation. This clearly is a loss to the book, but the absence of a direct contribution from the government should not be exaggerated. The book is essentially concerned with *alternative* approaches. This clearly implies some understanding of present government policy, but the focus is on critical analysis and change. It was felt therefore that the discussion of government defence policy contained in various chapters, especially those of Professor Freedman and David Greenwood, was sufficient.

Another possible criticism is that the alternatives looked at are not as radical as they might have been. This, of course, is a matter of debate. The range of prescriptions put forward by some of the contributors do cover a spectrum, of what could be described as left and right opinion. It might be thought, however, that there is only limited coverage of various options such as the pacifist approach or strategies based wholly on civilian resistance or guerrilla warfare techniques. Although the chapters by Lord Carver, Adam Roberts, Ken Booth and Dan Smith all deal with non-nuclear approaches to British defence policy it is true that none of these contributors recommends that Britain should rely solely on passive resistance or guerrilla techniques for her defence. The failure to deal with these 'alternatives' directly is due to a fairly widespread belief, especially among defence experts, that they cannot by themselves really be regarded as representing viable systems of defence against a ruthless and determined enemy.

It might also be felt by some that there should have been more discussion of the Gaullist option. In fact a chapter was written for the book by Alan Clark MP entitled 'Fortress Britain: Graduated Moves to Strategic Independence'. The chapter was, however, commissioned, written and delivered before the General Election of 1983 and his subsequent appointment to the Government. As a result of his appointment Mr Clark felt obliged under the conventions which govern Ministerial conduct in such matters to ask for it to be withdrawn.

The book is designed to reflect a spectrum not only of informed opinion but also responsible opinion – responsible in the sense that the alternatives suggested are likely to provide an 'effective' defence policy for Britain in the years ahead. There will, of course, be a great deal of debate about what an effective defence policy is. What one can say about the different options discussed in this study, however, is that they do attempt to come to terms with real defence problems rather than simply suggesting that Britain should 'opt out' or provide only token resistance to potential aggressors. Readers no doubt will make up their own minds on *how* effective they believe the various alternatives to be.

THE DEFENCE DEBATE

It is important to set the contemporary debate about the future of British defence policy into a wider historical context. Many of the issues that face defence planners today have recurred time and time again in the various defence reviews which have punctuated the period since 1945. Professor Freedman argues in his chapter that there have been three main questions in particular which have constantly preoccupied defence planners from the 1940s through to the 1980s. These are:

1. Should Britain concentrate on the Soviet threat to Europe or should it still be prepared to get involved in conflicts elsewhere in the world?
2. Within the NATO area, should Britain's main contribution be on land or at sea?
3. In addition to conventional forces, should Britain stay in the business of maintaining strategic nuclear forces?

Attempts were made in the 1960s and 1970s to settle at least the first and the third of these questions. It was decided to adopt an essentially Eurocentric defence policy and to improve the Polaris nuclear force through the provision of the new Chevaline warhead. The second question, however, was left largely unanswered, or at least no decision was really made on where the main priority lay. The importance of BAOR and the continental commitment had been stressed by governments since 1948, but equally Britain's maritime forces provided an important and unique contribution to Alliance defence. The main priorities of British defence policy were clearly laid out in the Mason defence review of 1974 which focused attention on the vital importance of four main areas: the strategic nuclear deterrent; defence of the home base; defence of the European Central Front; and the defence of the Eastern Atlantic.[1] Despite certain modifications of policy during the rest of the 1970s, it was essentially this framework laid down in 1974 by the Labour government of the day that the Tory administration of Margaret Thatcher inherited in May 1979.

As a number of the contributors to this book point out, the main problem facing the new government was that even with a continuation of the 3 per cent real increase per annum in defence spending (inherited from Labour) it was still not possible to sustain the existing defence programme. In the words of the government's 1981 White Paper, *The Way Forward*:

> even the increased resources we plan to allocate cannot adequately fund all the force structures and all the plans for their improvement we now have.[2]

The main reason for this was defence inflation. With the cost growth, especially in equipment, considerably outstripping the general level of inflation, even annual 3 per cent increases in real terms in the defence budget were not sufficient to allow the government even to implement the reduced defence plans of its predecessors. There was also the associated problem that more and more of the overall defence budget was being taken up with equipment purchases, with all of the obvious implications for other areas of defence (see Chapter 1).

Defence inflation, however, was not the only problem facing the government at the time. There was also the question of technological advance which the White Paper conceded was 'sharply changing the defence environment'. In particular this involved the increasing ability of 'modern weapons to find targets accurately and hit them hard at long ranges ... increasing the vulnerability of major platforms such as aircraft and surface ships'. To meet this, and indeed exploit it, the White Paper argued that the balance of investment between platforms and weapons needed to be altered 'so as to maximise real combat capability'. Thus the overall conclusion of the 1981 review was that Britain could not go on as before: 'substantial and uncomfortable changes' were necessary in certain fields.

Although the government argued at the time that nothing had been sacrosanct in the review, two of the four main defence priorities were singled out for continuing enhancement rather than contraction. In terms of the strategic nuclear force the government reaffirmed its determination to proceed with plans for Trident because, in its own words, 'no alternative application of defence resources could approach this in real deterrent insurance'. At the same time, plans were announced to improve the defence of the home base because of the government's concern that this vital area had been neglected in recent years: 'We need to do more, not less, in this field.'

It was clear from the White Paper that the major debates among defence planners had been over the relative priority between defence of the Central Front in Germany and defence of the Eastern Atlantic. Despite the financial pressures associated with providing a large land and air force on the Continent, the government decided that, for political and military reasons, this was an essential commitment which had to be continued in more or less its present form: 'this contribution is so important to the Alliance's military posture and its political cohesion that it must be maintained'. Echoing those like Field-Marshal Montgomery in the 1940s who advocated the need for Britain to accept the obligations of a continental commitment, the White Paper argued that: 'the forward defence of the Federal Republics is the forward defence of Britain itself'.

Despite this emphasis on the commitment to the defence of the Central Front the government still argued that it was important to retain a maritime contribution to Alliance defence: 'that such a contribution must continue, and on a major scale, is not in question'. At the same time, however, the White Paper indicated that the costs and increasing vulnerability of surface ships indicated that a shift in emphasis was necessary. The conclusion was that the most cost-effective maritime mix for Britain would be one that continued to enhance the maritime-air and submarine effort but accepted 'a reduction below current plans in the size of [the] surface fleet and the scale and sophistication of new ship-building' and broke away 'from the practice of costly mid-life modernization'. This would involve a reduction from fifty-nine to fifty destroyers and frigates (with eight withdrawn to standby).

Apart from these four main priority areas the White Paper also argued that, 'Changes in many areas of the world, together with growing Soviet military reach and readiness to exploit it directly or indirectly', made it 'increasingly necessary for NATO members to look to Western security concerns over a wider field than before', outside the boundaries of the NATO area. According to the White Paper this necessitated visits by a naval task group to the South Atlantic, the Caribbean and the Indian Ocean during the following year, together with various measures to enhance the 'out-of-area' flexibility of Britain's ground forces.

Although the priority given to such capabilities was certainly not as great as the other four areas, the government clearly recognised the need for some (albeit small) contribution to preserving Western global security interests.

Thus the overall defence posture laid down in June 1981 was based upon nuclear deterrence, the importance of the continental commitment, and defence of the UK itself, a modest enhancement of 'out-of-area' capabilities, and a switch of priorities away from large capital ships to maritime–air and submarine capabilities in the defence of the Eastern Atlantic. The four (and a half) main priority areas were therefore maintained from the defence reviews of the 1960s and mid 1970s, but an unbalancing and reduction was projected in naval forces for the future.

In the period since *The Way Forward* was published most of the priorities established at the time have been subjected to intense debate and considerable criticism from certain quarters. For some, the broad thrust of the review was largely correct, while for others, 'it was done in a hurry, involved pre-judgement, and was driven by short-term political, economic expediency rather than long-term strategic sense'. Sir Henry Leach, Chief of the Naval Staff and First Sea Lord, even went as far as to suggest in public in September 1982 that the government's defence policy was 'a major con-trick' involving 'a catalogue of half-truths'.[3] In his chapter in this book Lord Hill-Norton also describes the ideas contained in the 1981 review as 'demonstrable rubbish' (p. 117). These are strong words but they do reflect the intensity of the various debates that have been taking place in recent years, within, as well as outside, the defence community in Britain. It is hoped that this book captures the flavour of these strong feelings.

ALTERNATIVE DEFENCE POLICIES

Discussions about alternative approaches to British defence policy can take various forms. David Greenwood in his very useful opening chapter in the book charts the distinctive options put forward by the Conservatives, Labour and SDP/Liberal Alliance both before and during the British General Election of June 1983. He suggests that 'at the beginning of May 1983 it was possible to imagine that the next government might take one of four forms, each with somewhat different defence policies' (p. 47). These included a second Thatcher administration (determined to stick with its existing plans as far as possible); a Centrist administration (dependent for its parliamentary support on the

Liberal/SDP alliance; a Labour Government under Mr Foot; and a Thatcher-led government with a Gaullist tinge. Although Mrs Thatcher won a resounding victory in the Election, David Greenwood suggests that it is useful to look at the alternative defence policy which each would have been likely to pursue in office. This he suggests will give an indication, not only of possible modifications in the defence policy of the second Thatcher government, but also the criticisms likely to come from the opposition parties and an indication of their alternative policies should they win power in the late 1980s.

He begins by looking at the main outlines of the defence policy of the first Thatcher government and the changes which might be made to that policy between 1983 and 1988 as a result of economic cuts (which he believes will be necessary in the mid-1980s). The second Thatcher government committed to its present priorities, he suggests, might be expected to maintain the Trident force but might well slow down the submarine-construction programme. It might also modify policy in a number of other ways including delaying air defence modernisation; resuming the pre-Falklands timetable for surface fleet contraction; retaining One British Corps in Germany but locating three brigades in the UK; and perhaps cutting back on the Falkland garrison and 'out-of-area' capabilities generally (pp. 49–51).

Had a Centrist administration won the Election it would almost certainly have cancelled Trident. It would, however, have retained some form of nuclear capability pending arms-control agreements which made radical cuts in the Super Power strategic forces. In other areas of policy such a government would have been likely to continue the air defence modernisation programme; check the run-down of the fleet; make a continuing commitment to forces on the continent; and make reductions in the Falklands contingent and other 'out-of-area' capabilities (pp. 51–3).

In contrast the 1983 Labour manifesto argued for complete 'nuclearectomy' – phasing out all British-owned nuclear weapons and serving notice on the USA to leave all of its nuclear facilities in Britain. Whether or not a Labour government would have put into effect a genuinely non-nuclear defence policy must be open to question after the divisions which appeared in the election campaign. Such a government, however, would have been likely to try to move towards a more defensive deterrent posture with relatively greater stress on conventional forces. This would probably have included strengthening the defence of the UK itself; putting more emphasis on the fleet and a withdrawal and disbandment of a large proportion of One British Corps and the second tactical airforce in Germany; as well as scaling down the Falklands contingent and other 'out-of-area' capabilities (pp. 53–6).

David Greenwood also raises a fourth option which the present Thatcher government might conceivably move towards. This he describes as an essentially Gaullist defence policy. This would be likely to involve a continuation of the Trident strategic deterrent, accompanied by the search for indigenous technological competence for the future; added emphasis on safeguarding the homeland; a remodelled surface and submarine fleet for independent operations in European waters and elsewhere; reductions in Britain's contribution to the defence of Central Europe (perhaps with an Anglo–German agreement to station some forces in Germany); and an augmented capability for independent action outside Europe (pp. 56–8).

Useful as David Greenwood's approach is, it does not perhaps contain a complete spectrum of the alternatives open to Britain. Theoretically at least there would seem to be at least nine main options that the UK could choose if it so wished. These include:

1. *A nuclear, essentially continentalist strategy, within NATO*
   (Scaling down the naval and interventionist forces even more than at present);
2. *A nuclear, essentially maritime strategy, within NATO*
   (Withdrawing or significantly scaling down Britain's contribution to the Central Front and contributing more to the maritime defence of Western, and British, interests inside and outside the Alliance);
3. *A non-nuclear, balanced force strategy, within NATO*
   (Nuclear disarmament and a concentration on Britain's conventional contribution on land, at sea, and in the air to Western, and British, interests inside and outside the Alliance);
4. *A non-nuclear, continentalist strategy, within NATO*
   (Nuclear disarmament, a scaling-down of the maritime contribution to the Alliance, and a concentration on the conventional defence of the Central Front);
5. *A non-nuclear, maritime strategy, within NATO*
   (Nuclear disarmament, a scaling-down of the land/air contribution on the Central Front, and a concentration on maritime/air forces to defend Western, and British, interests inside and outside the Alliance);
6. *A nuclear, maritime strategy, outside NATO*
   (Withdrawal from NATO with a concentration on nuclear and maritime/air forces to defend British interests);

7. *A non-nuclear, balanced force strategy, outside NATO*
   (Nuclear disarmament, withdrawal from NATO and a concentration on national land, sea and air forces);
8. *A non-nuclear, unconventional strategy, outside NATO*
   (Nuclear disarmament, withdrawal from NATO and a concentration on guerrilla warfare and civilian resistance techniques);
9. *A passive resistance strategy*
   (Nuclear disarmament, withdrawal from NATO and abandonment
   of military forces relying on non-violent resistance).

These nine options are of some value in identifying different
distinctive models for Birtain's defence. There are, however, some
problems associated with such an approach. There is a tendency to beg a
number of questions – such as how nuclear disarmament is achieved and
what form a balanced force strategy would take. Some of the strategies
are not necessarily mutually exclusive – for example, passive resistance
and various unconventional techniques might be part of any of the other
alternatives. They are also very stark options. Consideration of the
defence debate in Britain reveals that the alternatives put forward by
various commentators are infinitely more subtle than these alternative
models suggest: the argument is invariably about degree. Thus some
favour British, but not NATO, nuclear disarmament; continentalists
usually accept the need for some form of maritime capability; and naval
lobbyists in most cases support the need for some British contribution to
the defence of the Central Front. The chapters in this book attempt to
reflect these subtle variations.

The book contains contributions of two kinds. There are the
essentially descriptive and analytical chapters, and chapters that are
rather more prescriptive in their approach. The contributions by David
Greenwood and Lawrence Freedman tend to fit into the former
category, analysing the major features of the debate without making
positive recommendations. The other chapters in the book attempt to
contribute to the debate itself by suggesting modifications or, in some
cases, radical alterations to existing policies. The issues discussed in
these more prescriptive chapters overlap, but in general they deal with
three main areas:

1. Britain's nuclear policy.
2. The continental commitment *v.* the maritime/air strategy.
3. Reserves, reorganisation and redeployment.

BRITAIN'S NUCLEAR POLICY

The decisions by the Conservative government in December 1979 to accept the deployment of 160 cruise missiles in Britain (unless progress was made in the Geneva INF talks with the Soviet Union by the end of 1983), and to purchase Trident missiles from the US in July 1980, have been the source of some considerable debate. Opinion in this book is divided between those who support Britain's nuclear strategy, those who reject the case for an independent British strategic nuclear deterrent but who support Alliance nuclear strategy (including the deployment of cruise missiles), and those who are basically opposed to a nuclear-based strategy of any kind.

The most positive support for Britain's nuclear strategy is expressed in the chapters by Lord Hill-Norton, Lord Cameron, John Wilkinson and Michael Chichester. The case presented by Lord Hill-Norton is that a British nuclear deterrent has utility in deterrent terms, both for the Alliance and for Britain, and also prevents Britain from becoming too dependent on the USA. In his words:

> the maintenance of the national strategic nuclear deterrent provides the ultimate signal to the Soviets that any attempt to isolate and then wage war against the UK itself would not be worth the certain and appalling consequences. It also ensures a continuing measure of military independence from the USA. In any superpower confrontation it also gives the Soviets another flank, and another centre of decision, to worry about; and it may, in times of doubt in the Alliance, provide a crucial stiffening of NATO resolve against any attempt at nuclear blackmail (p. 128).

For these reasons Lord Hill-Norton argues that it is 'entirely right' to accept the present government's arguments for acquiring the Trident D-5 system. His only criticism (not surprisingly for a naval man) is that the force should be 'unambiguously funded quite separately from the conventional sea, land and air forces' (p. 131).

Support for a British strategic deterrent in terms of its contribution to preserving the 'sovereign independence of the UK' is a theme in a number of other chapters in the book besides that of Lord Hill Norton. The need to preserve such independence of action reflects a certain anxiety felt by a number of authors about the declining credibility of the American nuclear guarantee to Britain and European NATO. This view is clearly expressed in the chapter by Lord Cameron in which he argues forcefully that:

> The stunning confidence some distinguished UK commentators have that the USA will still be prepared to give NATO full nuclear support in ten years' time is frightening. Who can tell what sort of a world we will have in ten years or even five? Their view that this country can safely get rid of its nuclear capacity or greatly reduce it because of this continued support by the USA makes little sense and many would wish for a better insurance policy than that (p. 113).

These views are very much at variance with those of another contributor to this book, Lord Carver. In his chapter Lord Carver argues forcefully that 'the *essential* ingredient' in preventing the recurrence of war in Europe 'is the presence of US armed forces in the Western half of it' (p. 80). It is this pressure that integrates American power in all its forms into the defence of Western Europe. According to Lord Carver the significance of the nuclear forces of both the USA and the Soviet Union lies only in mutual deterrence and, if ever this should break down, in preventing each from using nuclear weapons against the other. He argues that 'as long as both are clearly and physically linked to the security of Europe ... this mutual deterrence against war keeps Europe at peace, rigid, anomalous and unpleasant as it may be for many people' (p. 80). The conclusion that Lord Carver comes to from this analysis is that there is no reason why European countries, including Britain, should maintain their own independent nuclear weapons. 'Britain', he says, 'should waste no more money on nuclear weapons systems' (p. 89).

His case against Trident is, however, not only that he sees it as wholly superfluous to the American nuclear armoury. He also sees the force as lacking in credibility as a deterrent and dangerous to British security interests. In a much-quoted speech he made to the House of Lords in December 1979 he went out of his way to emphasise that his experience at the highest levels of the military establishment had convinced him of the futility of maintaining an independent deterrent force. He argued that:

> Over the years the arguments have shifted and I have read them all; but in that time I have never heard or read a scenario which I would consider it right or reasonable for the Prime Minister or Government of this country to order the firing of our independent strategic force at a time when the Americans were not prepared to fire theirs – certainly not before Russian nuclear weapons had landed in this country. And

again, if they had already landed, would it be right and reasonable? All it would do would be to invite further retaliation.

It could also be argued that Lord Carver's arguments about the redundancy of the British strategic force have been reinforced by President Reagan's decision in March 1983 to develop a new laser, and particle-beam-based ABM system. A similar Soviet system could well undermine the credibility of a small British Trident force towards the end of the century.

Lord Carver also sees the renunciation of Britain's independent strategic nuclear deterrent as helping to contribute to an overall lowering of the numbers of nuclear delivery systems and warheads in existence. He argues in his chapter that there are clearly too many nuclear warheads than are required for mutual deterrence. If by giving up her own nuclear delivery systems and warheads Britain can contribute to progress being made in the overall process of reducing the level of these armaments, he argues that she should do so.

This emphasis on a wider conception of security in terms of the need for arms control agreements alongside defence is also discussed in the chapter by Adam Roberts. He examines the strengths and weaknesses of both the unilateral and multilateral approaches to disarmament, and suggests that emphasis should be given to arms control measures designed to achieve greater stability. At the same time he argues that effective defence must not be neglected. Like Lord Carver, however, he maintains that stability is more likely to be achieved, and defence is more likely to be effective, if less emphasis is placed in British and Alliance policy on nuclear weapons.

Dan Smith is another of the contributors who argues forcefully against the British nuclear deterrent. He points out that his arguments are based on moral, political and strategic objections. In the case of the latter he rejects the case for a nuclear deterrent as 'a last resort weapon' and as a means of avoiding nuclear blackmail. If nuclear weapons are consigned to the role of deterrence in the last resort, he says, 'the obvious question is, what happens when you reach the last resort?' Do you then commit suicide? He does admit that 'the problem of a state without nuclear weapons facing a nuclear-armed adversary is a serious one which cannot simply be wished away' (p. 232). Such a problem, however, he argues, is not new. 'North Vietnam managed it against the USA, Yugoslavia against the USSR.' He also suggests that the threat of Soviet nuclear blackmail has been rather exaggerated anyway. In his view, 'for the USSR to threaten nuclear blackmail in time of peace would mean it would be breaking an inhibition that it recognises to be of great importance' (p. 232).

Yet another criticism of the British strategic nuclear deterrent is contained in the chapter by Ken Booth. Ken Booth also argues that his case against the deterrent is based partly on grounds of morality and partly on grounds of security. In questioning whether Britain has a rational strategy, like Dan Smith, he suggests that Britain's commitment to a policy of independent nuclear deterrence 'is based on the threat, in certain circumstances, of committing quasi-national suicide and quasi-genocide of the enemy'. This, he argues, is neither right nor prudent. In particular it makes little sense, he suggests, to base one's long-term security on threatening to destroy the nation in order to save it. Ken Booth concludes therefore that a non-nuclear strategy is the appropriate course for 'a physically small and densely populated middle power, with a complex and vulnerable cultural infrastructure' (p. 158).

The main thrust of Ken Booth's argument presented in his chapter is that to be effective a non-nuclear strategy requires Britain and the Alliance to possess larger conventional forces. In the case of Britain this requires, he suggests, the reintroduction of some form of national service. He appreciates the various difficulties of moving back towards conscription which was finally phased out in the early 1960s, but he regards the potential benefits as outweighing the costs. For Ken Booth, as for most of the authors in this book, the overriding issue of our time 'is that of nuclear war and how best to avoid it'. He believes strongly that national service can play its part in this task. Unilateralism alone is not enough. Security has to be maintained. National service, according to Ken Booth, is:

> part of the price the British community should be prepared to pay if it is serious about wanting to raise the nuclear threshold, reduce its unstrategic over-reliance on nuclear weapons in the event of war, strengthen the stability in Europe and generally improve the health of the Western Alliance. (p. 169)

Like a number of the other authors in the book Ken Booth's critique is aimed as much at NATO nuclear strategy as it is at the British strategic nuclear deterrent. For most of the writers, raising the nuclear threshold in Europe is a very urgent problem indeed. Ken Booth points out the dangers of early nuclear escalation inherent in NATO strategy as presently constituted. Should deterrence fail, he suggests, the heavy concentration by NATO on short-range 'battlefield' nuclear weapons would mean that military commanders on the ground would face considerable pressure to use their weapons before they were lost. The chances of rapid nuclear escalation would then be very high, with all of the horrific consequences that this would involve. According to Ken Booth therefore:

> the longer NATO forces are able to contain a Soviet attack by conventional means, the longer decision-makers will have to bring about that settlement – be it surrender, compromise or whatever – which would make all the difference between a bloody mess in the centre of Europe and the destruction of civilised society. (p. 160)

Hence the case for national service.

Concern over NATO strategy and the level of the nuclear threshold is a major theme running through this book. Lord Carver, Adam Roberts, Lord Cameron, John Wilkinson and Michael Chichester in their respective chapters also emphasise the need to improve NATO's conventional forces and thereby raise the nuclear threshold. The concern, however, of a number of these writers is to improve the conventional component within the spectrum of NATO's deterrent posture. They accept the need, albeit in some instances reluctantly, for a nuclear-based strategy.

Lord Carver's views on NATO's strategy are particularly interesting. In his chapter he is critical of the emphasis placed by the Alliance on nuclear weapons and nuclear deterrence. He argues that 'to initiate the use of nuclear weapons on the assumption that the other side would not rely in kind at all or would do so in such a limited way as not to inflict total disaster on Western Europe and Britain would be totally irresponsible' (p. 81). He therefore urges that the first priority for NATO is to improve the capability of its conventional forces, and that NATO 'should seriously consider giving up all dual-capable systems, particularly nuclear artillery' which blur the distinction between nuclear and non-nuclear systems. At the same time, however, although Lord Carver wishes to reduce the reliance by NATO on nuclear weapons – to push them on to the back-boiler – he is not suggesting that NATO or even Britain can give up nuclear weapons completely. He argues, both in his chapter and in a recently published book (*A Policy for Peace*) that as long as 'NATO decides that it must have some nuclear delivery systems based in Europe or in its surrounding waters', Britain should take its share of manning the appropriate delivery systems. In this respect he does not seem to be in favour of the closing-down of American nuclear bases in Britain or of cancelling the decision by NATO in December 1979 to deploy 464 cruise and 108 Pershing II missiles in Western Europe if no progress is made in arms control negotiations with the Soviet Union. The fact that these missiles are to be deployed further to the rear and that they are mobile puts them in a different category to the shorter-range battlefield nuclear weapons which he opposes.

These views are in some respects similar to those expressed by Adam Roberts in his chapter. Adam Roberts is particularly critical of NATO's threat to use nuclear weapons first in any conflict with the Soviet Union. Such a threat, he argues, is increasingly fanciful. The reason for this is that:

> The Soviet Union's potential for nuclear retaliation against Western Europe is so clear, and Western Europe is so crowded and vulnerable, that NATO first use has become a source of weakness rather than strength. (p. 196)

Because of this, Adam Roberts argues that there is an urgent need to get NATO strategy away from its present degree of reliance on nuclear weapons by putting much greater emphasis on conventional forces. He sees this approach as being 'tediously reformist', but realistic. He argues that such an alternative strategy would obviously not eliminate the role of nuclear weapons in NATO policy, but it would represent 'a move towards a view of them as weapons held in reserve, in case the adversary would be mad enough to resort to them' (p. 217).

In this respect Lord Carver and Adam Roberts are what Dan Smith describes in his chapter as 'Atlantic reformers'. Dan Smith argues that recent years have witnessed a crisis within the North Atlantic Alliance, and that figures like Lord Carver and presumably Adam Roberts (as well as Professor Freedman and Lord Zuckerman) are attempting 'to save Atlanticism from the mistakes made by NATO and the US administration' (p. 227). The crisis, he suggests, derives from a number of causes, not least of which is the inadequacy of NATO's strategy of flexible response. In particular he points to the concept of limited nuclear war, which 'is at the heart of flexible response' – accompanied by a commitment to terminate the war if possible by a display of resolution. Like a number of other contributors to the nuclear debate, Dan Smith expresses grave doubts about the logic of this doctrine. He argues that he is

> not convinced that such a mode of nuclear employment exists, nor that army commanders could find it in the thick of battle. The most

prevalent view today seems to be that NATO strategy has got it all wrong and that a nuclear war could not remain limited. (p. 227)

Dan Smith points out that Lord Carver's aim (and that of the other Atlantic reformers) is to advocate a strategy of minimal nuclear and strengthened conventional deterrence in order to overcome the inherent weaknesses in Atlantic strategy. He concedes that this approach does 'provide a much sounder strategy for NATO and a much safer situation for humanity'. However, he believes that these reforms fall short of what is required. They are inadequate, he suggests, for two reasons. First, because such a change in NATO strategy would involve less dependence by Western Europe on the USA, and the USA shows no desire to see such reduced dependence. He therefore accuses the Atlantic reformers of not having 'thought through the political meaning of their strategic nostrum'. Second, he argues that even minimal deterrence suggests that *at some point* the Alliance is still threatening to use nuclear weapons against an aggressor and this would result in mutual suicide. If this is the outcome of changing NATO strategy, he believes there is little point in the exercise (p. 230).

Dan Smith's solution is to do away completely with nuclear weapons and rely wholly on conventional deterrence. He suggests that this should involve a movement to a non-threatening defence policy that is part of 'a foreign policy which minimises confrontation as far as possible and is conducive to arms control'.[4] He argues that such a stance could well induce reciprocal steps in a similar direction by potential opponents. But even if it did not, the strength of conventional deterrence would remain, and that would be sufficient. Dan Smith accepts that such a course involves risks, but, in his words, 'none of them is as bad as those that attend trying to stay on the same dismal course as now'. In a sense, much of the argument does in the end come down to an assessment of risks. For most other contributors to this book the risks of moving to the kind of policy Dan Smith is advocating would be too great.

CONTINENTAL COMMITMENT *V.* A MARITIME STRATEGY

Apart from the nuclear question in British defence policy, the issue that has created most controversy in recent years is the debate between those advocating a continuation of the continental commitment and those suggesting a shift to a greater emphasis on maritime power. The essence of this debate is covered in the chapter by Professor Freedman. The case for the 'continentalist school' is put by Lord Carver, Lord Cameron and

Ken Booth, and the case for the 'maritime school' is put by Lord Hill-Norton, John Wilkinson and Michael Cameron.

Those contributors urging that the continental commitment should remain the first priority in British defence policy tend to stress a range of historical, strategic, political, legal and technological arguments in favour of such a posture. Lord Carver, for example, argues that, historically, British interests have been defended through a policy of ensuring that no single powerful European state dominated the Continent. This was the essence of the balance-of-power policy pursued by Britain and this was the 'fundamental reason why we welcomed the foundation of NATO' in 1949. He points out also that traditionally there have been those who advocate a 'blue water strategy', but such a strategy, despite some successes, had 'never been able to preserve our fundamental interests and security, if alliances on the continent of Europe have failed us' (p. 76).

In strategic terms it is argued that the Soviet Union poses the greatest threat to British security and the greatest concentration of Soviet military power is on the European continent. As *The Way Forward* pointed out, the defence of Britain cannot be disassociated from the defence of the Federal Republic. Lord Carver, Lord Cameron and Ken Booth all argue that the withdrawal or reduction of British forces on the Central Front would be likely to have serious military consequences in lowering the nuclear threshold and undermining NATO's strategy of flexible response. These writers therefore tend to agree with General Bernard Rogers's assertion that British forces are of critical importance to the balance of forces on the Central Front. Indeed the thrust of the arguments presented by most of these contributors is that they would wish to see an increase rather than a decrease in Britain's conventional contribution to continental defence.

Lord Cameron and Lord Carver in their respective chapters also echo the emphasis in the 1981 White Paper on the importance of technological change. Lord Cameron in particular highlights the growing vulnerability of surface ships and the difficulties of convoy reinforcement. In his words, 'the large, highly expensive surface ship presents a very attractive target – as indeed it always has. But new technology weapons have increased the magnitude of the threat and the vulnerability of this class of ship' (p. 101). Such vulnerability indicates to both ex-Chiefs of the Defence Staff that the need for convoy escorts is open to doubt. Lord Carver argues that reinforcements will have to be brought in before hostilities begin – emphasising the importance of existing forces and equipment on the ground in Europe. Once hostilities start 'it will be at least several weeks', he suggests, 'before the war against Soviet submarines had any chance of reaching a state in which, even with small escorts, it would be possible to start sailing convoys' (p. 84). He also expresses his doubt about whether a war in Europe between NATO and the Warsaw Pact would be likely to last longer than that anyway.

The political arguments tend to centre on the effect a run-down of Britain's conventional contribution to the Alliance would have on Britain's allies on both sides of the Atlantic. Ken Booth argues, for example, that a cut in BAOR would almost certainly have a far-reaching and detrimental impact on the perceptions of Western European states 'regarding the depth and character' of Britain's overall commitment to the defence of the continent. He quotes, in particular, the speech by General Robert Close, a senator in the Belgium Parliament, in which he claimed that 'If the British go, the Belgians go.' There is also, of course, the worry over the effect on the USA especially at a time when Senator Ted Stevens has been seeking to persuade his fellow senators to accept a cut in American troop levels in Western Europe. Once again Ken Booth argues that:

> It only requires a 'show of reluctance' on the part of the Europeans to meet their commitments – especially by major allies like Britain – and the US administration might find the pressures for reduction irresistible. . . . It could set NATO on a very slippery slope. Britain's attitude to its conventional commitment is therefore critical to the future of the alliance. (p. 168)

There is also the legal commitment that Britain entered into under the Brussels Treaty of 1954. In this Treaty (as subsequently amended), Britain accepted the obligation to station 55 000 men on the continent of Europe, plus the Second Tactical Air Force, until the late 1990s. The government's 1981 White Paper, *The Way Forward*, emphasised the need to stand by this pledge. Those supporting the continuation of the commitment point out that Britain's contribution to the defence of Western Europe under the 1954 Treaty remains important in the eyes of our Western European allies.

For all of these reasons continentalists like Lord Carver, Lord Cameron and Ken Booth believe that maintaining a high level of conventional forces in Europe is the highest priority for British defence policy. They do not, however, conclude that a maritime strategy can be neglected completely. Lord Carver argues that 'a degree of maritime warfare capability is essential to the security of Europe' (p. 83). He also recognises that Britain is best placed of all the European members of NATO, through her history and geographical position, to make a major contribution to NATO's maritime forces. This can best be done, he suggests, through submarine and long-range maritime aircraft. The continentalists agree, however, that provision of maritime forces 'must not be at the expense of an adequate contribution to a continental strategy' (p. 83).

This question of priorities is at the heart of the dispute between continentalists and supporters of a maritime/air strategy. Lord Hill-Norton, one of the leading members of the naval lobby, recognises the need for a permanent conventional presence in Europe. Such a contribution to Alliance defence, however, he argues, should 'flow from what can be made available after the first priority has been given to the creation of [maritime] forces of the right size and shape' (p. 130). Similar views are expressed by John Wilkinson and Michael Chichester in their chapter. Like Lord Hill-Norton they argue that BAOR should be reduced to around two divisions supported by a smaller tactical air force. The main responsibility for the defence of the Central Front and the flanks should then become 'the prime responsibility of those NATO members whose territories are situated within the confines of the European mainland'. According to Mr Wilkinson and Commander Chichester, Britain can then adopt a new role, which takes account of her

> unique geostrategic position as an offshore island base and energy supplier of major importance to the Alliance in war, of her maritime capabilities and expertise, and of her responsibility for the defence of the ocean approaches to Europe ... and of her possession of air mobile and amphibious intervention forces which can be used inside or outside NATO. (pp. 148–9)

In the same way that the continentalists, like Lord Carver, emphasise the historical justification for their view of priorities, so also the naval lobby looks to the past to reinforce its case. Lord Hill-Norton in particular points to the traditional emphasis on sea power in Britain's foreign and defence policy (p. 128).

In more contemporary terms the strategic case for a defence policy based on maritime/air power rests largely on the perceived global threat to Britain and Western interests. The military threat in Europe is seen as just one dimension of the worldwide threat posed by the build-up of Soviet military power in recent years. Following up the argument

presented in their book *The Uncertain Ally*, John Wilkinson and
Michael Chichester argue that the nature of the threat to NATO has
changed radically in the past thirty years. They see the development of
Soviet ability to project military power over vast distances as a major
threat to Western sources of energy and raw materials: a threat that is
outside the NATO area but that is vital to Alliance interests. For this
reason they argue that it is essential for the West to strike a new balance
in defence resource allocation between the historic NATO area and vital
interests further afield. As such they argue for a Western Strategic
Summit Conference to review NATO doctrine especially in terms of the
global threat posed by Soviet military power. At this conference, they
suggest, Britain should put the case to her allies for a reallocation of
Alliance defence resources between the defence of the NATO area and
other areas of vital importance: the aim being to achieve an agreement
on a broad division of labour within the Alliance, with Britain
concentrating on rapid deployment and intervention capabilities for use
inside and outside the NATO area.

The argument, however, is not confined to enhancing Western
interests as a whole. Those advocating a change in priorities away from
the continental commitment towards a maritime/air strategy also argue
that such a policy would reinforce Britain's own national interests. This
view has increasingly centred in Britain on a criticism of the North
Atlantic Alliance itself. For Lord Hill-Norton, John Wilkinson and
Michael Chichester NATO remains important, particularly to the
extent that Alliance and national interests coincide. The problem, they
argue, is that the march of events has reduced the situations in which
'this helpful coincidence of national and NATO interests can be found'
(p. 140). These writers point out that NATO is not particularly effective
in dealing with vital interests outside the Alliance area. Britain, however,
has many important remaining interests in the rest of the world which
need to be defended: 95 per cent of British trade is carried via the sea
and Britain has over 600 merchant ships at sea on any day. Lord Hill-
Norton, in his chapter, points to his experience in NATO which
confirmed his view that NATO was slow in reacting to new situations.
Such experience, he suggests, points most forcefully to the need,
certainly for Britain, 'to have a sufficient degree of military autonomy'.
It may be the best military alliance Britain has, but the need for the
attributes of independence remains. The Admiral even ends his chapter
by quoting from Palmerston: 'Britain has no permanent Allies, only
permanent interests.' (p. 137).

Although critical of the Alliance, most supporters of the maritime school accept that NATO enhances Britain's security interests. In their chapters, Lord Hill-Norton, John Wilkinson and Michael Chichester indicate not only their overall support for NATO but also their belief that Britain's allies can be persuaded through political argument (at 'the Strategic Summit') to accept a change in priorities within the Alliance. Lord Hill-Norton rejects the view of the continentalists that the Alliance would unravel if Britain reduced her contribution to the defence of the Central Front. He points out that it had faced and coped with far more radical moves by France and Greece. 'There would be', he suggests, 'a predictable initial outcry and then it would die down and NATO would accept change in British policy with sympathy and would even come grudgingly to welcome it as a move in the long-term interest of world security' (p. 134). This would be true of both the European members and the USA who would welcome Britain's contribution to meeting the global threat from the Soviet Union.

The political arguments of the maritime lobby are closely linked with their rejection of the legal commitment held up by the continentalists. Lord Hill-Norton in particular argues that the legal obligations under the Brussels Treaty are not as restrictive or sacrosanct as many suggest. He points out that the size of Britain's contribution has already been negotiated down from 77 000 to 55 000. There is also, he argues, 'a good rule concerning treaties called *rebus sic stantibus* which means that if the circumstances surrounding a treaty change, revision of the treaty must be sought' (p. 134). Such circumstances, he suggests, have changed dramatically.

Finally, in partial answer to the technological arguments put forward by those supporting a continuing concentration on the Central Front, John Wilkinson and Michael Chichester emphasise the importance of new weapons and military techniques which require fundamentally new tactical doctrines in Europe. New generations of weapons systems, they argue, will swing the battlefield balance more towards effective defence and this will facilitate more economical deployment of in-place forces within Europe in peacetime. New technology, new tactics and new deployment plans therefore will enable Britain to reduce her contribution to the defence of the Central Front.

For all of these reasons the naval lobby are highly critical of the cuts imposed on the Navy by the 1981 defence review, and urge, especially in the light of the lessons of the Falklands Campaign, an increase in resources allocated to the Navy, not a cut.

The Lessons of the Falklands Campaign

The debate between those supporting Britain's continentalist commitment strategy and a maritime/air strategy has not unnaturally tended to
focus in the recent past on the lessons of the Falklands War in April–
May 1982. Significantly both sides tend to argue that the campaign
justifies their particular point of view. Both sides also argue that the 1982
Falklands Defence Paper tends to favour their own position. Thus in
their chapter John Wilkinson and Michael Chichester argue that:

> The Falklands campaign showed that the defence of British and
> Alliance interests outside the NATO area requires flexible and mobile
> forces, naval and air forces with land forces capable of rapid
> deployment by sea or air and long-range air transport backed by
> inflight refuelling tankers. (p. 140)

Similarly Lord Hill-Norton suggests that the harsh realities of the
campaign to re-take the Falkland Islands 'brought home to the
government the need for flexibility and versatility in order to meet
unexpected challenges'. As such it demonstrated the 'strategic myopia'
of the 1981 review.

In contrast to these views, Ken Booth describes the Falkland affair as
a one-off episode which should not be repeated, 'especially since we are
becoming increasingly aware of the extent to which it was a close-run
thing' (p. 184). 'The extent to which it was a close-run thing' is also taken
up in vivid form in the chapter by Lord Cameron. He points out that
apart from the six ships that were sunk, ten others were hit by bombs
that did not explode. Sixteen of the twenty-three ships might have been
sunk. In Lord Cameron's judgement:

> if the conventional bombs that hit our shipping had all gone off, or
> one or both, of the Hermes and Invincible had been sunk there is little
> doubt that the Argentinians would have won a notable victory with
> considerable loss of face to the British. (p. 110)

His conclusion therefore is that the major lesson of the campaign was
that naval forces and shipping are desperately vulnerable to even
obsolescent air-, sea- or land-launched missiles and ordinary iron
bombs. Such vulnerability, he argues, would be even more pronounced
in a campaign in the Atlantic against vastly superior Soviet forces. 'We

would do well to bear this in mind', he suggests, 'when planning future equipment. The Navy must get under the sea as much as possible and also recognise that the day of the big ship is over.' (p. 111). According to Lord Cameron:

> The Falklands war and the very close call we had on that occasion must be taken to heart and not used as proving the point that we need a lot more naval forces. This would be money badly spent. (p. 116)

Which of the two schools of thought derives greatest satisfaction from the December 1982 Falklands White Paper is also a matter of some controversy. John Wilkinson and Michael Chichester argue, for example, that the White Paper effectively admits that the earlier reductions in the surface fleet (particularly *Fearless* and *Intrepid*) were too sweeping, and that the provision of 'a flexible and mobile force – to meet unforeseen challenges outside Europe – must now get a higher priority in the allocation of defence resources' (p. 141). They also suggest that the White Paper improvements are similar to those suggested in their book *The Uncertain Ally*.

Lord Hill-Norton on the other hand is not quite as convinced by the victory for the naval lobby. He welcomes the fact that the White Paper seems to have gone a long way towards recognising the need for flexible maritime power to meet unforeseen events, but he takes serious issue with the conclusion (often cited by the continentalists) that 'the lessons learned . . . do not invalidate the policy we have adopted following last year's [1981] defence programme review'. According to Lord Hill-Norton, 'both the campaign itself, and the whole body of the White Paper, do, specifically (and not surprisingly), invalidate that ill-conceived policy' (p. 118).

An interesting and well-balanced discussion of the Falklands Campaign and the subsequent White Paper is contained in the chapter by Professor Freedman. His general thesis is that although the broad strategic thrust of post-Falklands policy remains much the same as before, the revisions to the 1981 Defence Review contained in the December 1982 Paper indicates that the Royal Navy 'lives to refight the bureaucratic battles with another Minister, and possibly another government' (p. 66). Or, to put it another way, 'the 1981 Defence Review has been knocked off course and many of the bureaucratic battles that had been lost and won may now have to be refought' (p. 68).

RESERVES, REORGANISATION AND REDEPLOYMENT

The debates contained in this book between a nuclear and non-nuclear strategy, between a continentalist and a maritime/air strategy, and between a defence policy inside NATO and one outside the Alliance, as suggested earlier, are not as mutually exclusive as they sometimes appear. As the chapters in this book show, there are differences of emphasis within a particular school of thought and areas of agreement between alternative strategies. Many of these areas of dispute and consensus centre on the issues of reserves, reorganisation and redeployment of Britain's armed forces, particularly those in Germany.

One theme that comes up time and again in this book is the inadequacy of contemporary NATO strategy. Despite their differences, Lord Carver, Lord Hill-Norton, Ken Booth, John Wilkinson and Michael Chichester all criticise the present conception of flexible response, and they all emphasise the need for Britain and the Alliance to upgrade its reserve forces as one way of overcoming the deficiencies of Alliance strategy. Lord Carver, for example, argues that at present a dangerously high proportion of standing forces of all the allies in Germany are allotted to covering forces, intended to delay an invader until he reaches the main line of defence. The problem is, he argues, that there are practically no reserves – 'the pious and unrealistic hope being that covering forces will be able to withdraw through the main line and form a reserve' (p. 88). What is needed, he suggests, is more, and better use, of reserve forces. A similar point is made by John Wilkinson and Michael Chichester, who follow up the arguments contained in their book *The Uncertain Ally* by advocating the idea of total defence in which reserve forces would play a significant part (particularly in home defence and as a source for augmenting British forces in Germany). They urge a much greater commitment to reserve forces than at present. In his chapter in the book Ken Booth makes the case for a return to national service in Britain as one means of producing the reserves to improve NATO strategy. As part of his thesis, he argues that there is a wide consensus that the Alliance needs an enhanced capability to keep on fighting day and night: 'modern war is an extraordinarily greedy tyrant' (p. 163). National service, he suggests, would provide men in place or readily available and a large body of trained reserves, so important in allowing NATO to keep on fighting at the conventional level without resort to nuclear weapons.

The question of the reorganisation of Britain's armed forces is dealt with in different ways by the contributors. A great deal of the discussion not unnaturally centres on the Army. Not surprisingly perhaps the most radical suggestions on the restructuring of the land forces comes from a naval man, Lord Hill-Norton. He suggests that the concentration on national tasks implies the need to put increased emphasis on mobile, relatively lightly equipped forces with a high proportion of infantry. He suggests that:

> Armoured and armoured personnel carrier holdings would be progressively reduced as anti-tank and anti-air capability is increased. ... Training must move quite sharply away from the formation-related battle tactics of the North German plain to emphasise individual major-unit skills. (p. 132)

Similar views are also expressed by Lord Cameron, especially on the question of the tank. As far as he is concerned the tank is now nearing the end of its life in several roles. This is due, he suggests, to the accuracy of anti-tank missiles, guns, bombs, rockets and mines which have made the tank much more vulnerable than in the past. In his words, 'the old adage that the best way to fight a tank is with another tank goes off to the history books' (p. 112).

Predictably Lord Carver takes issue with these views. He does, however, admit that Britain does not possess a well-balanced army to fight an enemy who is wholly armoured. Britain's armed forces, he suggests, have a 'disproportionately high number of infantry' (p. 88). The campaign in Northern Ireland, however, he argues, necessitates this emphasis on infantry forces. As such there is no room for a radical change at present. He does suggest that more attention needs to be given to mobile reserves 'liberally supplied with man-portable anti-armour weapons' (pp. 88–9). In contrast to Lord Hill-Norton's and Lord Cameron's ideas, however, he argues forcefully that although such forces could make a significant improvement in NATO,

> they cannot replace the mobile tank, armoured infantry and artillery units which must be maintained and should if possible be increased. (p. 89)

In this respect, in response to John Nott's choice in favour of Trident over additional armoured forces, Lord Carver argues that an extra 300 tanks would indeed have a very significant effect in their own right on both deterrence and defence. To Lord Carver, therefore, the tank remains a vital component of NATO's conventional forces.[5]

Not surprisingly, perhaps, the debate about the need for various kinds of reorganisation of Britain's armed forces due to technological developments often tends to centre on inter-service perspectives. Thus, while Lord Carver argues that the tank still has a future, he is somewhat critical of various air defence, air transport and large surface ships programmes (pp. 84–7). Lord Cameron on the other hand points out the vulnerability of the tank and surface ships, but suggests that 'new generation of weapons will not render the aircraft obsolete' (p. 105) (although changes in concepts and tactics will have to take place). At the same time, Lord Hill-Norton urges the need for the reduction of the size of RAF Germany, by between one-third and one-half, and a movement away from armoured formations. To the Admiral the need for priority to be given to surface ships is clear – even though they might be medium-sized, much simpler and cheaper than current designs (pp. 131–2).

Closely linked to the debate about the reorganisation of the armed forces is the question of redeployment, especially in Germany. A number of contributors to the book emphasise the inadequacies not only of Britain's deployment of forces but those of the Alliance as a whole. In his hard-hitting chapter Lord Cameron points to the uncomfortable nature of NATO's strategy of flexible response which he argues is the product of political rather than military logic: in particular, West German insistence on forward defence as far to the east as possible. As a result he argues that the chance of NATO being able to hold a surprise Soviet attack by conventional means alone cannot at the moment be very great (p. 114). In line with the new air–land battle concept developed by the USA he suggests that the Federal Republic of Germany should be pressed by its allies to reconsider the 'concept of forward defence': 'they must be persuaded that it is the worst posture for a conventional defence, or indeed deterrence' (p. 114). In its place Lord Cameron argues that the 'concept of defence in depth' should be put forward as an alternative strategy. This would mean, however, that the present dispositions and deployment patterns would have to be changed – barracks, supply dumps, airfields and headquarters. Such a reform, however, he argues, would give SACEUR a chance to deploy his forces more easily not only against surprise attack but also to fight an effective battle against invading forces. Like many of the other authors, therefore, Lord Cameron believes that the time is ripe for a 'radical reappraisal' of NATO's existing strategic concepts.

What is 'radical' is, of course, open to debate. An even more radical suggestion is put forward by Dan Smith in his chapter. He argues not only for unilateral nuclear disarmament but also for a major change in Britain's (and NATO's) conventional force structure. According to Dan Smith:

> large armoured forces, the capability for long-range air strikes, sea-borne invasions or large air landings, whatever the strategic rationale behind them, all look threatening and can be taken as evidence of aggressive intent whatever the declaratory policy. (p. 234)

He urges, therefore, a policy of defensive conventional deterrence which would replace the obviously offensive components of present defence policy with 'relatively short-range defensive capabilities in the air, on land and at sea'. Dan Smith argues that modern technology, particularly precision-guided munitions, would allow Britain to design forces that were able to undertake 'mobile and dispersed action' and capable of inflicting major damage to an invading force, while at the same time being 'effectively incapable themselves of mounting offensive actions over significant distances' (p. 235). The major characteristics of such forces, he suggests, would be their ability to operate in dispersed, relatively independent units – avoiding concentrated targets for tactical nuclear attacks. Thus the aim of defensive conventional deterrence, according to Dan Smith, would be to put up the cost to an aggressor and deny him the fruits of victory without 'accentuating the confrontation and tensions which themselves could be the occasion for war' (p. 235).

One of the major questions for Dan Smith is whether having adopted such a defence policy Britain would be able to convince her allies in NATO to restructure and redeploy their forces in line with the concept of defensive conventional deterrence. This, he suggests, would be of crucial importance in deciding whether Britain should stay in the Alliance or not. Dan Smith wishes to see Britain co-operating with her Western European allies and sees a continuing place for Britain in NATO. That continued participation in NATO, however, he suggests, must be made conditional on the Alliance moving towards defensive deterrence. But he accepts that the Alliance might not be prepared to accept such conditions, and if that was so, 'after allowing a reasonable period for the assessment of the proposals in other countries', Britain should withdraw, at least from NATO's integrated command structure and from the continent. He admits that this is not the most desirable outcome, but he argues that:

> remaining fully committed to NATO while objecting to its basic

assumptions would raise a series of contradictions within both defence and foreign policy which would ultimately be unbearable. (p. 237)

DEFENCE POLICY AT THE CROSSROADS

The chapter by Dan Smith which raises serious question marks about Britain's continued membership of NATO is perhaps the most radical in this book. All of the other (prescriptive) contributions, however, contain criticisms of existing policy in varying degrees. The time therefore would seem to be ripe, as one of the authors says, to engage in a 'full examination of Britain's proper place in the world' (p. 157) and to return to first principles and try and develop a rational strategy for Britain for the future. The questions raised in this book are numerous. They include:

1. Should Britain remain a nuclear power or provide herself with an essentially non-nuclear capability?
2. Should Britain concentrate her defence in Europe or be prepared to intervene elsewhere in the world?
3. Should Britain stay fully committed to NATO, withdraw from the military integrated structure, or pull out completely from the Alliance?
4. Should Britain stay fully committed to existing NATO strategy or seek some form of revision?
5. Should Britain continue to emphasise the American defence connection, move towards a Western European defence grouping, or adopt an essentially independent stance?
6. Should Britain make structural changes in her armed forces as a result of new technological changes? If so, what form should they take?

The growing pressure on Britain's defence budget means that answers to questions such as these are urgently required. The problem, however, is even more profound than this. As Ken Booth points out in his chapter in this book:

The debate was never more important, for we are at a crossroads. Whatever we decide, we will have to live with our answers for a very long time; or we may have to suffer through them; and some of us, perhaps many of us, may even die by them. (p. 157)

NOTES

1. *Statement on the Defence Estimates 1975*, Cmnd 5976.
2. *The United Kingdom Defence Programme: The Way Forward*, Cmnd 8288.
3. Sir Henry Leach, *Journal of the Royal United Services Institute for Defence Studies*, September 1982.
4. For a similar discussion of 'non-provocative, non-nuclear defence of Western Europe', see Frank Barnaby and Egbert Boeker, *ADIU Report*, vol. 5, no. 1, January–February 1983. See also D. Smith, *Non-nuclear Military Options for Britain*, Peace Studies Papers No. 6 (London: Housmans). See also The Alternative Defence Commission, *Defence without the Bomb* (London: Taylor & Francis, 1983).
5. The question of the reorganisation of NATO forces and the utilisation of new technology is, of course, very much at the heart of the American air–land battle concept.

1 Economic Constraints and Political Preferences

DAVID GREENWOOD

This chapter is divided into three parts, reflecting its threefold purpose.

It begins with a sketch of the United Kingdom's defence programme and budget, as these had taken shape by the final year in power of the Thatcher government which took office in 1979: in other words, with an account of that administration's legacy to the second Thatcher government formed in June 1983. The aim here is to furnish a point of reference for discussion of alternative approaches to security provision. In defence policy-making and planning, you start from where you are and facing in a certain direction. So it is sensible to look at where the UK stands in 1983–4, and at where the country is heading, by way of preparation for appraisal of the ideas on other paths to security which are put forward by later contributors to this volume.

The second part of the chapter is an analysis of the economic factors that limit the freedom of choice on alternative defence postures. The purpose here is to show that, squeezed between a nether millstone of rising real costs for manpower and military materiel and an upper millstone of budgetary constraint, the Ministry of Defence's programme-in-being is well nigh certain to undergo modification as the decade unfolds. It is entirely appropriate, therefore, that thought should be given to alternatives. At the same time, any options for change that are canvassed must be examined in the light of their feasibility in the likely economic circumstances of the years ahead.

The third part of the chapter is a survey of the 'options for change' which the principal political groupings in Britain seem to favour, as inferred from formal statements – and the less formal pronouncements of their leading lights – made during 1982 and 1983 (with the General Election in mind). Among other things, this exercise shows that quite a number of notions for alternative approaches to defence provision are already on the political agenda, so to speak. On the other hand, it also reveals that several of those elaborated in this book are not (though some could, of course, find a place there in the not-too-distant future).[1]

THE PROGRAMME-IN-BEING

'You start from where you are': that is, with the pattern of current and planned future provision on which Mrs Thatcher's first government had settled by the beginning of 1983. For all practical purposes this means the blueprint for defence in the 1980s which emerged from the defence review of January–June 1981 – and was published then, as a White Paper entitled *The United Kingdom Defence Programme: The Way Forward* (Cmnd 8288) – as elucidated in subsequent policy statements and as amended after the contretemps with Argentina in the South Atlantic during 1982.

TASKS

To begin with, what are the principal tasks to which the defence effort is directed? A key paragraph in *The Way Forward* reads as follows:

> We have now four main roles: an independent element of strategic and theatre nuclear forces committed to the Alliance; the direct defence of the United Kingdom homeland; a major land and air contribution on the European mainland; and a major maritime effort in the Eastern Atlantic and Channel. We also commit home-based forces to the Alliance for specialist reinforcement contingencies, particularly on NATO's European flanks. Finally, we exploit the flexibility of our forces beyond the NATO area so far as our resources permit, to meet both specific British responsibilities and the growing importance to the West of supporting our friends and contributing to world stability more widely.[2]

That is a slightly eccentric formulation. The 'theatre nuclear forces committed to the Alliance' are so committed because of the third and fourth 'main roles', and the use of home-based forces for 'specialist reinforcement contingencies' on NATO's flanks is related to these also. So there is curious elaboration there. In contrast, forces are actually stationed 'beyond the NATO area' as well as being periodically deployed afar, while some troops geographically within the Alliance's area of interest – as formally defined by the North Atlantic Treaty – are there for purely national reasons. So there is really an additional role: fulfilment of extra-European or non-NATO commitments (now including what was not foreseen in *The Way Forward* – protection of the Falklands).

If these qualifications are accepted, the result is a fivefold categorisation of defence tasks. These are:

1. Provision of a *strategic nuclear force*, committed to the Alliance as the quoted paragraph records but in important respects independent.
2. *Protection of the home base*, not only because it is the 'homeland' of the official formulation, but also because it is (a) in the front line for maritime operations in the Eastern Atlantic and (b) an important rear area for land–air warfare on the European continent – in other words, invaluable real estate from a NATO standpoint and for fulfilment of the third and fourth roles.
3. The major contribution of naval and maritime–air forces for the implementation of Alliance strategy in the *Eastern Atlantic* (and also the Channel).
4. A major contribution of ground and tactical air forces to NATO's order of battle for land–air warfare in the *European theatre*, principally on the Central Front but also on the flanks (especially the northern).
5. Fulfilment of a variety of *non-NATO commitments*, many of them 'out of area' and all of them 'extra-European' (practically, if not strictly, speaking).

For some years this last task has been regarded as a residual one, rating a lower priority than the others. But that is changing, as will be made clear presently.[3]

MONEY

The first Defence Estimates prepared after the appearance of *The Way Forward* were those for 1982–3. The amount allocated to defence for that fiscal year was £14 100 millions; and my own notional attribution of that sum to principal roles is shown at Table 1.1.

As it stood on the eve of General Galtieri's ill-advised and ill-fated invasion of the Falklands, the forward programme embodied a pattern of priorities broadly similar to that depicted in this tabulation. It was recognised that the acquisition of a next-generation strategic nuclear

TABLE 1.1   *The defence budget (estimates) 1982–3 (notional attribution to principal roles)*

Role	1982–3* £m	%
1. Strategic nuclear force	1 050	7·4
2. Protection of the home base	3 100	22·0
3. Eastern Atlantic (naval/air)	3 250	23.0
4. European theatre (ground/air)	5 650	40.1
5. Non-NATO commitments	350	2.5
Service pensions	700	5.0
TOTAL	14 100	100.0

* Original Defence Estimates 1982–3 (March 1982) (cash).
Source: author's calculations.

force, based on the Americans' Trident D–5 missile, would produce a discrete lump of capital spending – for new nuclear-powered ballistic missile submarines (SSBNs) and a warhead development programme, in addition to the purchase of the missiles themselves – and that when this entered the reckoning in the later 1980s and early 1990s the share of the budget taken by line item 1 would be temporarily raised. It was expected that, with the contraction of the surface fleet foreshadowed in *The Way Forward*, the expense of the Eastern Atlantic role might loom less large in future budgets. But the allotment of some 20–25 per cent of annual funding to protection of the home base, of around 40 per cent to forces for operations in the European theatre, and of a comparatively trivial 2–3 per cent for non-NATO tasks – these were regarded as the more or less constant components of planned provision.

What impact, then, did the Falklands Campaign have on the budget for 1982–3 and the plot for future years? Put simply, in *1982–3* actual operations cost around £500 million, a further £200 million was spent on immediate replenishment of depleted stocks and re-equipment, while establishing the garrison and a naval presence in the South Atlantic entailed outlays of another £200 million (mainly in the second half of the financial year) – all of this, totalling £900 million, being expenditure that the government had neither bargained nor budgeted for. However, largely because of the upheaval associated with and resulting from the campaign, the Services were unable to use approximately £600 million which *had* been voted. That is to say, there was an 'underspend' of this order on the baseline programme for which the 1982–3 Estimates were originally prepared. Actual outgoings in the fiscal year therefore ended up a net £300 million higher than planned, at £14 400 million rather than the budgeted £14 100 million (cf. Table 1.1).

So far as *subsequent years* are concerned, plans and financial projections were affected in several ways. Ministers had to find room in the procurement budget for extra spending on (a) making good equipment losses and (b) acquiring additional hardware to equip and sustain the Falklands garrison and a naval patrol in the South Atlantic. They also had to accommodate provision for the latter's running costs over a number of years. On top of this, they chose – in the light of the Falklands experience – to enhance the armament of selected ships and the 'out of area' capability of the 5th Infantry Brigade. Initial estimation of such Falklands-related expenditure for the mid-1980s put the equipment bill at around £300 million per year and that for the garrison at more than £400 million in the first full year (1983–4), falling to around £200 million in later years.[4]

The domestic political climate being what it was in the autumn of 1982, the Ministry of Defence succeeded in persuading the Treasury that all these outgoings – the net overspending of £300 million in 1982–3 and annual sums, in the bracket £500–700 million, for subsequent years – should be met by additional funds over and above the provision for the so-called baseline programme drawn up following the previous year's defence review. And confirmation of this came with the publication, early in 1983, of the government's expenditure plans for 1983–6. These showed appropriate additions for 1983–4, 1984–5 and 1985–6 to the spending figures as projected twelve months previously with funding of the baseline programme only in mind.[5]

The reason for this diversion into the minutiae of post-Falklands defence budgeting can now be revealed. The defence programme-in-being embodies what was foreshadowed in *The Way Forward* (cf. Table 1.1 and commentary thereon), and elaborated in subsequent policy statements (for example, the Memorandum on *The Trident Programme* which was tabled when the decision to acquire D–5 missiles was announced), with adjustments as outlined in the December 1982 White Paper, *The Falklands Campaign: The Lessons*, and later pronouncements. It is summarised in Table 1.2, a presentation that is an extended version of Table 1.1 elucidating provision and plans as envisaged at the beginning of 1983. Incorporating as it does all those post-Falklands modifications to the earlier blueprint which have just been discussed, this tabulation is the most concise statement available of the legacy of

TABLE 1.2 *The benchmark programme*

Role	1982–3 £m	1983–4 £m	1984–5 £m	1985–6 £m	1986–7 £m	1987–8 £m
1. Strategic nuclear force	1 000	1 100	1 300	1 500	1 800	2 400
2. Protection of the home base	3 000	3 575	3 800	4 075	4 225	4 700
3. Eastern Atlantic (naval/air)	3 100	3 600	3 850	4 100	4 350	4 750
4. European theatre (ground/air)	5 400	6 000	6 500	6 800	7 500	8 000
5. Non-NATO commitments	1 200	975	1 050	975	900	850
(of which Falklands)	(900)	(650)	(700)	(600)	(500)	(300)
Service pensions	700	750	800	850	925	1 000
TOTAL	14 400	16 000	17 300	18 300	19 700	21 700

the first Thatcher government and hence of its successor's inheritance. It is, therefore, the benchmark by reference to which alternative approaches to defence provision can most usefully be considered.[6]

THE BENCHMARK PROGRAMME

A line-by-line commentary on Table 1.2 will serve to pave the way for such use.

Beginning with the bottom line, i.e. the money, the Defence Ministry and the armed forces expect their budget to increase by an annual 3 per cent in real terms, not counting the supplementary Falklands funding. The year-by-year totals of Table 1.2 exhibit a rising trend which reflects this. The precise year-to-year percentage changes incorporate both the 3 per cent real increase and the anticipated inflation rate (as foreseen by the Treasury at the turn of the year 1982–3), budgetary projections being presented on a cash basis these days.[7] Whether the sums shown in the tabulation, and plausible extrapolations to the later 1980s and beyond, really are sufficient to pay for everything in the forward plans – that is another matter. Whether it is reasonable to expect such amounts to be forthcoming is yet another. These are among the themes to be taken up presently.

Regarding the actual content of the programme, or inheritance, it is well known that whether large (and increasing) sums should be committed to the *strategic nuclear force* is, and promises to remain for some time, the single most controversial issue in the domestic politics of British defence. Each of the alternatives has its constituency: total renunciation of strategic nuclear armament, retention but not replacement of the Polaris force, acquisition of a less capable and/or less costly system than Trident. The issues are fully debated in several of the contributions to this text.

In contrast, that there should be provision for *protection of the home base* – on the sort of scale planned – is not in dispute. 'We need to do more, not less, in this field' was the judgment recorded in *The Way Forward*, prior to a listing of improvements in train. Notable among these are

- procurement of new mine hunters for the Royal Navy and new minesweepers for the Royal Naval Reserve
- expansion of the Territorial Army and establishment of a new Home Service Force
- completion of the major improvement plans for the air defence of the

UK, involving modernisation of ground-based radars and communications networks, introduction of the AEW version of the
Nimrod aircraft, retention of older interceptors (Phantoms) plus the
introduction of new ones (Tornado F2s), and expansion of the
tanker force (without which the fighters are embarrassingly short-
legged).[8]

The question is: should even more attention be paid to this major role?
There are those who *would* do so; and they exist in all parties and
factions. The idea of a home base made most difficult for an aggressor to
assail has obvious attractions for those on the Left who favour
'defensive deterrence', allowing the renunciation of nuclear weapons. It
appeals also to those on the Right who think that the UK should assume
a Gaullist stance, founded on independent nuclear capabilities, adequate naval capacity and a well-defended homeland.[9] These arguments,
and other views on the 'proper' place for this role in the pecking order of
defence priorities, are a further recurring theme in the following pages.

In the early 1980s, the biggest rows about defence priorities were those
surrounding the national contribution to NATO's forces for the *Eastern
Atlantic*. The provision in the programme-in-being reflects the outcome.
How much for these naval and maritime–air capabilities as opposed to
the ground and tactical air subscription to the Alliance in Europe was a
central, if not the central, issue in the debate surrounding the 1981
review. The question recurred during and immediately after the
Falklands campaign because the prominent part played by the Fleet in
that operation demonstrated the flexibility and versatility of naval
forces, highlighting the fact that any diminution of provision in and for
the NATO area implied a loss of capability for contingencies beyond the
North Atlantic. And the argument is not over. For the moment, though,
suffice it to note two things. First, the prescription in *The Way Forward*
was for important changes in how the maritime tasks should be
discharged. The key elements in it were: enhancement of the
maritime–air and submarine effort; but a reduction in the size of the
surface fleet and in the scale and sophistication of new ship-building,
permitting closure of one major dockyard and contraction at another, as
part of a general attempt to alter the 'balance of our investment between
platforms and weapons . . . so as to maximise real combat capability'.[10]
Second, the modifications to the forward programme made following
the Falklands campaign involved amending the timescale of the
rundown (and dockyard contraction) together with some 'quick fix'
improvements to the armament of selected vessels. But that is all.

Ministers did *not* fundamentally revise their ideas about the Royal Navy's place in the national order of battle.[11]

In other words, notwithstanding the clamour during 1982 for a shift of emphasis in defence priorities in favour of the maritime contribution to NATO at the expense of the continental, the government stood fast. At the conclusion of the 1981 defence review it had this to say about the *European Theatre* role.

> Despite all the financial pressures on our defence effort ... this contribution is so important to the Alliance's military posture and its political cohesion that it must be maintained.[12]

Eighteen months later, in a clear riposte to the naval lobbyists, the part of the post-Falklands White Paper dealing with 'The Future' reaffirmed the Ministerial view of 'the major threat to the security of the United Kingdom, which comes from the Soviet Union and its Warsaw Pact allies'. And the document continued with the reminder that it was (and is) 'in Europe that we and our Allies face the greatest concentration of Warsaw Pact forces'.[13] What was mapped out in *The Way Forward* is, therefore, still what is in store – and in the programme – for BAOR, RAF Germany and their back-up in Britain. That is to say, behind the figures for this line item in Table 1.2 lie plans for (a) maintenance and modernisation of the now-remodelled Rhine Army; (b) bringing the RAF's front line in the Federal Republic and the UK up to date, subject to resolution of a few outstanding procurement problems (like what, if anything, should be bought to replace the Jaguar force and what missile systems should be developed to arm the aircraft of the later 1980s and 1990s); and (c) completion of the reorganisation of the home-based army.[14] Even so, as noted, the last has not been heard of the 'maritime *v.* continental' argument. Moreover there are strong currents running in the Alliance, and in British domestic politics, favouring revision of NATO's concepts of operations for the defence of north-west Europe. Thus it is not at all certain that what is intended *will* in fact be realised; and more than one contributor to this book would argue that it *should not* be!

Finally, what of the task which in the 1980s will feature in the debate on defence priorities as it never did in the 1970s – fulfilling the UK's non-*NATO commitments* (including *protection of the Falklands*)? Present provision and plans may be summarised as follows.

● It is intended to 'continue as necessary to sustain specific British responsibilities' in Hong Kong, Cyprus, Gibraltar and Belize, at trifling expense.[15]

● It is intended to maintain a sizeable garrison in the Falklands and a significant naval presence in Falklands waters, at considerable cost.

● It is intended to carry through a series of improvements in the ability of the Services to operate worldwide, including some measures decided upon before the Falklands fracas and some extra ones decided upon after it. (Much of this – especially the transformation of the 5th Infantry Brigade into a properly constituted force for rapid deployment 'out of area' and the preservation of a true amphibious capability for the 3rd Commando Brigade – looks like the establishment of a 'special capability' for extra-European contingencies, notwithstanding the claim that in fact it is in line with the policy – which dates back to 1968 – of maintaining only a 'general capability' for such purposes.)[16]

Because of the Falklands-related expenditure, the immediate prospect is of spending on this fifth (and supposedly minor) role on a par with that for the strategic nuclear force, at least until the Trident bills start to come in during the later 1980s. For that reason if for no other the Fortress Falklands policy must be put to the question. And the appropriate priority for non-NATO commitments generally is a matter that invites scrutiny too. In fact these are among the most difficult issues with which Mrs Thatcher's second government – and whoever rules in the final years of the decade – will have to deal.

ECONOMIC CONSTRAINTS

They will be that much harder to handle, as will all the other problems concerning the content of the programme, because there must be doubt about the ability and willingness of future governments to find the sums in the bottom line of Table 1.2; and there must be doubt about the assumption, implicit in the tabulation, that the Defence Ministry can actually do all it has planned with that kind of money.

There must be doubt for two reasons. No one has yet found an answer to the rising real cost of defence inputs, as a result of which you get less defence for your money as time goes by. No one seriously believes that the UK's economic fortunes are about to take a decisive turn for the better, so the allotment of less money for defence than present plans envisage must be the realistic expectation.

LESS DEFENCE FOR YOUR MONEY

What are the reasons for believing that (a) outlays on personnel and equipment – the principal defence inputs – will go up faster than the general rate of inflation, so that (b) the cash allotted for the programme-in-being may not suffice to pay for all that it is supposed to pay for?

On the personnel side, the short answer is that having opted for all-volunteer forces British governments are now obliged to provide remuneration for Servicemen and Servicewomen that compares favourably with what is obtainable in civilian occupations. For a year or two, of course, anxiety about manning levels is unlikely. On present plans, defence's uniformed labour force is to contract. Reductions of between 8000 and 10 000 for the Royal Navy, of about 7000 in Army numbers, and of some 2500 in the strength of the Royal Air Force, were foreshadowed in *The Way Forward*; and, though the timescale for this contraction has been adjusted because of the Falklands campaign (and commitment), contraction there will still be. But an offsetting influence will come into play. The proportion of the traditional recruiting-age cohort required by the Services to sustain even the reduced strengths will stay high, because of the changing age distribution of the population. As for the non-uniformed workforce, although the number on this payroll too should fall during the mid-1980s, the chances are that the civil servants – white-collar and blue-collar – will fare well in the pay stakes, as they have hitherto. Then there is the matter of pensions. Both Service and general public-sector retirement benefits are generous on any reckoning, and the former are a direct charge on the defence budget.[17]

The solid underpinning of the 'less defence for your money' thesis comes, however, from the rising real cost of military equipment. The Ministry of Defence acknowledges that the extent of it is 'difficult to calculate with precision'; but procurement records apparently suggest 'an average annual figure, over and above inflation, of 6 per cent to 10 per cent on capital production costs of major equipments'.[18]

The explanation of the phenomenon lies in the mechanism of interlocking vicious cycles which is a characteristic of the weapons acquisition process nowadays.

Cycle No. 1 is the straightforward technical competition between adversaries. More effective systems fielded by one nation – usually in response to an observed (or feared) advance by the protagonist – are regarded by this rival as increasing the threat, stimulating further technological advance which duly evokes a response from the first nation, and so on. It is not self-evident that such competition must inevitably be associated with rising unit costs. In many civil fields, technical progress finds expression in better *and cheaper* products: to cite just two examples, today's electronic calculators and 'personal stereophonic sound systems' offer improved performance for less expense than yesterday's, by and large. The problem in the defence field is that the impulse is almost invariably to harnessing science in order to get the maximum capability within reach. *Cycle No. 2* comes into play when higher development costs lead governments to fund new projects less frequently. The technological 'leaps' which then have to be attempted typically make for a more protracted development process and even higher costs.

Cycle No. 3 operates when, in conditions such as these, governments find it increasingly difficult to decide which projects to pursue, and spend more time on studies and assessments (and in deliberation on these), which in turn prolongs development and leads to yet higher costs. When higher unit production costs are experienced, *Cycle No. 4* gets under way: tight budgets mean that fewer systems can be acquired, which reduces the scope for learning economies in production and thus adds further to average costs. *Cycle No. 5* operates when, because of small numbers, there is a reduced incentive to embark on productive investment (tooling), limiting the scope for economies of scale and so adding yet further to the unit cost of production. (A pictorial representation of the foregoing is possible, which bears an uncanny resemblance to a pentagon stood on its head.)

Needless to say, each of the cycles described exhibits what control engineers call 'positive feedback'. Together, therefore, they produce a faster rate of increase in the unit cost of acquisition than that which would result from the increased performance and effectiveness demanded in new weapons systems.[19]

It is natural to ask why, if this phenomenon is indeed well understood, policy-makers and planners do not do something about it. Two observations are in order here. The first is that the Ministry of Defence *is* 'introducing a range of measures to keep costs in check'. In fact, recent policy statements have yielded an impressive prospectus.[20] But the second observation is this: a cynic would say we have heard it all, or most of it, before; and a realist would point out that, even if the authorities do all that they say they will do, the economics of procurement cannot be transformed overnight. In the short-to-medium run it is permissible to hope for some amelioration of the 'less defence for your money' condition but idle to expect complete relief.

LESS MONEY FOR DEFENCE

What are the reasons for believing that governments in the 1980s, of whatever hue, will probably be prepared to allot less money to defence than present plans envisage; that is to say, less – in the event – than the sums in the bottom line of Table 1.2?

Essentially there are two. The uncertain growth prospects for the British economy mean that the availability of resources for all purposes – public and private, military and civil – may well not turn out as expenditure planners have presumed. And even if there were a spectacular recovery the defence budget might not be the most favoured beneficiary. In fact the country received notice in the summer of 1983 that, in her second term as Prime Minister, Mrs Thatcher might subject all public spending – including that for defence – to more radical revision than was ever attempted in her first stint.

On the general economic outlook, not surprisingly there is no consensus among experts about the prospects for a sustained recovery, any more than there is agreement among them about the true causes of present distress or the best means of promoting revival. Certain facts are indisputable, however. For instance, all the statistics confirm that the British economy has been in the doldrums for a decade. According to data prepared by the National Institute of Economic and Social Research (NIESR), there were average annual increases in Gross Domestic Product (GDP) of almost 3 per cent in the 1960s. But the rate slowed to less than 2 per cent a year in the 1970s; and from 1977 to 1982 there was virtually no growth at all. At the beginning of 1983 there was a whiff of recovery in the air, but little confidence that it would be long-lasting.[21]

It has been the same elsewhere. Since 1973 there has been a remarkable slow-down in labour productivity, unprecedented, common to almost all advanced nations and to all sectors within their economies, and, although perhaps exaggerated by some measurement biases, emphatically not a statistical illusion. Demand has been generally slack – and consciously checked in many places to restrain inflation – discouraging investment, innovation and structural change. The latter has been further impeded by rigidities of one kind and another: job preservation legislation, protection and subsidies for firms in the greatest difficulties, and so on. As for investment and innovation, many commentators believe that the effect of inadequate demand has been exaggerated by secular factors.

> The 1950s and 1960s were characterised, like earlier booms, by an unusually rapid rise in investment ... This was artificially prolonged by the tendency of governments to grant increasingly large subsidies to investment. The result was an exhaustion of the best investment opportunities ... and a fall off in the rate at which the capital stock was increased.[22]

What produced the deficient demand in the first place is a key question. The oil-price rises of 1973–4 and 1978–80 had a lot to do with it, for they affected real demand not only directly but also indirectly (by strengthening inflation and so leading to restrictive actions by governments). On the supply side, some role should also be assigned to what economists call 'catch-up': the scope for growth depends on how far you are below the frontier represented by best practice; and the international differentials here have been narrowing.

Against this background, the presumption must be that the distressed condition of the British economy – and many others – is not a temporary malady but, rather, a deep-seated malaise. Most of those who study economic growth and fluctuations concur in this assessment, expecting recovery to be slow and fitful. 'Only an extreme optimist would expect the growth rates of the 1950s and 1960s to be regained ... in the foreseeable future' is one such analyst's view.[23] Assessments of the immediate economic outlook for the UK are in line with this general expectation. At the end of 1982 the NIESR was forecasting growth in real GDP of '1.5 per cent a year on average over the next five years ... barely sufficient to absorb the underlying rate of increase in productivity and maintain employment at its current level'. Furthermore, the National Institute noted that the prolonged recession had given rise to conditions unfavourable to well-founded recovery.

> Renewed investment activity on any very large scale is unlikely when adequate capacity already exists for a considerably increased volume of production. It is also possible that ... the recession has made firms cautious, hesitant to launch new ventures and unwilling to tie up funds in long-term investments.

At the beginning of 1983 the Organisation for Economic Co-operation and Development (OECD) entered a similar set of judgments, registering 'considerable doubt as to whether the basis for a strong economic recovery exist[ed]'.[24]

In sum, a lengthy convalescence may be necessary before the UK's economy is properly on its feet again. Even then there is doubt as to how nimble the patient might be. For, according to one distinguished scholar, 'with age, British society has acquired so many strong organisations and collusions that it suffers from an institutional sclerosis that slows its adaptation to changing circumstances and technologies'.[25]

The significance of such a prospect for the allocation of resources to defence is obvious. In conditions of slow (or no) growth, the commitment of funds as envisaged in present plans – the profile of expenditure outlined in Table 1.2 – implies the absorption by military spending of progressively larger shares of GDP; and this at precisely the time when, to prompt recovery, the impulse to boost consumption, investment in the private sector and civilian public works must be especially powerful. No government is likely to countenance that for very long, with the possible exception of one unreservedly willing to accord defence a high, rising – and, indeed, an overriding – priority among claims on national output. And not even an ultra-dry Conservative administration would fall into that category.

In fact, what these broad inferences from the general economic outlook suggest regarding the 'less money for defence' hypothesis is if anything reinforced by such indications as politicians have given of late concerning their views of defence's place in national priorities. Starting on the Left, one of the few things that unites all the contesting factions within the Labour Party is a desire to see military spending absorb fewer resources. Bringing the proportion of GDP allotted to defence in the UK more into line with the average for NATO's European members is the expression of this aspiration for which the Labour leadership has opted in the past, and with which it will probably persevere (if only because the formulation is imprecise and, therefore, does not divide the Party). Moving to the Centre – if that is an appropriate description of where the Social Democratic Party (SDP) and the Liberals stand – the position is more or less the same. A greater stress on seeking security through arms control is a distinguishing feature of this political partnership's stance and that implies a somewhat reduced defence effort. So too does the commitment to numerous programmes of social improvement which is another plank in its platform.

That leaves the Conservatives, who formally support the allocation to defence of a high – and, if need be, rising – share of total resources, but whose tune may be about to change. One of the most remarkable episodes in British politics during 1982 was the 'leaking' — first to *The Economist* newspaper and thereafter to the rest of the media – of an exercise, approved by Ministers, to identify options for achieving during a further term of Tory rule a decisive reduction in the proportion of the nation's resources taken by public expenditure as a whole. Although conducted by the Central Policy Review Staff – the 'think tank' – this study was disavowed by Mrs Thatcher, principally because of the furore that arose when it was learnt that it contained suggestions for innovations like student loans (to ease the burden on the education budget) and compulsory private medical insurance (to ease that on the health budget). Be that as it may, what prompted the inquiry was a recognition among leading Conservatives, including the Prime Minister herself, that to lower – rather than simply check the growth in – the share of aggregate public expenditure in GDP would require radical new approaches to definition of the limits of collective provision. This is still an important strand in Thatcherite thinking. The study was set aside in 1982. It was not buried and forgotten. It will be resurrected, assuredly, in the not-too-distant future.[26]

The significant point for present purposes is that the 'think tank' had things to say about provision for defence: things which, but for the outcry caused by its ideas on civil programmes, would have received more attention than they did. Essentially, its argument ran, the commitment to real annual increases in military spending of 3 per cent or thereabouts would have to be adandoned if there was to be any hope of getting and holding government expenditure below, say, 40 per cent of GDP.[27]

Combining the 'less defence for your money' and 'less money for defence' arguments yields a clear conclusion. The Ministry of Defence is likely to find that it cannot do all that it has planned for the 1980s with the sums that it has been allotted, as depicted in Table 1.2 above. In other words, a squeeze on the defence programme is implicit in this spending profile. On top of that, the ability and willingness of future governments actually to find these sums is open to serious doubt. The implication is that before long Mrs Thatcher's second government is likely to be in much the same position as her first was, back in 1980: unable to 'fund all the force structures and all the plans for their improvement we now have' (to use words employed in the opening paragraphs of *The Way Forward*, to explain why the 1981 review was necessary); and, therefore, impelled to modify the programme-in-being.[28]

POLITICAL PREFERENCES

But how will it alter things; and for what alterations to the programme will the Parliamentary opposition, and critics in the country, be pressing? To shed light on this question, consider the alternative futures which were sketched just before and during the General Election campaign of 1983. At the beginning of May 1983, it was possible to imagine the governance of Britain passing to any one of the following:

● a second Thatcher administration
● an administration of a Centrist cast, dependent for its Parliamentary support on the Liberals in harness with the Social Democratic Party (SDP)
● a Labour government, determined to shift the emphasis in British defence dispositions towards a non-nuclear posture
  and, not to be omitted from the reckoning
● a Tory government with a Gaullist tinge, and prepared to amend priorities accordingly.

In the event, the country elected a second Thatcher government. But to elucidate the issues then, and still, in contention among the parties, suppose we put back the clock and look, as one might have done before the June 1983 poll, and consider the alternative prospectuses for the nation's defences then on offer. Is it possible to infer how the different contenders for power (or influence) in the June 1983 Election would have altered the programme in being, given the chance?

It *is* possible, because something like this has been done already (by the present writer, with Peter Hennessy's help, in a series of articles for *The Times*, published in October 1981). It is instructive to undertake a similar exercise now, for the purposes of this book, in order to illuminate – albeit cryptically – those alternative approaches to defence provision which early in 1983 were actually being canvassed by key political groupings. And, indeed, entering into the spirit of 'putting back the clock', to speculate as one might have then, before Mrs Thatcher's resounding win, on the different possibilities.[29]

For a start, it is useful to take a synoptic view of the programme in being. This is provided in Table 1.3, which is no more than a summary representation of the so-called benchmark programme, as elucidated in the first part of this chapter. If it were the practice for British governments to produce not Defence White Papers but Defence White Postcards, this is what the 1983 edition would have looked like![30]

Because of what has been said already it would be superfluous to

TABLE 1.3   *The programme-in-being*

Resources	1983–4	1985–6	1987–8
Defence budget (£000 millions)	16.0	18.3	21.7
Defence manpower (thousands)			
Service personnel	325	315	300
MoD civilians	225	200	195

Roles and forces (with share of 1983–4 budget)	Mid-to-late 1980s
Strategic nuclear force (7 per cent)	4-boat Polaris force in-being.
	4-boat Trident force in-the-pipeline.
Home base (22 per cent)	Greater emphasis on Reserves for coastal and territorial defence: improvements to air defence (including air defence Tornado).
Eastern Atlantic (22 per cent)	Reduced surface fleet of 3 carriers, 42+ escorts plus smaller types (1985) with cheaper frigates (Type 23) to be built to replace remaining Leanders.
	Fleet submarine force building up to 17 (in 1990), and new conventional class entering service in later 1980s.
Europe (38 per cent)	1 (British) Corps remodelled: 3 divisions (but one brigade located in UK).
	RAF Germany contracting: Tornados, with Harriers and other existing types, in service; new Harrier in-the-pipeline; Jaguar replacement undecided.
	United Kingdom land/air forces for reinforcement and rotation.
Non-NATO commitments	Residual garrisons, plus Falklands contingent and improving capacity for composing *ad hoc* forces for extra-European operations.

comment at length on this synopsis. What is of interest is how different the tableau *might have looked* – or if we really do now imagine an evaluation penned prior to the 1983 poll – how it *might look* under new management. (Imagine what follows as an extract from an analyst's evaluation, composed sometime in the first quarter of 1983.)

A SECOND THATCHER ADMINISTRATION

Of the 'new management' possibilities worth considering, this first would entail the least change, perhaps no more than whatever marginal adjustment to plans and budgetary projections might be necessary to accommodate those economic pressures identified in the second part of this chapter.

Having said that, however, *exactly* what a second Thatcher administration would alter in such circumstances is really anybody's guess. Once they have formally committed themselves to policies – which, naturally, they have represented as the 'right' policies and as durable policies – governments do not, as a general rule, spend time specifying what they would do if things were to go wrong. It is plausible, though, to indicate the options for adjustment which would probably commend themselves if it were indeed to become apparent in the mid-1980s what became apparent in 1980–1: that the Defence Ministry was 'attempting too much and achieving too little', leading Ministers to conclude (as they did in 1981) that 'we cannot go on as we are'.[31] These options are shown in Table 1.4 here, which may be regarded as the rough notes for a mid-1980s White Paper which may even now be lying under the blotting-pad of a prudent bureaucrat in the Ministry's programme and budget division.

The part of this tabulation labelled 'Resources' indicates the scale of the adjustment which is being assumed, for the sake of argument. If impelled to revise budgetary (and manpower) projections downwards to this extent a second Thatcher government would probably opt for the kind of amendment to plans suggested in the 'Roles and Forces' part.

It would not abandon the Trident programme. But it might exploit whatever room for manoeuvre there is in the procurement timetable. It could choose, for instance, to acquire the missiles, and build the new SSBNs for taking them to sea, at a slower rate than is currently envisaged. Options for rephasing re-equipment exist elsewhere also. The construction programme for new frigates, the Type 23s, and that for new conventionally powered submarines, could be stretched. So, too, could the schedule for introducing into service the Tornado and improved Harrier aircraft, the Nimrod airborne early-warning plane and several of the Army's weapon systems. Other 'savings' might be made by earlier withdrawal of older items of equipment, like some of those surface ships that are to be paid off anyway, the more long-in-the-tooth armoured fighting vehicles and such venerable aircraft as the Buccaneers and Lightnings.

TABLE 1.4 *A second Thatcher government (squeezed)*

Resources	*1983–4*	*1985–6*	*1987–8*
Defence budget (£000 millions)	16.0	17.5	20.0
Defence manpower (thousands)			
Service personnel	325	310	290
MoD civilians	225	195	190

Roles and forces	*Mid-to-late 1980s*
Strategic nuclear forces	4-boat Polaris force in-being.
	4-boat Trident force in-the-pipeline (but with, say, rephased missile acquisition and submarine construction).
Home base	Delayed air defence modernisation (including slower introduction of Tornado interceptors).
	Reduced manning levels.
Eastern Atlantic	Resumption of pre-Falklands timetable for surface fleet contraction and for introduction of more up-to-date weapons.
	Rephased new construction programmes.
Europe	Strength of 1 (British) Corps in Germany cut (one brigade *per* division located in UK): postponement of some re-equipment.
	RAF Germany's strength cut by early withdrawal of older aircraft types.
Non-NATO commitments	Residual garrisons; Falklands contingent cut to, say, battalion group plus air defence, with only nominal naval presence in South Atlantic; enhancement of general 'out of area' capabilities slowed down.

In any search for further economies, Ministers would have to look to the British contribution to NATO in Germany and to the British Army of the Rhine (BAOR) in particular. The remodelling prescribed in *The Way Forward* – involving adoption of a three-division/nine-brigade format with one brigade stationed in Britain – could be carried a stage further (in theory, at least), to yield a set-up in which each division had one home-based brigade in normal times. Alternatively, retention of the nominal order of battle but a dilution of equipment scales and a diminution of unit establishments might be preferred.

Taking the lion's share of the money as they do, European theatre forces are the obvious target, should retrenchment be necessary. But 'out of area' provision is another. Second thoughts on the feasibility of a Fortress Falklands policy were being aired, within the Conservatives' ranks, even before the first anniversary of the islands' liberation. Once longer-range transport planes are available the option of a relatively small, but rapidly reinforcable, garrison could begin to look very attractive. In addition, it is an open question whether that enthusiasm for boosting the Services' ability to operate worldwide, which was discernible just before and immediately after the operations in the South Atlantic, would endure in the face of intense budgetary pressure, especially if the Treasury were to insist that special provision for funding post-Falklands expenditures could not (or should not) be made beyond, say, 1985–6.

A CENTRIST GOVERNMENT

If the mould of British politics has indeed been broken by the foundation of the SDP and the simultaneous revival in the Liberal Party's fortunes, the prospect must be entertained of defence programme management in the hands of a Cabinet if not actually led by a politician sporting Liberal/SDP colours then one at least dependent on this partnership's support in Parliament.[32]

It is unlikely that such a Cabinet would choose, or be allowed, to pour more money into arms and armed forces year in year out. It would assuredly not want, or be permitted, to pick up the £10 000 million-plus bill for a new strategic nuclear force. At the same time there is no basic aversion to expenditure for military purposes at what may be becoming the centre of gravity in British politics, any more than one discerns there a disposition to alter fundamentally the security relationship with the USA and NATO. So the options for change most likely to find favour in these circumstances are the ones set out in Table 1.5.

TABLE 1.5   *The centrist administration*

Resources	1983–4	1985–6	1987–8
Defence budget (£000 millions)	16.0	17.5	17.5
Defence manpower (thousands)			
Service personnel	325	310	280
MoD civilians	225	195	180

Roles and forces	Mid-to-late 1980s
Strategic nuclear forces	4-boat Polaris force in-being but perhaps not for long.
	Cancel Trident but retain some nuclear capacity, maybe in the form of cruise missiles in submarines.
	(More energetic approach to arms control.)
Home base	Continue air defence modernisation.
	Possibly restore regular strength.
Eastern Atlantic	Fleet rundown checked.
	Dockyard closure plan re-examined.
Europe	Reduce British Forces Germany marginally
	OR
	Maintain existing force level but seek fresh offset agreement.
	(More flexible approach to MBFR talks.)
	Possibly restore regular strength in UK-based forces.
Non-NATO commitments	Residual garrisons, but reduced Falklands contingent and South Atlantic presence and no boost to extra-European capability generally.

Looking, first, at *resources*: the course of action that a Centrist government would probably find most attractive, if given responsibility for a £16 000–18 000 million defence budget, is that which incoming Labour governments adopted in 1964 and 1974: not to slash appropriations wildly, but to set a budget ceiling at the existing expenditure level and cut the nation's military coat according to this amount of cloth.

For *roles and forces* that might mean the sort of change spelt out in the lower part of Table 1.5. Stopping the Trident programme would head the list. Gratuitously discarding the UK's existing nuclear weaponry – including the Polaris force – would not feature there however, partly because the opportunity to try exacting some *quid pro quo* from the Soviet Union has a certain appeal (difficult though it is to imagine why Moscow should respond), and partly because there could be interest in lower-cost alternatives to Trident among this fraternity (whose real objection to the latter system is to its expense and, particularly, to its opportunity cost in degradation of Britain's ability to perform non-nuclear tasks). Within the domain of conventional capabilities, a positive preference for concentration on the UK's maritime role might assert itself. That would be consistent with the criticisms that some of the Centre's luminaries have levelled at the Conservatives' plans for axeing the surface fleet to pay for the Army's re-equipment. Reducing both elements of British Forces Germany, i.e. Rhine Army and the air force there, or asking the West Germans to consider some new offset scheme – these are definite possibilities. A renewed attempt to make headway in the talks on Mutual and Balanced Force Reductions (MBFR) in Europe would certainly stand high on the agenda. On the other hand, if the European *Communautaire* spirit is alive anywhere in British politics it is among Liberals and Social Democrats. Brutal surgery on the explicitly European elements in the UK's defence effort would, therefore, be unlikely. In fact, at the end of the day, an administration of a Centrist cast might find itself disposed to leave unchanged more than it altered. Provision for extra-European and non-NATO commitments would be the exception here: modification of the Fortress Falklands stance and critical examination of anything smacking of Imperial recidivism would, one feels, be among the first items of defence business for such a government.

LABOUR'S PRIORITIES

What has just been discussed amounts to a deliberate, pragmatic, cautious approach to shifting defence priorities, and defence's place in national expenditure priorities. According to its public pronouncements in 1982–3, the Labour Party wants none of this. What, then, might occur if it were to win an overall majority in Parliament and form an administration, led by someone like Mr Foot, committed to a nuclear-free posture for the UK, less than wholehearted about an Alliance whose strategic doctrine rests on posing the threat of nuclear devastation, and (presumably) sceptical about spending on arms and armed forces generally?

At a guess such a government would come up with something like the main lines of policy summarised in Table 1.6, involving a defence budget of no more than £16 000 million by the later 1980s and perhaps less, with Service strengths at around 200 000 – which is three-fifths of the present number – and defence's civilian labour force numbering, say, 175 000.

Over a period – 'in the lifetime of a single Parliament' if the Party's rhetoric is to be believed – strategic nuclear capabilities would be excised from the defence programme, both the Polaris force-in-being and the Trident system in-the-pipeline. A complete 'nuclearectomy' would also require (a) getting rid of stocks of free-fall nuclear bombs and depth charges; (b) ending the 'dual key' arrangements with the USA which cover the warheads for BAOR's Lance missiles and, also, some cannon-launched munitions; and (c) telling the Americans to leave Holy Loch in Scotland and several sites in England and Wales, taking their weapons with them (including any cruise missiles that might have been emplaced here).

In line with the ideas on 'defensive deterrence' which the more thoughtful of Labour's spokespersons have begun to articulate recently, prominent among the other programme choices that a Foot-led administration might make would be strengthening the protection of the UK itself. The purpose would be to present a would-be attacker with the prospect of pain out of all proportion to the possible pay-off from invasion. Action would include enhancing the home base's coastal, territorial and air defences. On the naval side, that would mean greater stress on mine-hunters and fast patrol boats at the expense of provision for bigger ocean-going warships. It would mean regarding 'home defence' as the most important of the Army's roles, and therefore the prior claimant on resources for equipment and time for training. It would mean having the Royal Air Force accord top priority to providing an air defence system as good as, and preferably better than, that now undergoing overdue updating. It would mean spending perhaps two-fifths of the budget on these tasks, compared with the 20–25 per cent allotted to them in the programme-in-being.

On the other hand, dissociation from NATO's concept of operations for defending north-west Europe would be favoured. That might mean reducing the British Corps in Germany to a token force of (say) 10 000 men, or even making preparations for withdrawing ground troops altogether. Certainly it is hard to envisage a place in the rubric of

TABLE 1.6   *Labour's priorities*

Resources	1983–4	1985–6	1987–8
Defence budget (£000 millions)	16.0	16.0	15.0–16.0
Defence manpower (thousands)			
Service personnel	325	275	200
MoD civilians	225	200	175

Roles and forces	Mid-to-late 1980s
Strategic nuclear forces	NONE
	Cancel Trident programme and pay off Polaris boats progressively.
	Serve notice to quit on all American nuclear-related facilities.
Home base	Maintain and perhaps enhance coastal, territorial and aerial protection: keep home defences up-to-date and up-to-scratch through re-equipment and intensive training.
Eastern atlantic	Continue rundown of fleet, but not dockyards.
	Increase emphasis on smaller ships for coastal defence (mine counter-measures and anti-submarine warfare).
Europe	Progressive phasing-out of theatre and battlefield nuclear weapons.
	Withdraw and disband large proportion of 1 (British) Corps, as part of dissociation from NATO's concept of operations for defence of north-west Europe.
	Withdraw and disband some squadrons from RAF in Germany (for the same reason); buy fewer Tornados and improved Harriers.
Non-NATO commitments	Prepare to abandon most residual garrisons, reduce the Falklands contingent and plans for composing forces for extra-European missions.

'defensive deterrence' for the kind of armour-heavy divisions that Rhine Army has at present or for the longer-range artillery that goes with them. Nor does the concept provide a solid rationale for the sixty new Harriers scheduled to be bought for the RAF in Germany.

With the future of naval provision, principally for the Eastern Atlantic, the Party would have a problem. From the criticism levelled at the Conservatives' prescription of diminution in the surface fleet one would infer that Labour would favour the restoration of many cuts. By no stretch of the imagination, however, could the lukewarm support that the Opposition front bench gave to the Falklands operation afford any comfort to the maritime lobby. Therefore the odds are that, if the Party were to get sufficient Parliamentary support to enable it to ignore the voices of moderation in its ranks (which is what is being assumed here), it would be content to let the naval contraction take its course, and might in fact countenance a more rapid rundown as part and parcel of a rejection of the Tories' recidivist inclinations on 'out of area' provision.

To contemplate recasting the defence effort along these lines is radical, and entails running risks. But it is not ridiculous. The trouble is that it probably does not represent what a majority on the Left would prefer. Many, if not most, of the Labour Party's activists are people who, having discarded the existing apparatus for deterrence and defence would shy from putting any other in its place. In particular, they would baulk at paying the price of 'defensive deterrence' because *any* military provision would be at the expense of funds for desired social and economic transformation. This is the danger of the radical alternative. Indeed, since the repercussions of a decisive electoral success for a Party committed to unilateralism would shake NATO to its roots, one fears that such an eventuality would heighten the very risks the New Romantics seek to lessen.[33]

THE GAULLIST OPTION

Finally, what of the fourth of the 'new management' possibilities identified earlier: an administration inclined to give fuller vent to that whiff of Gaullism which was discernible in much of Mrs Thatcher's rhetoric during and after the Falklands campaign, and, on that basis, prepared to fashion 'a defence for Britain which is a British defence' (to paraphrase the late General)?

In that eventuality the dispositions favoured would probably be of the kind set out in Table 1.7. By way of commentary on this presentation, two initial observations on the figures are in order. First, the cost of

TABLE 1.7 *The 'Gaullist' option*

Resources	1983–4	1985–6	1987–8
Defence budget (£000 millions)	16.0	18.0	20.0–21.0
Defence manpower (thousands)			
Service personnel	325	310	290
MoD civilians	225	195	190

Roles and forces	Mid-to-late 1980s
Strategic nuclear forces	RETAIN
	Maintain Polaris force and Trident acquisition plan under bilateral arrangement with the United States.
	Establish technological base for independent provision in future.
Home base	Maintain existing coastal, ground and air defence provision, and improve it steadily as time goes by.
Eastern Atlantic	Remodel surface and submarine fleets to enhance capabilities for independent operations in European waters and elsewhere.
Europe	Retain own theatre nuclear systems.
	Develop technological base for independent provision in future.
	Reduce elements of 1 (British) Corps and RAF in Germany; retain remaining ones under bilateral agreement with West Germany (or withdraw).
Non-NATO commitments	Retain residual garrisons including Falklands contingent; augment capacity for independent operations wherever national interests may require.

'standing alone' would be no less than that projected for current arrangements, mainly because of a need for costly equipment acquisitions and provision for technological independence in the longer run. Second, the posture would probably require almost as much manpower.

Maintaining a strategic nuclear deterrent force would be the top priority. There would also be a place in this *national* order of battle for theatre nuclear forces, to give some credibility to the notion of *unilateral* flexibility in response and to permit some measure of *independent* graduated escalation in the face of any challenge. Such nuclear provision would pose problems, because Britain's existing and planned systems are of American origin. Bilateral arrangements would be necessary for the life-span of the Polaris and Trident forces. Consideration would have to be given to developing indigenous technological competence for the future.

So far as non-nuclear forces are concerned, there would be added emphasis on safeguarding the homeland. The air defence of the UK would rate a particularly high priority, even if that meant buying more Tornado interceptors (at £16 million apiece). In Europe, though, reduction or withdrawal of troops might not be part of the design. It would depend on what Anglo–German security relationship were forged as formal Alliance links were recast. And even if a decision were eventually reached to have no divisions permanently stationed in Germany the capability to deploy forces there would have to be retained, for nothing would have happened to alter the fact that Britain's first line of defence lies on the continent.

Nor would a Britain 'standing alone' reduce its naval might as a Left-led nation 'opting out' might do. Rather the contrary: a well-balanced fleet would be required, certainly including vessels like the *Invincible* class and perhaps even 'proper' aircraft carriers, preferably mustering enough escorts to sustain not only a presence in the Eastern Atlantic, the North Sea and the Channel – and in the South Atlantic for as long as necessary – but also task groups for regular deployment beyond European waters. In general, more rather than less attention would be given to capabilities for protecting perceived national interests outside the NATO area.[34]

CONCLUSION

It goes without saying that this speculative *jeu d'esprit* could be prolonged. But the essential point has been made. The defence programme-in-being – described in the first part of this chapter – will come under economic pressure before too long, as the argument of the second part of the chapter showed. In considering options for change the striking fact is that, in contrast to the position in the 1960s and 1970s (and even at the beginning of the 1980s, when Secretary of State for Defence John Nott conducted the exercise that yielded *The Way*

Forward), the range of imaginable choice for the United Kingdom is extremely wide. Judgements and assumptions concerning security policy, posture and provision, about which there was once a degree of consensus, have been put to the question in recent years as never before. Consequently, there was greater variety in the prospectuses for defence offered by the main political parties in the General Election of 1983 than in just about any previous election since 1945. These have been examined, by means of the device of microcosmic Defence White Papers incorporated in an imaginary evaluation of the political prospect as it appeared before the second Thatcher government took office. That evaluation has more than curiosity value, however; for it may be assumed that – in general terms if not in every particular – critiques of whatever priorities are favoured by the Conservatives in the years to 1987–8 will follow the lines defined in their opponents' 'prospectuses'. Decisive though the Tory's triumph was, there will be – and it is right that there should be – wide-ranging examination of 'alternative approaches' and that serious professional and popular attention should be paid to it. For we should never forget that these are, or could be, quite literally, life-and-death matters.

NOTES

1. Throughout the chapter I have drawn on material prepared for my own book-length study of British defence priorities in the 1980s and beyond, written for the Royal United Services Institute for Defence Studies. At this juncture I must also record my thanks to those colleagues at Aberdeen with whom I have discussed from time to time the topics dealt with here; and to Margaret McRobb, without whose secretarial help I would have been lost.
2. *The United Kingdom Defence Programme: The Way Forward*, Cmnd 8288, para. 7 (p. 5).
3. See Table 1.2 and the commentary thereon.
4. The information in these paragraphs is taken from the *Statement on the Defence Estimates 1982*, Cmnd 8529-I, 8529-II, and *The Falklands Campaign: the Lessons*, Cmnd 8758, plus news stories in *The Times* and *The Financial Times* (London) on 2 February 1983.
5. *The Government's Expenditure Plans 1983–84 to 1985–86*, Cmnd 8789 (2 vols) and news stories on 2 February 1983.
6. It must be noted that in Table 1.2 only the *totals* to 1985–6 are official figures. The breakdowns by major tasks/roles represent my own calculations; and the aggregate spending figures for 1986–7 and 1987–8 are extrapolations.
7. For 1983–4 the Treasury made allowance for inflation of 6 per cent on non-pay items and of 3 per cent on pay. The planning totals for 1984–5 and

1985–6 appear to assume inflation (overall) at 5 per cent and 3 per cent respectively.

8. See Cmnd 8288, paras 11–15 (pp. 5–6).

9. For example, the group who early in 1983 launched the 'Defence begins at Home' campaign (with Lord Hill-Norton in their number).

10. Cmnd 8288, paras 21–31 (pp. 8–10) and also para. 5 (p. 4) from which the quoted phrases come.

11. See Cmnd 8758 and my article on this White Paper in *The Sunday Times*, 19 December 1982.

12. Cmnd 8288, para. 16 (p. 6).

13. Cmnd 8758, para. 302 (p. 31).

14. Cmnd 8288, paras 16–20 (pp. 6–8).

15. Cmnd 8288, para. 36 (p. 11).

16. Cmnd 8758, paras 303–4 (pp. 31–2).

17. Civil servants' pensions are not. They would have added around £250 million to the defence budget for 1982–3, according to figures in Cmnd 8529-II (table 2.2 on p. 11).

18. Cmnd 8529-I, para. 403 (p. 27).

19. I am indebted to Messrs D. Kirkpatrick and P. G. Pugh for sight of the text of their presentation 'Towards the Starship Enterprise – are the current trends in defence unit costs inexorable?', given to a Workshop on Spiralling Unit Costs in Defence – Causes and Countermeasures, held under the auspices of the Management Studies Group of the Royal Aeronautical Society on 30 November 1982. In this part of my exposition I have drawn freely on this material.

20. See, for example, Cmnd 8529-I, paras 407–34 (pp. 27–31).

21. *National Institute Economic Review*, no. 102, November 1982, Statistical Appendix, Table 1 (p. 81) and *passim*; but note also the Chancellor of the Exchequer's remarks in his 1983 Budget speech (as reported in *The Times*, 16 March 1983).

22. R. C. O. Matthews (ed.), *Slower Growth in the Western World*, Joint Studies in Public Policy No. 6 (London: Heinemann 1982) (for three institutes) p. 7.

23. Ibid, p. 17. There are, however, some economists who foresee more rapid recovery: one is Yves Laulan (see his paper for the International Institute for Strategic Studies' Annual Conference, 1982).

24. *National Institute Economic Review*, no. 102, November 1982, ch. III ('The British Economy in the medium term') p. 47; and *The Financial Times*, 11 February 1982 (on the OECD's *Economic Survey of the United Kingdom*, Paris: OECD, 1983).

25. M. Olson, *The Rise and Decline of Nations* (New Haven: Yale University Press, 1982). See also, C. Freeman *et al.*, *Unemployment and Technical Innovation* (London: Frances Pinter, 1982).

26. On this episode see *The Economist*, 18 September 1982 and subsequent stories in *The Observer*, 26 September 1982 and *The Times*, 6 October 1982. (That the issue was emphatically not 'buried and forgotten' is clear from a news item in *The Times*, 25 March 1983.)

27. See *The Economist*, 18 September 1982.

28. Cmnd 8288, para. 4 (p. 4).

29. See *The Times*, 27, 28, 29 and 30 October 1981. This final part of my chapter is, in effect, a revised version of these articles.
30. This text went to press *before* the appearance of the *Statement on the Defence Estimates 1983*. The contents of Table 1.3 are therefore derived from the earlier argument of this chapter rather than from an official source.
31. Cmnd 8288, para. 6 (p. 4).
32. Remember this is an analyst's evaluation *circa* March 1983.
33. On 'defensive deterrence' and the kind of force structure and force levels that might be required to support such a doctrine, see also D. Smith, *Non-nuclear Military Options for Britain*, Peace Studies Papers No. 6 (London: Housmans, for Bradford University's School of Peace Studies).
34. That concludes the analyst's imaginary evaluation.

2 British Defence Policy After the Falklands[1]

LAWRENCE FREEDMAN

On 15 June 1982, the Argentine garrison in Port Stanley surrendered. The war[2] of the Falkland Islands was over after two and a half months of intense activity, including six weeks of heavy fighting during which well over 1000 men died. For the British Army this was the heaviest fighting since Korea – for the Royal Navy since the Second World War. It was an unexpected and rigorous test of the British services from which, by and large, they emerged with credit. The government, too, gained in popular standing from the conflict. This was despite the fact that the outbreak of the war could be seen as a result of a major foreign policy failure and the reliance on the Royal Navy in its prosecution as an indictment of established defence policy. It also presented a challenge to a defence policy that had only been forged some nine months earlier.

BRITISH DEFENCE POLICY

The history of British defence policy is of an attempt to reconcile the mismatch between resources and commitments. The reconciliation is often achieved temporarily but it never seems to last. The inexorable rise in equipment costs pushes up the price of defence while the economy refuses to generate the extra funds necessary to keep pace. The problem can only be managed by the government allowing defence spending to grow at a rate faster than that of the overall economy or by reducing forces. The first Thatcher government followed both these methods: the defence budget was growing by something close to 3 per cent a year at a time when other public expenditure was held down and the growth in GDP was negative.[3] Yet, despite this comparatively generous allocation, the government still found it necessary to take hard decisions on defence priorities. After a sharp debate in the spring of 1981, the Secretary of State announced a revised programme that came out in favour of sustaining the British Army of the Rhine at the expense of the maritime contribution to the Eastern Atlantic.[4]

The reviews that have punctuated defence policy-making with some regularity throughout the post-war period have all revolved around three distinct issues: should Britain concentrate on the Soviet threat to Europe or should it still be prepared to get involved in conflicts elsewhere in the world? Within the NATO area, should Britain's main contribution be made on land or at sea? In addition to conventional forces, should Britain stay in the business of maintaining strategic nuclear forces?

Over time, the logic has pushed successive governments towards stressing the 'continental commitment'. For the defence reviews of the mid-1960s and mid-1970s, the greatest scope for savings came with a geographical contraction – in particular, relinquishing defence responsibilities 'East of Suez'. In 1979, the new Conservative government appeared to hanker after a renewed involvement in military activities outside the NATO area. It devoted some space in its first Defence Estimates to a consideration of the need for a greater intervention capability. In February 1981, the Prime Minister even appeared to promise substantial involvement in the Rapid Deployment Force (RDF) planned in the USA. However, in Parliament, the Secretary of Defence, John Nott, explained that the government was considering only 'modest use of force to protect the interests of friendly local states and the West in strategic regions'.[5] In June 1981, in *The Way Forward*, the main nod in the direction of wider defence interests was in provision for improving parachute assault capabilities and a special equipment stockpile, and also in announcing a resumption of substantial naval task groups being sent on long detachment for visits and exercises in the South Atlantic, Caribbean, Indian Ocean and further East.

The government resisted the temptation to expand Britain's defence commitments overseas. This ensured that the budgeting problem it faced was not exacerbated. However, there was no scope for contraction in this area and that had to be found by choosing between the continental and maritime contributions to the Alliance. In June 1981, it was decided that there was to be a reduction in the numbers of destroyers and frigates from about sixty to fifty (including eight to be withdrawn to standby) and also in dockyard capacity. One divisional headquarters of the British Army on the Rhine (BAOR) was to be removed. Only the

RAF escaped lightly while the Navy took 57 per cent of the cuts in planned expenditure.

It was thought by many at the time that these cuts had been made necessary by Trident. Certainly the government's determination to replace Polaris with the latest generation of submarine-launched ballistic missiles did push the strategic nuclear force into a prominent position in the budgetary projections. This prominence was in itself quite novel. In the 1957 Defence White Paper, the stress on nuclear forces was seen as a way of reducing the burden of conventional arms, almost as the substitution of an unusually efficient form of firepower for a less efficient one. By the defence reviews of the 1960s and 1970s, the allocation to the nuclear force was so minimal (under 2 per cent for much of the 1970s) that there was little financial incentive to reconsider nuclear policy.

It has only been with the capital cost of replacement of Polaris that the question of priorities between conventional and nuclear forces has had to be faced. However, the profile of expenditure on Trident meant that it did not loom large in the short term, and so its cancellation would not have made it possible to avoid the choices among conventional capabilities that were made in 1981. The last defence decisions made prior to the Falklands War were in March, when the government announced a decision to buy the more advanced D-5 version of Trident (as against the C-4).[6] Although, along with inflation, this raised the capital cost from £5 billion to £8 billion, it also changed the incidence of cost so that the main burden is now to fall later in the 1980s, with expenditure of only about £300 million by 1984.[7] A later decision, announced in September 1982, promised further savings through the servicing of the Trident missiles in the US.

THE DEBATE

Thus defence policy prior to April 1982 can be seen as following NATO orthodoxy by concentrating on land and air forces capable of blocking a conventional invasion of West Germany, backed up by a nuclear deterrent. Therefore, the most significant feature of the Falklands War was that it was fought well out of the NATO area and with the Royal Navy the lead service. It was precisely the war for which Britain was planning least.

In an age of deterrence, there would be something terribly wrong if it came to be necessary to fight the war for which one was planning most.

Nevertheless, the unexpected nature of this war and the reliance on the service that the government was about to run down, inevitably led to accusations of strategic myopia. The Falklands War was presented as a lesson in the nick of time, before the senior service was rendered wholly incapable of coping with such eventualities.[8]

The experience has encouraged a revisionist critique of government policy which argues that some way must be found of preserving and even enhancing the surface fleet. Conservative revisionists would prefer this to be done by increasing defence spending; Labour revisionists by scapping Trident. Revisionists in both parties seem prepared to see substantial cuts in BAOR if necessary to fund the navy.[9] Labour front-bench spokesmen are very much of this opinion. Britain now appears to be the only country in which the left-wing party is the Navy party.[10] This perhaps is because the Navy is the service most associated with a capacity for independent action and this nationalist appeal strikes a chord in the modern Labour Party, as well as the more mundane fact that most shipbuilding constituencies are represented by Labour MPs.

During the Falklands War, the Secretary of Defence insisted that the 'broad strategic thrust' of government policy was to be maintained. As an act of defiance after the conclusion of hostilities, he published an unamended Defence White Paper which took no account of the events of April, May and June (including listing as operational a number of ships sunk by Argentina) and consists largely of spelling out the detail of established policy. Nevertheless it soon became clear that the war would have important consequences for defence policy irrespective of any changes in the broad strategic thrust.

The first threat to established defence policy was the possibility that a good part of the war would have to be paid for from Ministry of Defence funds. Although it was suggested from the start that the cost of the war would be met from the government's contingency funds, by the time it ended there was some concern that MOD might be expected to fund the replacing of some of the lost assets. As it was, the Treasury agreed, with its customary lack of enthusiasm, to pay all the bills, including the cost of establishing and maintaining a garrison on the reconquered islands.

The cost of the war up to September 1982 was put at £700 million. Much of this can be accounted for by consumables, fuel, ammunition and other stocks, as well as by requisitioning and chartering of merchant ships. A figure of £970 million over three years to replace the lost equipment has also been mentioned. The direct costs of the fighting will within a few years be overtaken by the costs associated with the establishment and maintenance of the Falklands garrison. The final form of this garrison has yet to be agreed but it will involve some four thousand troops and supporting staff, with one squadron of Phantoms and a hunter-killer submarine and a couple of frigates close at hand. It will be the largest overseas garrison after Germany and, unlike Hong Kong and Brunei, none of the costs will be met by the host country. Indeed an additional injection of funds is necessary to keep the Falkland Islands economically viable. The cost of the post-war protection has been put at around £250 million for 1982–3, £424 million for 1983–4, and in multiples of a hundred million pounds for some time thereafter.[11]

Apart from the Treasury's enforced generosity, the burden of the immediate costs was made easier by the fact that the Ministry was managing to achieve a substantial underspend in its non-Falklands budget during 1982–3. This was a result of an over-zealous application of new procedures for controlling procurement, introduced as a result of the embarrassing overspends of the previous years, and as a result of defence contractors having to take on urgent Falklands work at the expense of other MOD business.

In planning its expenditure on the Falklands, the Ministry of Defence sought to invest as little as possible themselves, but to use as much of the additional expenditure allowed for the garrison to purchase equipment that could be employed for a variety of alternative purposes. Purchases announced in December included twelve extra Phantom aircraft, Rapier units, Chinook helicopters and wide-bodied transports. Also, some £200 million of the expenditure during the war was on equipment and improvements that will have lasting value to the forces. So, in the short term, rather than weaken the armed forces the war has made possible a slight but significant expansion.

Furthermore, the post-Falklands revisions to the 1981 Defence Review have allowed the Royal Navy to live to refight the bureaucratic battles with another Minister, although with the same Prime Minister. It is also being hinted at in MOD that some of the financial projections behind the 1981 Review were unduly pessimistic and that there is some room for manoeuvre.

Prior to the December 1982 White Paper some of the Navy cuts had been restored. In order to keep up numbers while the replacements for the four ships lost are built over the next few years, three old destroyers, *Fife, Glamorgan* and *Bristol*, which were to be taken out of service, are now to be retained. Two symbols of the campaign have been rescued. HMS *Endurance*, the ice-patrol ship whose withdrawal, announced in 1981, is widely believed to have sent the wrong signal to Buenos Aires as to British intentions, is to continue its patrols in the South Atlantic. It is not altogether clear why this is necessary for defence purposes if there are now to be patrols by frigates and submarines. More significant, the government has agreed with the Australian government that the latter's planned purchase of the Anti-Submarine Warfare Carrier, HMS *Invincible*, which was a vital component of the Task Force, will not go ahead. Keeping HMS *Invincible*, along with its two sister ships, the recently completed HMS *Illustrious* and HMS *Ark Royal*, which is currently under construction, involves a substantial change of policy. Instead of having two carriers, there will now be three, so that two can always be on patrol. The role of these carriers was central to the whole debate over the 1981 Defence Review. Mr Nott made little secret of his view that their construction had been a mistake because this left very little money for the weapons to be placed on these carriers or the escorts required to accompany them.

The White Paper[12] confirmed that the Navy had convinced the government that the replacement ships should be Type 22 Frigates rather than the cheaper Type 23s which are still in the development stage. In order to sustain patrols around the Falklands the total number of destroyers and frigates is to be held at fifty-five, instead of the fifty envisaged in the 1981 White Paper, with possibly a smaller number than eight in reserve. The policy of no mid-term replacement also seems to have been reappraised. While there remains the intention to revert to the 1981 plan once a continuous presence is no longer required in the South Atlantic, no date can be put on that revision. Britain is therefore going to have a larger and more modern Navy than had been envisaged.[13]

In addition to other lessons, such as the need for as large a stock of ammunition and other consumables as possible and the role of civilian assets in military emergencies, the government has also decided to improve the 'out-of-area' capability represented by the 5th Infantry Brigade. With some of the equipment purchased for the Falklands garrison there will be a much greater capacity to intervene in conflicts outside of NATO.

Thus, while the government still insists that its main focus is on the Soviet threat to Europe, the aftermath of the war and the need to protect the reconquered Falkland Islands has resulted in a total defence policy with a much less regional image than that described only nine months prior to the Argentine invasion. This may be financially manageable in the short term because of the Treasury agreement on Falklands costs and the adoption of the Trident D-5 missile, which means that the expenditure burden of the new nuclear force is delayed by a few years.

Indeed, MOD officials are currently remarkably optimistic about their medium-term future.

However, it is hard to avoid the conclusion that there will be a full-scale budget crisis over the next few years. This is still assuming – and it may be a large assumption – that the government will wish to follow current expenditure plans of annual rises in defence spending of 3 per cent in real terms up to 1986 and 1 per cent thereafter. The 1981 Defence Review has been knocked off course and many of the bureaucratic battles that had been lost and won may now have to be refought. The Ministry of Defence has suddenly taken on an overseas garrison second in size only to Germany and located in a much less hospitable part of the world. It may well be that the long-term cost of protecting the Falklands, and the Islands' lack of economic viability, will encourage some settlement with Argentina. If not, then the garrison will have to be maintained out of the defence budget.

PRIORITIES

The battle for defence resources, which appeared to have been settled decisively against the Navy in 1981, may not only be refought but another turn of the budgetary screw may force it to be even more intense. Before considering the revisionist critique that argues for a reversal of priorities in the conventional area, we will consider the possible relevance of the Falklands to the argument for a reversal of priorities between conventional and nuclear forces.

Only CND appears to believe that any conclusions can be drawn from the fact that Polaris was irrelevant to the Falklands War. Given reports of Argentine work on nuclear weapons, those searching for scenarios to justify a British nuclear force might find one in some horrific twist to a future Falklands War. In general, however, the strategic issues in the Trident debate remain the same as before. If my analysis is correct concerning the financial pressures, then it may be that the factors working against Trident will intensify. It will never be the case that money released by abandoning Trident will support for long substantial conventional forces. The government has suggested that future Soviet leaders are more likely to be deterred by an invulnerable second strike SLBM force than by 'two additional armoured divisions with 300 extra tanks', given that the Warsaw Pact already outnumbers NATO in tanks by some 30 000.[14] Mr Silkin, for the Opposition, has spoken of two dozen carriers or fifty frigates, which looks fine until one considers recurring operational and manpower costs, which would soon dwarf capital expenditure.[15] It is also the case that, in the short term, expenditure on Trident is not sufficiently high for its cancellation to provide substantial savings. However, the picture may look a lot different later on in the decade, as the government of the day faces the budgetary crisis postulated earlier in this article just as the main burden of Trident expenditure begins to hit the defence budget.

This question of short-term savings has also helped to save BAOR in the past. Large-scale reductions of forces would cost money in the short term because of the need to either make men redundant or build new barracks. If they are to be accommodated in Britain, yet still assigned to Germany, then there would be the question of maintaining facilities and pre-positioned stocks in Germany. Nevertheless, after a few years, there could be significant savings and there would be immediate benefits in terms of the balance of payments. A sharp deterioration in the value of the pound against the mark would substantially alter the financial considerations. It is not really good enough to justify BAOR simply on the basis of the perverse short-term impact on expenditure of attempting to scale it down.

There are both military and political arguments to support BAOR. The military arguments point to the Soviet preoccupation with Central Europe and its build-up of arms facing NATO, and the value of forces-in-being. The Navy may be vital if reserves are to reach the front-line, but only if the front-line can hold long enough for the battle not to have been lost by the time the reserves arrive. The political arguments turn on the symbolic importance of a British contribution to the defence of Germany by other members of NATO. It may be that a cut-back of, say, 20 000 of the 55 000 troops could be tolerated, but less so if this triggered a proportionate US response. There are once again powerful political pressures building up in Washington for cutting back US forces in Europe. Many Senators would be anxious to follow a British example.

The revisionist case has also rested on a political assessment – of the ease with which an understanding could be reached with the allies on shifting the main burden of Britain's defence effort and of the character of the contemporary Soviet threat which makes it necessary to look beyond Europe to other potential trouble-spots. For those of this opinion, the Falklands War added another argument: the Navy is the only service with the ability to carry a substantial force to another part of the globe to respond to unexpected threats.

THE 'LESSONS' OF THE FALKLANDS

This brings us to the 'lessons' of the Falklands.[16] There was undoubtedly much discovered about the performance of individual
weapons or types of command structure and about the validity of
peacetime training and tactical analysis. Our concern here is with
whether there are any lessons to guide defence policy at a more
fundamental level.

There is a tendency to look at any conflict for pointers to some
decisive trend in modern warfare – for example, demonstrating that a
particular category of weapon is on the ascendancy. The Falklands War
did confirm suspicions of the vulnerability of the surface fleet to almost
any kind of air attack. However, it is probably unwise to generalise too
much from the experience: there are too many specific factors of
geography, climate and terrain and too many variations in qualities and
capabilities for confident statements. It was not always the advanced
weapons that did the damage – much was done with machine-guns and
gravity bombs. Where technical edge was important was in coping with
the most lethal instruments of the modern offence: hunter-killer
submarines (SSNs) and aircraft with stand-off ground-attack missiles.
The relevant equations involve capacities for detection, interception and
protection. The one dramatic use of torpedoes from a submarine (the
sinking of the Argentine cruiser *General Belgrano*) demonstrated that
the Argentine Navy had none of these capacities when facing SSNs, and
so thereafter it prudently stayed in port. The British had something in
each capacity for dealing with aircraft, with the major deficiency being in
detection (early warning). This was sufficient to avoid disaster but not
enough to avoid severe casualties.

The most interesting 'lessons' are in the reminder of how important
the factors of location, terrain and climate remain and how decisive the
human factor can be. It is a reminder not to get overawed by lists of
forces purporting to represent a military balance (or imbalance) or by
'laws' that dictate the proper ratios of attacking to defending forces if
the former is to succeed. We were shown what can be achieved by
training, physical stamina and tactical ingenuity. The war, therefore, did
not signal a revolution in warfare. Indeed, it is hard to imagine under
current conditions a less revolutionary war!

Nor is there any reason to suggest that a new pattern is in the process
of being set at the level of grand strategy. It certainly represented a break
in the pattern of recent British campaigns. Despite a common view that
British forces have been reasonably idle since Suez, except for Northern

Ireland, they have, in fact, been quite busy – Northern Ireland represents a continuation of the sort of campaigns with which the Army had already become familiar. These campaigns – in Kenya, Cyprus, Aden and Borneo – had involved intervention on behalf of civil authorities in conflicts that have typically been highly charged politically. The enemy has had to be found in jungles or separated out from the civilian population. Casualties have often been severe but sustained in dribs and drabs over time rather than in single engagements.

By contrast, the Falklands War was short and sharp, with comparatively distinct and unambiguous political and military dimensions. The enemy was of a sort almost designed to secure maximum political consensus in Westminster; a white, fascistic military dictatorship with reasonably sophisticated forces, whose only powerful friend was more friendly with Britain. At issue was British territory and all the symbolism of sovereignty rather than something vaguely referred to as 'vital interests'. Allies helped, but this was a national matter and was dealt with by national means. In the fighting itself, civilians only became a complicating factor towards the end, and then much less than had been feared. For both sides, the war had to be limited, not only because for neither was the survival of the nation at stake, but also because of geography. Argentina was fighting at the limit of its air range and could not pour extra men and equipment into the conflict. Britain was even more constrained by range and the size of the available task force. This was never going to turn into a prolonged war of attrition.

It was, therefore, a war that Britain had to fight alone because only British interests were involved and, because it was inherently limited, Britain could fight alone. It supports the view that one must always prepare for the unexpected because trouble can pop up anywhere, yet on reflection it is hard to imagine many other circumstances in which Britain would be so uniquely implicated in such an unusually limited and winnable war. To the extent that such circumstances can be imagined, they involve the Caribbean and Latin America where are to be found most of the remaining territories administered by Britain, as well as Belize on which a garrison remains after independence to help defend it against Guatemala.

THE REVISIONIST CASE

To what extent, therefore, can the case against the 1981 Defence Review draw on the Falklands War for compelling arguments? The case against the 1981 Review has not, on the whole, been based on a fear of the unexpected but on an assessment of the Soviet threat: that through the expansion of its own Navy, the USSR is in a position to threaten not only NATO's supply routes across the Atlantic but also the vital oil supply routes from the Gulf to the West. The preoccupation is with the Indian Ocean rather than the South Atlantic, with the USSR rather than with adventurist Juntas, and with threats to the West as a whole rather than just to Britain.

The Falklands War gives no support to this case. The importance of the images of 'Britishness' evoked by the assault on the Islands and the sending of the Task Force raise questions as to the ease with which there could be a similar rallying of support to send men to Arabia to keep oil flowing. The extent to which sending such a force would be absolutely dependent on concerted action with our allies has implications for force requirements. A point can still be made about the flexibility of navies but not too much. As a concession to this global view of the threat, *Invincible* and other ships vital to the success of the Task Force were destined to travel off to the Indian Ocean after Easter 1982 to 'show the flag'. If General Galtieri had delayed a little, the assembly of the Task Force would have taken much longer and it would have arrived in even more inclement weather. The delay might well have been decisive.

The vital role of the Navy in carrying to the South Atlantic the wherewithal to retake the Islands would not necessarily be duplicated in other conflicts. In more land-locked conflicts, it would be necessary to rely on RAF transport or, more likely, US transports. Moreover, the war leaves substantial anxieties concerning the vulnerability of the surface fleet. With the exception of the few Exocets, the Argentine Air Force was not particularly well prepared for anti-ship operations. By dint of the bravery of the pilots as much as the quality of the weapons, they were able to score a number of hits. If their bombs had exploded when they ought to have done, the consequences could have been disastrous. The undoubted British successes against the Argentine Air Force cannot hide the fact that this was by no means the most advanced threat the Royal Navy must prepare to meet, nor that the two Type 42 Destroyers lost were advanced in design and assigned to air defence roles.

In the USA, the Secretary of the Navy, John Lehman, has countered arguments against his massive naval shipbuilding programme by arguing that his ships would never be so vulnerable. The reason, he explains, is the extended air cover to be provided by the large *Nimitz*-class carriers. It is probably the case that, with more aircraft of longer range than the Sea Harriers with the Task Force, casualties could have been severely reduced. But this is of little comfort to the Royal Navy. The last large aircraft carrier, HMS *Ark Royal*, left service in 1979. Whatever changes in direction are achieved in the British defence budget, there will be no room for the £2 billion apiece *Nimitz*-class carriers. The options for numbers of destroyers and frigates are within the range of forty, as envisaged in 1981, and possibly some sixty to seventy by 1990 if the Royal Navy was extremely lucky. Whatever the decisions of the next few years, there will be severe limits in the future to the tasks that the Royal Navy can take on without the benefit of either land-based air cover or the forces of allies. For the Navy the answer is therefore not to allow its supporters to exaggerate its potential flexibility or independence of action, but to stress what it can do when working with the navies of our allies.

The Falklands War has opened up the debate concerning the balance of Britain's military capabilities, and has disturbed the financial background to that debate. I have argued in this chapter that it does not provide in itself any reason for changing the basic direction of British defence policy, which is not to say that there are no reasons for such a change. One unhelpful after-effect of the war is that a certain unreality may be entering the debate as to what Britain can achieve alone in the military sphere. The benefits of alliance are being taken too lightly. It may be that Britain's allies would welcome a greater stress on maritime forces, even at the expense of BAOR. It may be wise to explore this possibility, though the evidence suggests that the allies share the 1981 view of Britain's defence priorities. The allies may also want to know if we expect comparable distractions to the Falklands in the future. There would be no justification for a series of unilateral measures taken in the belief that, as an island with a fine maritime tradition, we know how to look after ourselves without the help of others.

NOTES

1. An earlier version of this chapter appeared in *The World Today* (September 1982).
2. War was not officially declared as is now normally the case. The desire to avoid the full legal and political implications of a declaration of war led to the extensive use of euphemisms to describe the conflict. What happened clearly *was* a war, if the term is to have any useful meaning at all, and that is how we shall describe it.
3. By way of illustration, this financial year (1982–3) will be the first since

1968–9 when expenditure on defence is higher than that on education. *The Government's Expenditure Plans, 1982–83 to 1984–85*, Cmnd 8494-II, March 1982, pp. 91–2.

4. *The United Kingdom Defence Programme: The Way Forward*, Cmnd 8288, June 1981.

5. *Hansard*, 17 March 1981.

6. Statements on the Defence Estimates 1981, Cmnd 8212-I, April 1982, pp. 30, 32.

7. See my analysis of the Trident II decision appended to First Special Report from the Defence Committee Session 1981–2, *Strategic Nuclear Weapons Policy*, HC266, April 1981.

8. In fact, of the forty-two warships deployed in the task force, only six were on the disposal list. *Hansard*, col. 236, 6 July 1982.

9. Conservative MPs with sea-faring constituencies are to the fore of the revisionist ranks. See, for example, the article by Alan Clark, MP for Plymouth, in *The Times*, 10 July 1982. See also the series of editorials entitled 'No end of a lesson' in *The Times*, 2–5 November 1982, and a response by David Watt on 12 November. There is also a distinct Gaullist strand in the opposition to BAOR. See the book by Michael Chichester and John Wilkinson, MP, *The Uncertain Ally: British Defence Policy, 1960–1990* (London: Gower, 1982). Wilkinson became Parliamentary Private Secretary to the Secretary of Defence, which is curious in that his book was by and large an attack on Mr Nott's policies. An earlier version of the anti-BAOR case is found in James Bellini and Geoffrey Pattie, *A New World Role for the Medium Power* (London: Royal United Services Institute, 1977). Mr Pattie is now Under-Secretary of State for Defence Procurement.

10. In the Parliamentary debate on the Defence Estimates, the former Prime Minister, James Callaghan, observed approvingly, 'When I listen to my own Front Bench, I begin to feel that we are becoming a Navy party', to which the Front Bench Defence Spokesman, John Silkin, replied 'We are.' *Hansard*, col. 176, 6 July 1982. The only senior Labour MP to speak against this trend was Dr John Gilbert, a former Deputy Secretary of Defence.

11. See Bridget Bloom, 'Realities behind the rhetoric', *The Financial Times*, 18 November 1982.

12. Secretary of State for Defence, *The Falklands Campaign: The Lessons*, Cmnd 8758, December 1982.

13. For a contrary appreciation of the White Paper, see David Greenwood, 'Don't be fooled by the White Paper', *The Sunday Times*, 19 December 1982. Greenwood argues that: 'All that is involved is adjustment of the programme for the short-to-medium term and *not* a radical reordering of priorities'. That is certainly the government's view, but the cumulative impact of the adjustments and the fact that much may have happened politically and economically before the adjustment back to the 1981 baseline, gives them greater significance. However, it is important to note that without new warship orders quite soon, the age of the hulls could force the numbers downwards.

14. *Statement on the Defence Estimates, 1982*, Cmnd 8528-I, June 1981, p. 3. The government may be overstating its case here. Elsewhere in the Defence White Paper it takes pride in the number of manned tanks in Germany rising

from 469 to 590 since 1979 (p. 9), but the derisory way it talks of an extra 300 provides argument for those questioning existing force levels in Germany. If it makes little point to have 900, why bother to have 600?

15. *Hansard*, col. 1076, 1 July 1982.
16. I have dealt with questions relating to the actual conduct of the war in more detail in 'The War of the Falkland Islands, 1982', *Foreign Affairs*, vol. 61, no. 1, Fall 1982.

3 Getting Defence Priorities Right

FIELD-MARSHAL LORD CARVER

For centuries the basis for the protection of the interests of Britain has been the need to ensure that the continent of Europe is not dominated by a power that is unfriendly towards us. That was the basis of opposition to France in the time of Louis XIV and XV and of Napoleon Bonaparte, and to Germany under Kaiser Wilhelm II and Hitler. It is the fundamental reason why we welcomed the foundation of NATO, the threat from Germany having been replaced by that from the Soviet Union. Throughout our history a rival view of the priority for our strategy has been urged: that we should turn our backs on the continent and concentrate our efforts on securing trading advantage and access to raw materials across the oceans, in the Pacific and Indian Oceans, the South and Western Atlantic. That strategy brought some significant successes, as well as some notable failures; but it has never been able to preserve our fundamental interests and security, if alliances on the continent of Europe have failed us.

Today we are much more vulnerable than in previous periods, both because modern weapons have reduced the Channel to the equivalent of a small ditch, and also because we have become much more dependent on supplies from overseas, not just for our prosperity, but for our very existence, while our economy has withered to a degree which makes us less capable of providing for our own security. We never could stand alone, but the strength of our economy relative to that of other European nations made it possible for us to subsidise their war effort, while limiting our own. It is as well to remember that, of the 56 000 soldiers who were led to victory at Blenheim by Marlborough and Eugène, only 9000 were British, and, of the 170 000 under Wellington and Blücher at Waterloo, 24 000 only were British, and many of the latter were Irish. In the 1980s we cannot subsidise our allies, and must therefore make an appropriate contribution ourselves.

But we must face the reality that the cost of the strategy of keeping Europe friendly to us has been high. In terms both of casualties and of the effect on our economy, the two World Wars of the century cost us a great deal. We have recovered from them, although not to the same position that we held relative to other nations. That is particularly true of the Second World War. We would be ruined, as would the rest of Europe, by another war of the same kind. The Yom Kippur Arab–Israel war of 1973 and the recent fighting in the Lebanon have brought home to us the destructiveness of modern conventional weapons. But far more sinister than that is the existence of nuclear weapons. If they were used – and there are thousands of them on both sides in Europe – we should not recover. A process that resulted in their use on this country and in Europe generally could not be called defence or security.

We must therefore prevent such a war from taking place: that must be our first priority. There are fundamentally two approaches as to how this can be achieved. One is to balance the power and presence of the armed forces of the Soviet Union in Europe by the presence of American armed forces in addition to West European, at the same time balancing the Soviet nuclear armoury with the American. The other approach is to try and make Europe west of Russia's frontier as neutral as possible, getting rid of the armed forces, conventional and nuclear, of the two giant powers from that area.

Those who advocate the latter maintain that there is no potential *casus belli* between the states west of Russia's border, and that, if only the armed forces of the great rivals in the cold war were to keep out of the area, all would be sweetness and light. The more extreme exponents of this view maintain that, in that event, the only armed forces that those nations would then need, if any at all, would be ones that were sufficient to deal with the possibility of internal unrest. That view – even the less extreme version – seems to me to be unrealistically naive. There are a great many potential sources of dispute, traditional, racial, material and political, between the nation-states west of Russia, and between them and Russia, which could not only lead to war between them, but, in the absence of the forces of the USA, to intervention by the Soviet Union in order to see that the dispute was resolved in a way that suited her interests. The division of Germany is an obvious one: recent events in Poland and their repercussions in neighbouring nations, including within the Soviet Union, clearly point to another source.

Less-starry-eyed supporters of US–Soviet disengagement from

Europe recognise this, but believe it can be insured against by the nations having armed forces of the Swiss or Swedish model, or by relying on some form of home guard. Others suggest reliance on guerrilla warfare, and others on non-violent or passive resistance. Armed forces of the Swiss or Swedish type (they are not the same), particularly if supplemented by a form of home guard, might be effective in deterring, or, if that failed, containing – even perhaps defeating – an incursion by a neighbouring nation of similar size, using the same type of forces; but none of these solutions would deter or could contain, certainly not defeat, the immensely strong armed forces of the Soviet Union, which would not be inhibited in their use by any sensitivity to international or domestic opinion. Reliance on guerrilla warfare or armed resistance movements would not only be ineffective against their forces, but carries with it the grave disadvantage that it tears a nation apart and causes great hardship and suffering to the populace, caught between the two sides and under pressure from both. The supporters of passive resistance point to what they claim as its success against the British in India, and against the German occupation in certain countries in the Second World War, notably Norway, as well as in earlier times within the Ottoman and Austro-Hungarian Empires. But, although it helped to preserve national identity and culture, in no case did it force the occupying power to leave. It has not achieved that in Afghanistan.

There are those who recognise these realities, but would still like to see Western Europe defend itself without the presence of American forces, some of them believing that, with their departure, the Soviet Union could be persuaded to withdraw its forces into Russia, and that, without nuclear weapons Western Europe would no longer be a potential target for Soviet nuclear attack. Others, who share the same wish, believe that, even if Soviet troops remained east of the Iron Curtain, a combination of British and French nuclear deterrence and the possible return of US forces in the form of a 'rapid deployment force' would suffice to prevent war. In favour of the former it can be argued that one of the principal aims of the Soviet Union for many years has been to get rid of US forces in Europe, and that, if they went, she would withdraw hers to Russia. But the principal purpose of her forces between the Iron Curtain and her frontiers is to ensure that the countries within that zone remain closely linked to her and protect the mother country against the possibility of any recurrence of 1812 or 1941. She is most unlikely to withdraw them voluntarily, and, even if she did as part of a bargain to ensure the removal of US forces, there would be nothing to prevent her, as has already been pointed out, from returning swiftly if events looked like moving in a direction that she did not like.

In answer to the latter view, although it is true that, in terms of manpower and gross domestic product, the European members of NATO, including France, could provide conventional forces which should suffice to deter any Soviet aggression across the Iron Curtain, one has to consider what the chances are of its happening. The links that bind the European members of NATO together are not especially strong, in several cases weaker than the links each separate nation has with the USA. From the moment that it appeared that the decision had been made, or was likely to be made, to withdraw US forces, the tendency would almost certainly be for the different European members of NATO to look different ways. Norway and Denmark would almost certainly opt to join Sweden in a Scandinavian neutral block; France would emphasise her independence; Spain and Portugal would seek a bilateral arrangement with the USA, as would probably Turkey also. Greece and Italy might opt for a neutral stance. The key country is the Federal Republic of Germany. The American link has been of especial importance to her. If it were broken, she would almost certainly look eastward, for an accommodation with the Soviet Union in a new *Ostpolitik*. Divided and neutered, the rest of Western Europe would inevitably drift in that direction also.

The possession by Britain and France of their independent nuclear forces is not likely to convince their European colleagues to stick together and face the armed might of the Soviet Union under the protection of that umbrella. If they had had doubts about whether the Soviet Union would be deterred from aggression, when it would immediately have involved her in hostilities against the USA with its vast nuclear arsenal, how much greater would be their doubts if it clearly did not? It would then involve the Soviet Union in hostilities with Britain, if she maintained her forces on the continent, but doubtfully with France. If they had feared that the USA might not risk nuclear retaliation on its own country by using its nuclear weapons in defence of Norway, Germany or Turkey, would they not reasonably fear that Britain and France would be actuated by the same motive? The argument that the British Government uses is that although the Russians might doubt whether the USA would use its nuclear weapons (in spite of the fact that its forces on land, in the air, and presumably at sea also, were involved), they would have no such doubts about the British because they are Europeans. This has never seemed to me to be convincing. Britain is relatively much more vulnerable to nuclear attack than either the USA or the USSR, and it would be absolute folly for her to initiate a nuclear exchange. The Soviet Union would certainly have reason to doubt whether France would start a nuclear war, as it has often been stated as her policy that she would not do so unless directly attacked herself. As to reliance on the return of US forces by air and sea in an emergency, few European members of NATO are likely to have much confidence that, even if they did return, they could do so in time to prevent the Soviet forces from occupying most of Western Europe before they arrived. A war of liberation would not then be an experience to be welcomed, even if it were likely to be successful.

All these considerations lead one to the conclusion that the essential ingredient to prevent the recurrence of war in Europe is the presence of US armed forces in the Western half of it. This is not only, nor even principally, because of the additional strength in conventional land, air and naval forces that she provides, but because it integrates the power of the USA in all its forms into the defence of Western Europe; its political and economic power and the power of its armed forces, conventional and nuclear. The physical presence of the former on this side of the Atlantic is of much greater significance than that of the latter. The significance of the respective nuclear armouries of the USA and the USSR, since the latter acquired the capability to retaliate at every level, lies now solely in the fact that they deter these two giants from fighting each other, and if that were tragically to fail, from using nuclear weapons against each other. As long as both are clearly and physically linked to the security of Europe, the USA west and the USSR east of the Iron Curtain, this mutual deterrence against war keeps Europe at peace, rigid, anomalous and unpleasant as it may be for many people, particularly for those east of the Iron Curtain.

It is not necessary for other European countries to have their own independent nuclear weapons to buttress these two pillars of security – the presence of US forces, and the fact that the USA has a powerful nuclear arsenal, which includes an invulnerable retaliatory force in her ballistic missile submarines. But it is very necessary for the Europeans to have adequate conventional armed forces, particularly land and air, for two good reasons. The first is to persuade the Americans that they should keep significant land and air forces based in Europe; that they stand a chance of success, and are worth reinforcing in an emergency; and that the Europeans are carrying their fair share of the burden. The second is that, if the mutual nuclear deterrent to war were to fail, it is of vital importance to contain any military operations, bring them to a halt and initiate negotiations, before either side is tempted to use nuclear weapons to redress what it sees as an unfavourable or hopeless conventional warfare situation.

For it would not redress it. Whatever assumptions one may make as to the limits that it might be possible to achieve in a nuclear exchange, on the assumption that both sides use approximately the same number and type of weapons, NATO is almost certain to end up worse off than the Warsaw Pact. This is partly because the population of Western Europe is concentrated in a smaller area in larger cities and conurbations than that east of the Iron Curtain; partly because its armed forces are dependent on fewer and more vulnerable installations, and partly because the Warsaw Pact's total available forces, certainly armies, are much larger. Even if the damage inflicted on the armed forces of both sides by the exchange is equal (and it is likely to be greater to NATO's), the Warsaw Pact will be left with more troops when it is all over.

The West would therefore not avert a conventional defeat by initiating a nuclear exchange: it would merely suffer a nuclear defeat on top of a conventional one. The argument used by those who favour NATO's current nuclear policy of 'flexible response' is that the shock of introducing the weapon in a limited way would bring the other side to its senses and cause them to stop and parley for fear of further escalation, and that, as the war had been embarked upon, it is assumed, in order to extend Soviet power and influence over Western Europe, they would not wish to ruin the area in the process. But these somewhat specious arguments must be balanced against the repeated Russian assertions that, once nuclear weapons were used, they would exercise no limitations and go all out to emerge better off than NATO when it was all over, grim as the state of Europe and the whole Northern Hemisphere would then be. To initiate the use of nuclear weapons on the assumption either that the other side would not reply in kind at all, or would do so in such a limited way as not to inflict total disaster on Western Europe and Britain in particular, would be totally irresponsible. To threaten to do so, and to train one's forces on the assumption that almost as soon as things go wrong they can assume that nuclear weapons will be used, is as misguided as it is dangerous. To act on the assumption that one can compensate for an inadequacy in conventional forces by having nuclear weapons available, up to the scale from artillery shells to intercontinental ballistic missiles, is the height of folly. Nevertheless that is what NATO's European members have done for the last thirty years, in spite of pressure on them by influential Americans like Robert McNamara and Henry Kissinger to shake themselves free from that illusion.

The first priority for NATO therefore is to improve the capability of the conventional forces that its European members contribute to the Alliance, and for Britain that means the army and air force that we station on the continent, with all that is necessary to see that they are made fully operational in a period of tension which threatens the possibility of war. It is only such forces that can stand guard as a deterrent and warning to the Warsaw Pact and a source of confidence to our allies, European and North American, encouraging them to make adequate contributions themselves. To withdraw our army and air force from the continent, breaking the pledge we made in 1954, which made possible the rearmament of Germany and her entry into NATO, would be to court disaster.

However, no more in defence than in other fields can one allow a matter of the highest priority to override all other considerations. We have other interests, which, if not as fundamental as that of averting war in Europe, are nevertheless of great importance, and we have minor ones also which, if not essential to our security, yet need to be protected and if necessary fought for, as the Falkland Islands affair has shown. In this important category lie the integrity of the United Kingdom, threatened by events in Northern Ireland, and our great dependence on imports from overseas, notably oil from the Middle East and minerals from southern Africa, a dependence we share with the whole of the Western capitalist world. Our direct responsibility for territories overseas has dwindled to a handful, and their security is not a major issue in our defence planning.

The major issue is often posed as the choice between a maritime and a continental strategy. It has already been argued that we must not abandon a continental strategy, as the highest priority in our defence, but we cannot abandon a maritime strategy either. The difficult question to answer is what that strategy should be and how it should be implemented. One must first consider the part that maritime warfare has to play in the defence of Europe. It is clear that if the Russian navy were free to operate unchallenged in the Mediterranean, the Baltic, the North Sea and the North Atlantic, as well as in oceans further afield, the Soviet Union could bring Western Europe to its knees without facing the risks involved in a land/air war, with its greater danger of escalation to a nuclear exchange. But if her navy is liable to be opposed, on, above and below the surface of the sea, it would be imprudent in the extreme for her to initiate a war at sea anywhere in the oceans of the world, unless she were prepared to face war in the other elements at the same time. She would merely have given clear warning of her aggressive intentions, provoking the West to take all the steps necessary to meet aggression, which would deprive the Soviet Union of many of the military advantages that she normally enjoys. She would forfeit the invaluable asset of surprise. A degree of maritime warfare capability is therefore essential to the security of Europe. By geography and history Britain is best placed of all the European members of NATO to make a major contribution, but it must not be at the expense of an adequate contribution to her continental strategy, bearing in mind the limitations placed by the economy on finance and by voluntary recruitment on manpower, and the political factors that determine both.

The space covered by the sea is vast. Navies, even the largest ones, are very small in relation to that space: anyone who has tried to find a ship at sea away from the main shipping routes realises this. Under the sea it is much more difficult. There is almost no theoretical limit to the desirable size of one's maritime warfare capability. Aircraft, whether based at sea or on land, are now an even more important element than ships and weapons like missiles and torpedoes fired directly from them. Unlike land forces, which can be related to the area of land to be defended and the size of force that the enemy can reasonably be expected to deploy in that area, navies, and the air forces associated with them, are much less easily related either to space or to the enemy's naval and air forces. To complicate the problem of assessing what NATO as a whole, and Britain in particular, should provide, there is a considerable difference of opinion about the relative parts that surface ships, submarines and aircraft should play. There is also debate about the balance between fixed- and rotary-wing aircraft, and the degree to which the former should be land-based or carrier-borne. In enclosed seas, like the Mediterranean, the Baltic and the Persian Gulf, and in open seas adjacent to land areas where there is no restriction on the stationing of land-based aircraft, the latter have many advantages over carrier-borne. With the increased use of in-flight refuelling, the objections to reliance on land-based aircraft to provide maritime air capability are much less convincing than they used to be. At the same time, the value of the VSTOL (Vertical or Short Take-off and Landing) aircraft, operated from platforms at sea, has been demonstrated in the Falkland Islands operation. The combination of the nuclear-powered submarine and the long-range maritime aircraft, the latter not just for reconnaissance patrols but also as a strike aircraft against both surface ships and submarines, clearly holds promise. In comparison, the area over which a surface ship and its weapon systems, even when extended by a helicopter, can bring its fire-power to bear is very limited and more subject to weather and the state of the sea. As a counter to the Soviet maritime threat in the waters surrounding Britain and the Eastern Atlantic, it is clear that this combination has a major part to play.

Those who wish to preserve a large surface fleet use two arguments: the need for frigates as convoy escorts; and the requirement to employ the navy to preserve our interests, including those we share with NATO and the Western capitalist world as a whole, in the South Atlantic, the Indian and the Pacific Oceans, for which it is suggested that aircraft carriers and amphibious assault ships, with the necessary afloat support and escorts, are required. The need for convoy escorts is certainly open to question. No responsible military man would deny the importance of moving American forces and their supplies across the Atlantic to Europe before hostilities have broken out. However, if they have not been moved before war begins, convoys and escorts for them are not needed. Successive NATO Supreme Commanders Atlantic (who are also commanders of the US Atlantic Fleet) have emphasised that, as soon as hostilities do start, it will be at least several weeks before the war against Soviet submarines has any chance of reaching a state in which, even with escorts, it would be possible to start sailing convoys. One has then to ask if it is possible to imagine a war in Europe between the Warsaw Pact and NATO lasting longer than that time. If it had started as a result of some misunderstanding or miscalculation, it would surely have been possible to bring it to a halt and start discussions: NATO's conventional forces would be adequate to contain that type of situation. If it had been a deliberate invasion, designed to overrun Europe, it would either have been halted or would have led to the situation in which one side or both contemplated using nuclear weapons. If that in itself did not bring matters to a halt, it would have made nonsense of plans to move supplies across the Atlantic, even if the forces to be supplied or reinforced, and the ports through which those supplies would have to move, still existed. Convoy escorts cannot therefore be regarded as a high priority.

A surface fleet of larger vessels, capable of operating as far afield as the Indian and Pacific Oceans, carrying its own air support, is an attractive idea at first sight; but one must ask what its objectives might be. It is generally thought of as a contribution to a principally American rapid deployment force, in order to assert Western access to the oil supplies of the Persian Gulf in the face of local opposition (possibly Iranian or Iraqi) perhaps backed by the Soviet Union. Even for the US Navy, with its huge aircraft-carriers, operating within the Gulf would be a hazardous business against a land-based air force, certainly that of the

Soviet Union. The addition of British Harrier-carriers and assault ships would make a negligible real military difference. The most rapidly deployed and effective type of force for such a purpose would be strike and reconnaissance aircraft, based on and operating forward from Akrotiri in Cyprus. The US Air Force would probably wish to fill existing airfields in the area to capacity with their own aircraft. There would seem to be little point in sending British soldiers or marines, except possibly to occupy the islets of Tumbs and Abu Musa, if the US Marines were fully occupied elsewhere.

Where else (except for a reconquest of the Falklands, if we let them go) would such a force be suitable? Not as a reinforcement to Hong Kong. It cannot be defended, if the Chinese choose to attack it, and it would take ages for such a force to get there. Do we contemplate reassertion of our sovereignty over the Seychelles or Mauritius, if their governments pursue policies hostile to our interests? That is hardly conceivable. We still have a commitment to defend Belize, although it is independent; as long as we have troops and aircraft there, reinforcement by air is much quicker and more effective than by sea, and with the sympathy of the USA and Canada, as is likely, there is no difficulty in getting there. A South Yemeni threat, backed by the Soviet Union, to close the Straits of Bab el Mandeb, the southern exit of the Red Sea, is one that is conjured up. But the French at Djibouti and the Americans at Diego Garcia are better placed than we are to deal with that, and our interests are not more directly threatened than theirs by such action. The Suez Canal route is no longer one of our 'vital interests'. So those who favour emphasis on a larger surface fleet, including Harrier-carriers and assault ships, fall back on the need for 'power projection'. But in these days of air transport, gunboat diplomacy, by appearing at a country's principal port after a long voyage, no longer exercises the influence that it did in the days of the Pitts or of Rudyard Kipling. Nuclear-powered submarines and long-range maritime aircraft, combined with land-based strike and reconnaissance aircraft, all of which are suitable for the defence of Western Europe, would be our most valuable contribution to any international force that, linked to the preponderant power of the USA, might be required to provide a military presence beyond the North Atlantic.

These principles should guide the future of the Royal Navy and the contribution of the Royal Air Force to maritime warfare. What of the latter's other tasks? What used to be called ADGB (Air Defence of Great Britain) has become a much more complicated problem than it was when that acronym was used at the time of the Battle of Britain.

Aircraft need not get nearer than perhaps 200 miles from their target in order to release a missile which may be directed to its destination by a variety of electronic or other means. It is not even necessary to use aircraft at all. The missile, ballistic or cruise, may be launched from the land or from a platform on or under the surface of the sea. A purely anti-aircraft system would not therefore, however much money was spent on it, provide a complete defence, and there is no practicable one against ballistic missiles. Point defence of vital installations on which our defence depends, that tries to destroy the missile or the warhead as it nears its target, would seem to cater for most forms of attack, but would not serve as a defence to large cities. To provide a high degree of defence over the whole country would be impossibly expensive. The problem has to be looked at in the light of the defence of the NATO area as a whole against air and missile attack.

As long as even the most rudimentary air defence is maintained, there is little to fear from enemy airborne troops. Even in the Second World War transport aircraft were so vulnerable to air defence systems that one could not contemplate airborne operations on any scale unless they had been almost totally suppressed. Today the relative vulnerability of transport aircraft, both to air-to-air and ground-to-air weapon systems, is far greater. Nor are seaborne expeditions and amphibious assaults sensible undertakings unless the enemy's airstrike force has been significantly reduced or is operating at its extreme range. Making provision against airborne or seaborne landings in the UK is therefore a waste of effort. As long as the defence of the NATO area holds, the threat is negligible. If it does not, territorial army battalions and home guards will be irrelevant.

The danger with air defence programmes is that one can spend a great deal of money to provide what is at best only a partial defence; but to fall back on the well-worn air-staff view that the best form of defence is attack raises almost as many problems. Attack of airfields, on which aircraft are kept in shelters, can be an unrewarding affair, particularly if it involves a deep penetration into the Warsaw Pact's air defences. As airfields are fixed targets, one often wonders why it is thought that aircraft and not missiles are the best method of delivering weapons to attack them.

The essence of air power is its flexibility. The more our aircraft can be designed and organised to switch from one role to another, capable of being deployed not only in the NATO area, but outside it also, the better value will be obtained from the very large sums of money that are devoted to them. Air equipment of all kinds (including that for the navy and the army) absorbs 43 per cent of the production element of the defence procurement programme for 1982–3. Not all aircraft, of course, are combat aircraft: some provide transport – fixed-wing and rotary. Those who favour 'power projection' outside the NATO area suggest an increase in airborne and airportable troops, and in the transport aircraft, fixed-wing and rotary, to take them to their destination and supply them on arrival. The objection to this is much the same as that applying to a naval rapid deployment force. Whereas the latter may have no problems in sailing to its objective, other than the long time it takes to get there, an air-transported force faces many problems, diplomatic and practical, in establishing and maintaining its route. One has only to think of what the problem would have been in the Falkland Islands operation if Ascension Island had not existed, or had not been British, or had not fortunately had a large US Air Force airfield built on it. The employment of a parachute-dropped force involves very large numbers of aircraft, the crews of which have to kept well trained in the technique. Before it can be dropped, the enemy's air defence has to be almost completely suppressed. When the force lands, it is immobile and weak in fire support, vulnerable and ineffective against a force equipped with heavy weapons, as Arnhem demonstrated. Such a force is not suitable for use in Europe, where the air and air defence situation would rule it out, as it also would an amphibious assault force. Britain's Royal Marines and airportable troops are a useful reinforcement for NATO's Northern Region, but one must be under no illusion that they could move to their destination by airdrop or amphibious assault after hostilities had started. They must get there first, and their specialised assault techniques, which it is valuable to preserve on a small scale, are not needed for that. Nor is helicopter lift an economic method of moving troops, weapons and stores on a European battlefield. Helicopters are very expensive machines – to buy, to train men to fly and to keep flying – susceptible to poor weather conditions and with a limited lift capability. They come into their own when surface methods of movement are exceptionally difficult, which they are not in central Europe. Present levels of fixed- and rotary-wing air transport are adequate to provide for a flexible general purpose force. It would be a mistake to increase them, when the requirement has diminished with the reduction in our defence commitments outside the NATO area.

It is those reductions that have led to the significant shrinkage in the size of the army, and in particular of the infantry, in the quarter of a century that has passed since the Suez fiasco. Not counting the reservists called up for that operation, it then stood at 400 000 men, almost equally divided between regulars and national servicemen. Its strength today is 158 000 and is due to be reduced to 135 000. In addition it contains about 9000 Gurkhas. The latter provides the bulk of the garrison of Hong Kong, for which an extra battalion is to be raised, and all of that in Brunei. Other overseas commitments, for which the principal need has been infantry battalions, are reduced to Gibraltar (one), the Sovereign Base Areas of Cyprus (one and a half) and Belize (one), to which the Falklands Islands has now been added, the implications of that affair no doubt affecting the declared intention to withdraw from Belize. Nevertheless, in spite of these considerable reductions, there are fifty-one regular British infantry battalions, thirty of which are in the UK, and thirty-eight Territorial Army ones; while there are only fifteen field and heavy artillery regiments (five in the UK) and eleven tank regiments, of which the two in England are training units, one providing a squadron of tanks in Berlin and the other a demonstration squadron at the School of Infantry. That is not a well-balanced army to fight an enemy who is wholly armoured. It has a disproportionately high number of infantry. But, as long as the commitment in Northern Ireland, actual or potential, continues, it could be imprudent to reduce further the regular infantry component. One of the influences that keeps the army in this traditional shape is the much greater cost of producing and maintaining the equipment for tank and artillery units. Assuming that in the near future it would not be possible to make a radical change in the balance between infantry and other arms, we must seek to make the best use of what is available, both regular and reserve.

The key to that could lie in a radical revision of the part to be played in the war plans of NATO's Central Region in Germany by reserve forces. At present, a high proportion – dangerously high – of the standing forces of all the allies stationed in Germany is allotted to a 'covering force', intended to delay an invading enemy until he reached the main line of resistance, held tenuously by almost all of the standing forces that remain. There are practically no reserves, the pious and unrealistic hope being held that the covering force will be able to withdraw through the main line and form a reserve. What is needed is to make more and better use of the reserve of German ex-conscripts, supplemented by a local home guard, formed from those whose reserve commitment has expired. They could take over responsibility for manning both delaying measures and the main line, especially the creation and control of obstacles. This could free more of the standing forces to form mobile reserves. Surplus infantry, regular and territorial, from Britain could be used to supplement these forces. All of them should be liberally supplied with man-portable anti-armour weapons. Such measures could make a significant improvement in NATO's conventional capability; but such forces cannot replace the mobile tank, armoured infantry and artillery units, which must be maintained, and should, if possible, be increased. The 1982 Defence White Paper compared the cost of the Trident system to replace Polaris as Britain's independent strategic nuclear strike force with that of providing two additional armoured divisions with 300 tanks, and poured scorn on the suggestion that the latter could have an equivalent deterrent effect against Soviet aggression. Considering that Trident is wholly superfluous to the American nuclear armoury, an increase of one-third in Britain's contribution to the conventional defence of West Germany would indeed have a very significant effect both on Soviet perception of NATO's determination to defend itself and the latter's confidence in its ability to do so.

Britain should waste no more money on nuclear weapon systems. There are already far too many nuclear warheads and methods of delivering them, many more than are needed to provide the mutual deterrent to war between the USA and the USSR. There are also more than are needed to prevent the use of nuclear weapons if deterrence should fail, which is all that the great nuclear arsenals now do. Constantly trying to match the numbers and types that the other side deploys, a striving for a numerical and technical superiority at every level, adds nothing to the deterrent effect and merely fuels a seemingly endless nuclear arms race. We should put our efforts behind trying to reverse this trend and encourage NATO to accept that all 'forward based systems', including Britain's, should be included in the arms control talks that have been initiated at Geneva. If progress to reduce the number of nuclear delivery systems and warheads could be helped by Britain giving up producing and maintaining her own warheads, she should do so. NATO should seriously consider giving up all dual-capable systems, particularly nuclear artillery. Stability would be helped by making a clear definition between those systems intended to deliver nuclear warheads and those intended to deliver conventional warheads.

If NATO is to continue to have land-based theatre nuclear systems, cruise missiles and Pershing IIs are preferable to aircraft, particularly the Pershings. Both types of missile are mobile and independent of fixed bases. They are therefore less of a temptation to pre-emptive attack. A declaration that aircraft would not be used to deliver nuclear weapons in Europe would help stability in the nuclear balance and itself be something of a confidence-building measure. Having given up our ballistic missile submarines when they had ceased to be operable as a long-range theatre nuclear system, and also our aircraft-delivered weapons, we could offer to take over all or part of the manning of whatever missiles it is agreed, as a result of the Geneva talks, are to be based in this country. In principle the Pershing II is preferable to the cruise missile, as the possibility of providing a defence against it is small. It is therefore less of a spur to a defence-*v*.-offence arms race. The fact that it takes a shorter time to reach its target than longer-range ballistic missiles seems to me irrelevant to the threat it poses.

It follows from what I have written about nuclear weapons generally and nuclear artillery in particular that I see no point in producing the enhanced radiation weapon (the neutron bomb). Its principal disadvantage is that it is even more likely to blur the distinction between conventional and nuclear weapons in the minds of those who wish to use the latter, than other types of warhead. It therefore makes it more likely that somebody will commit the unforgivable folly of thinking that it can be used without the danger of nuclear retaliation by the other side. Our minds should not be concentrated on the introduction of new types of warhead and delivery systems, but on reducing the grossly exaggerated number of both.

An effort to extend and achieve progress in measures of arms control, nuclear and conventional, should be accompanied by a determined and imaginative drive to develop confidence-building measures. A promising start was made in this field at the 1975 Helsinki Conference on Co-operation and Security in Europe. Results have been disappointing, and the French made some useful suggestions at the 1981 Madrid follow-up conference. The introduction of mutually tolerated satellite photography has been the most significant development. Real progress in this field could reduce the danger of exaggerated fears, misinterpretation of intentions and consequent escalation of tension which could lead to war, as it did in 1914, when neither side really intended or desired it. A degree of mutual trust, established by this means, is probably an essential prerequisite to effective arms control.

NATO's forces should now cease to train and think in terms of having recourse to nuclear weapons as soon as the conventional battle, in the air, on land or at sea, looks like going badly. They should concentrate their thoughts and efforts on how to improve the conventional capability of all their forces, regular and reserve, so that the Warsaw Pact will appreciate that NATO will fight to defend itself and is capable of doing so. NATO itself should have that confidence. If, unfortunately, that did not prevent the outbreak of a war in Europe, it could be brought under control quickly, without NATO having to threaten the use of nuclear weapons and face the terrible decision as to whether it would in fact do so. For to start a nuclear war would not be defence: it would be suicide.

4 Alternative Strategies: Strategy, Tactics and New Technology

MARSHAL OF THE ROYAL AIR FORCE LORD CAMERON

> Tactics and strategy are two activities mutually permeating each other in time and space, at the same time essentially different activities, the inner laws and mutual relations cannot be intelligible at all to the mind until a clear conception of the nature of each activity is established.
>
> Clausewitz

This book has as its aim the discussion of alternative strategies. This particular contribution is designed to cover technological developments and how they are affecting and will affect strategies, tactics, and equipment. The nature of each activity is dynamically affected by the surge of new technology. The actual changes are often delayed by the bureaucratic machine and the conservative thinking and conceptions of the armed forces whose ideas are often hindered by fighting the last war, or being led astray by a different type of operation such as Vietnam or, in some ways, the Falklands.

It is the fashion at the moment for defence analysts, commentators and politicians to centre their discussions on how to break the nuclear stalemate between the superpowers. This is admirable. However, obsessive concentration on 'no first use', 'nuclear free zones', 'unilateral nuclear disarmament' and the like result in too little attention being paid to the conventional option and its development. It should be remembered that 51 million people were killed in the Second World War by conventional weapons.

NATO strategy is one of flexible response. It was adopted in 1967 largely at American urging, because that nation wanted a longer period to make up its mind and assess the scene before putting American cities on the line as part of the strategic nuclear exchange in support of NATO. In essence, flexible response means forward defence – on the political urging of the Federal Republic of Germany. A conventional phase of fighting is to be maintained as long as possible so that reinforcements for NATO can arrive from America and elsewhere and battlefield nuclear weapons would be used first if NATO conventional forces can no longer hold the ring. Then the use of Long-Range Theatre Nuclear weapons would complete the ladder of escalation before the strategic nuclear exchange. That is the theory. It all sounds very clinical and there is much doubt on whether it will happen that way at all.

Henry Kissinger has said:

> NATO is reaching a point where the strategic assumptions on which it has been operating, the force structure that it has been generating and the joint policies it has been developing will be inadequate for the 1980s.

Well, what has changed to give rise to such a statement? First the Soviets have reached a state of nuclear parity and shortly marginal superiority to the USA. In 1967 there was little sign that the US would lose its nuclear dominance. Clearly the US President now has a different equation to consider when contemplating strategic nuclear action in support of Europe. Second, we have seen a degree change in the quality and offensive nature of the Soviet Armed Forces. They have always had a considerable quantitative superiority, but they have now added the quality equivalent to the West, including an aggressive posture. Third, NATO has always relied on large-scale reinforcement convoys coming to Europe by sea but not arriving until about thirty days after the start of operations. Because of the great improvement in the Soviet maritime capability these convoys will be extremely vulnerable and this vulnerability applies to transport aircraft as well as surface ships.

Fourth, the Soviets have so organised themselves that NATO is likely to get much less warning-time of attack compared with the lengthy period expected when flexible response was evolved. Depending, as we do, so much on reinforcements, there is a good deal of doubt whether they will arrive in time, or even at all. Last, the decade is seeing the introduction of a wide range of new technology to the military scene. Some aspects like electronics and 'precision-munitions' are going to have a profound effect on strategy and tactics.

For these reasons and others it is time flexible response was examined to see if it still stands up to the demanding criteria of the 1980s and beyond. It is the range of new technology and its effect on traditional military strategy, tactics and structures that will be the main subject of this chapter.

NEW TECHNOLOGY

It must first be asked whether the impact of new technology is evolutionary or revolutionary – a question that continues to exercise military thinkers. For two main reasons it seems to fall more into the revolutionary category. First, there have been many incremental improvements over a whole range of weapon technologies which, when taken together, add up to a most dramatic change in overall weapon effectiveness. Second, weapon technology is moving ahead so fast that concepts and tactics are being left behind. In certain areas of weapon technology we have already had a quantum jump in weapon effectiveness which merely gives a warning of what can eventually be achieved.

For these reasons there is a necessity for a full reappraisal of how the introduction of new technology is going to affect the future. Could some aspects of new technology radically alter concepts and tactics to the clear advantage of the Alliance? This is possible, but in certain circumstances it might be the Warsaw Pact who would benefit.

The first task therefore is to highlight some of the important characteristics and limitations of new generation weapons; to give a general indication of how they impinge on future concepts, tactics and resource allocation; and to conclude by posing some questions surrounding their application.

Also, as nuclear weapons form the touchstone of deterrent philosophy – and nothing is likely to replace them as the ultimate strategic weapon – the discussion is restricted to an examination of conventional weapon technology, since the wider aspects of a full war scenario, including consideration of chemical and biological weapons, would require more than this chapter.

HISTORICAL PERSPECTIVE

Many earlier attempts at crystal-gazing failed because those concerned did not recognise the full potential of new developments. For example, in 1937 a study on technological trends and national policy overlooked a number of military developments which included helicopters, jet engines, nuclear weapons, electronic computers, inertial navigation systems and rocket-powered missiles, all of which were operational within twenty years and the majority within a decade.

Many people in 1945 failed to anticipate ICBMs, men in space, solid-state electronics, to say nothing of micro-electronics and computers. However, the past difficulties in forecasting should not inhibit acceptance of the present challenge; rather it makes it all the more necessary to take a bold approach, though one should not underestimate the difficulties of the task.

From the military point of view technology has always been recognised – sometimes belatedly – as an important factor in warfare, and the technological prowess of opposing forces has often been critical in determining eventual victory or defeat. Also, of course, many of the more important technological developments have been fundamental in moulding political intentions and ambitions.

One of the main characteristics of new technology systems, in whatever historical perspective they are viewed, is that when introduced they provided an element of technological surprise. This, in fact, is true whether technology was applied in a new and formerly unforeseen direction, or to improve or upgrade the performance of an existing system. It is also true, of course, that existing technology can be used in radically new ways and still provide an element of technological surprise.

The key fact that emerges is that it is not just the existence of new technology itself that is relevant, but the recognition and awareness of its impact – and decisiveness in exploiting it. Throughout history there are many examples, from the long-bow to the tank, where victory in battle can be attributed to a technological innovation that had long been waiting for recognition and effective application.

An important conclusion that may be drawn from current technological progress is that the time/distance equation is becoming compressed, making tactical surprise both easier to achieve and more telling in its ultimate effect. This, in turn, places an enormous premium on rapid recognition and response. Such is the rate of advance that developments in weapon effectiveness are tending inevitably towards making the first battle decisive.

THE SOVIET POSITION

Since technological surprise and tactical innovation are major and complementary factors affecting the military balance, and are not the exclusive preserve of the Western powers, technological advances made by the Soviet Union must be closely monitored and their implications for the Alliance assessed with the greatest care.

Traditionally the Soviets have lagged behind the West in nearly all aspects of technology. However, this situation is changing, and changing rapidly, as the Soviets place greater importance on the advantages of technology – a situation brought into sharp focus by the late President Brezhnev's statement that progress made in the development of science and technology in competition (with the West) would be of such decisive significance that the issue had become of central economic and political importance. Particularly significant is the fact that Soviet R & D expenditure is still expanding and is currently more than twice that of the US and UK. With such concentration of effort progress is inevitable.

Although the Soviets are still lagging in several areas of technology, notably advanced electronic processes, in other fields such as charged particle devices, high energy physics and mobile ballistic missiles, their achievements owe nothing to the West. Thus the Soviets must not be underrated and, when assessing what damage new weapons and techniques can inflict on forces of the Warsaw Pact, it would be prudent to assume that their capability against the West will at least be comparable.

The potential for advanced technology to provide a destabilising factor in a carefully balanced strategic situation is significant. The West should therefore be prepared to use technology to exploit the enemy's weaknesses, in which context lead-time can be significant. This we have frequently failed to do for several reasons – often political.

AREAS OF CHANGE

ELECTRONICS REVOLUTION

In attempting to isolate developments in technology, few would dispute the importance of the electronics revolution. Advances in computer technology, data processing, information assimilation and dissemination, and micro-miniaturisation have given us the ability to design equipment that is light, cheap, rugged, reliable, but above all small enough to be of practical use.

Many examples could be used to illustrate this trend in electronics but a comparison of the computer in, for instance, the cancelled US Skybolt missile of 1960 with an equivalent system in a cruise missile is perhaps as good as any. Weight and power consumption have been reduced by a factor of 100 while speed of function has been increased some 200 times. Even more significant is the fact that costs have been reduced over this same period of twenty or so years to 1 per cent of the former level, and are continuing to fall for a constant capability. This is a most remarkable development cycle and one that appears likely to continue.

Permeating all theatres of conflict is the disruptive effect of electronic warfare. Reflecting Soviet Admiral Gorshkov's view that the next war will be won by the side which best exploits the electro-magnetic spectrum, the Soviets have developed an ECM capability vastly superior to the West. Nevertheless the West has a clear lead in micro-circuitry and data-processing techniques, and this is an asset that must not be squandered.

SURVEILLANCE

Historically one of the most difficult military tasks in war has been to locate the enemy. With the surveillance sensors now becoming available using radar, radio, infra-red, optical and other associated equipment from airborne and satellite vehicles, the movement of major military concentrations will be more easily detected and monitored. This will become increasingly significant in all environments, but particularly at sea where it will become extremely difficult for surface shipping to pass unobserved.

With continuing improvements in sensor resolution, target identification and monitoring on a much finer scale will be possible. This will affect tactics at sea and also in the land/air battle. In the sub-surface environment continuing developments in improving the sensitivity and selectivity of sensors, when allied to expanding and even more sophisticated data-handling techniques, suggests the possibility of the sea becoming increasingly translucent.

SPATIAL ORIENTATION

Until recently, one of the major factors limiting the effectiveness of a whole range of weapons systems such as strategic aircraft, ICBMs, submarines, and cruise missiles, has been the lack of absolute spatial orientation. It has not been possible to calculate target, launch-platform and weapon positions with sufficient accuracy to make optimum use of warhead capabilities. These limitations are now rapidly being overcome, and when, for instance, the Global Positioning System becomes operational, accuracies of 20 ft in latitude, longitude and altitude at intercontinental ranges are forecast. The ability to know one's absolute and relative position to this degree of accuracy will have a most profound effect on a number of current operational concepts.

No less dramatic are the developments that have taken place in the field of onboard inertial navigation and weapon-aiming systems. In the delivery and navigational capability of tactical and strategic aircraft, as well as in the performance of cruise missiles, the achievements of integral orientation systems are already clear. As equipments continue to reduce in size so the prospect of introducing this technology into other areas of military operations (such as tank forces) expands, and in all battle environments it will be imperative to be capable of fighting a full twenty-four-hour, all-weather battle. Such a change will have a particular effect on the land battle where human judgement and manpower availability are likely to be limiting factors in sustaining the intensity of operations.

WEAPON CHARACTERISTICS

The prime characteristic of the new generation of weapons is their high lethality. The stage is steadily being approached when, with certain weapons, a target that can be seen – and there will be many ways of seeing a target – can be hit. With the wide selection of weapon heads and delivery modes now available, a hit will almost certainly guarantee destruction.

Furthermore, a notable feature of new technology weapons is that accuracy of delivery need no longer be a function of range: a characteristic that allows considerable freedom of manoeuvre to the user. Also, the new generation of precision-guided munitions, or terminally-smart weapons, is cheap in terms of weapon effectiveness; many of them are virtually 'operator proof' in that they are self-contained; accuracy is not a function of operator skill; and they are sufficiently small to encourage high intensity use.

CHANGING DOCTRINES

SURVIVABILITY

With the ever-widening range of sensors becoming available, the means of detecting concentrations of men and equipment will be greatly simplified, and the need for concealment, deception and dispersal will be of paramount importance. Concentrations of men, vehicles, ships and aircraft will become easy targets. This points to a need for a large number of small and highly mobile formations. For similar reasons it will be unwise to concentrate a great deal of military value in one place, or in a single complex weapon system.

The overriding requirement will be to provide systems survivability, whether through physical protection, concealment or deception. But while dispersal of forces will serve to complicate the targeting problem, and hence aid survivability, it could also complicate, in some cases, the concentration of force for attack.

COMMAND AND CONTROL

As mentioned earlier, the hub of technology around which most of today's impressive developments revolve is that of applied electronics. The most obvious application for these developments has been in the area of Command and Control and Information Systems. As has been indicated, it is in the field of micro-electronics, data handling and synthesis of information that the West is ahead of Soviet technology. But the lead is not an unassailable one, and it must be assumed that the Soviet Union is capable of reaching comparability in its own micro-electronics industry which, in turn, could have profound implications for their overall capabilities.

The position has now been reached where it is possible to handle more and more information of ever greater complexity, over a wider area, at a faster rate, and with cheaper and cheaper equipments. Given this situation it is tempting to insist on the all-embracing system without pausing to apply objectivity to operational requirements. But the Alliance needs to determine what information is really required, by whom, in what detail, and in what time-scale, before plumping fully in this direction.

With the ability of commanders to involve themselves in distant conflicts at an ever-lowering level of command, the difference between command and control will need to be more clearly defined. Certainly the ability to side-step the accepted 'chain of command' has its apparent advantages in terms of resource allocation, but it would effectively stifle initiative and restrict flexibility at the lower levels, while, more importantly, over-control could hinder the timely use of high technology weapons.

Although the new generation weapons have a high lethality, their effective use is largely conditional upon accurate and up-to-date target information being available to the weapon operator. This will require a reappraisal of the resource allocation procedures currently employed. In fact, if command and control procedures are not adjusted to match the capabilities of the new weapons, then the latter are unlikely ever to realise their full potential.

This view will be particularly applicable to the timely provision of tactical target information to weapons that operate beyond visual range. This information may need to go direct from the sensor or surveillance system to the operator and perhaps only be monitored at an intermediate decision centre. The balance between the delegation of decision or the adoption of a highly centralised system of control is clearly a matter of fine judgement, though it is absolutely essential that the issue be correctly resolved. Pertinent to such consideration is the need to guard against any tendency to swamp commanders with a plethora of information with the consequential risk of delaying vital decisions. Additionally, whatever the theoretical attractions which centralised control may offer, total dependence on such a system could prove disastrous in the event of it breaking down or being severely impaired. The need for commanders at all levels to be trained and capable of fighting on, in accordance with broad directives, will remain of paramount importance.

LOGISTICS

Theoretically, because of the high lethality of each weapon, fewer will be required to destroy a fixed number of targets and it should be possible to make corresponding reductions in logistic and support requirements. The balance would come in assessing weapon requirements and hit-probabilities relative to the expected threat and specific target groups, and to provision stocks accordingly. However, while, in practice, the weight of munitions delivered to specific targets should be greatly reduced, the number of targets worthy of attack could multiply significantly. Equipment holdings and quantities of re-loads will therefore need to be carefully evaluated, taking into account system performance, operational degradation factors, and an allowance for unforeseen circumstances.

While improved weapon effectiveness should lead to a reduction in the weight and volume of ordnance to be moved from storage areas to the user, this benefit could be eroded by demands arising from the multiplicity of targets likely to be presented. But the ability to launch terminally-intelligent weapons from well to the rear of the battle zone should reduce the requirement for logistic supply and movement in the immediate battle area.

Although precision-guided munitions can be mass-produced, they are nevertheless highly sophisticated. They take time to manufacture and production rates cannot be altered arbitrarily. Thus, in any future conflict, one of the West's greatest historical strengths – the capability of its industrial base – may not have time to become a telling factor in the military balance.

Against these considerations must be set the vulnerability of storage depots and supply lines to attack by guided munitions. In this regard NATO would seem to be at greater risk with its large, complex and highly centralised storage and distribution structure, while its growing network of forward storage sites could well become no less vulnerable. A rearward and widely dispersed multi-plex storage system might be more appropriate to NATO's longer-term needs.

CHANGING ENVIRONMENTS

Having touched briefly on some of the military capabilities and implications of new technology weapons it will be logical to consider how NATO's operational concepts, tactics, equipments and force structures might be affected.

MARITIME

With the detection, identification and tracking of surface vessels becoming a relatively simple task, and with even well-defended ships becoming vulnerable to a growing range of target-locating and terminally-intelligent sea-skimming missiles, the presently accepted concept of surface fleet operations involving the projection and transfer of power by naval forces and their associated aircraft merits close review.

Certainly the large, highly expensive surface ship will present a very attractive target – as indeed it always has done. But new technology weapons have increased the magnitude of the threat and the vulnerability of this class of ship, with the result that the emphasis in future must surely be towards smaller ships in greater numbers. It should be added that some sort of aircraft carrier may have its place in the naval inventory, if it can be afforded, principally because of its flexibility in a variety of situations short of open conflict. But does it still have a credible role to play in all-out war against a major enemy?

The traditional constraining factors in the development of naval vessels have often been the conflicting requirements of range, speed and sea-keeping. Developments in hull-support technology, increased automation with reduced on-board maintenance, and the introduction of weapon systems of increasing range but decreasing dependence on launch platform stability seem bound to alter the relative importance of these interacting parameters, and hence lead to a change in ship construction and size.

Convoy techniques that served adequately in two previous wars were based on three particular factors: sustained convoy speed was higher than sustained submarine speed; the convoy could be operated as a defensive moving fortress having local sea control; and the whole convoy could elude the enemy by evasive manoeuvre. Satellite surveillance, long-range acoustics, stand-off weapons and high-speed nuclear submarines have eroded these factors, despite an almost doubling of convoy speed since Hitler's war. With the influence of new technology weapons running counter to the traditional roles of the surface ship, a review of future methods of undertaking reinforcement and resupply tasks would appear to be justified.

While traditional methods of submarine detection and monitoring have relied on acoustic sensors, the status quo was unlikely to remain indefinitely, but any breakthrough in non-acoustic detection methods, by either East or West, would be of incalculable strategic significance. While, in the shorter term, the balance of advantage lies with the submarine – and hence the emphasis must be towards sub-surface operations – in the longer term, and without international controls to guarantee the integrity of the sea, the West's dependence on this medium in the strategic equation must increasingly be questioned as technology develops.

Perhaps the greatest single perturbation in the evolution of maritime operations will stem from the significance of the modern mine. The Soviets have both massive stocks of mines and the ability to lay them and, in consequence, the approaches to naval bases and international choke-points could be denied the West. In contrast, NATO's countermeasure force is woefully inadequate.

In many respects the mine and new technology were designed for each other. Today's mine is not the ungainly spiked sphere of the last war but a weapon of tremendous sophistication and selectivity. Further advantages are that it can be deployed covertly, targeted selectively and controlled remotely, while the traditional international freedom of the seas facilitates its peacetime deployment.

With the dependence of NATO nations and many other countries of the world on free access to the seas, the Soviets have developed a capability of such potential that denial of the sea would have far-reaching consequences for these nations, but with only limited disadvantage to the Soviet Union.

An early review should be conducted into the desirability of making mining the subject of an international arms agreement. There is also a parallel and urgent need to review NATO mining policies, both offensive and defensive.

LAND/AIR

Technology will also fundamentally affect the land/air battle. New surveillance techniques will make it easier to monitor movement and hence give forewarning of enemy deployments, dispositions and strength. Against this must be weighed the lethality of new technology weapons and the need for forces, including headquarters, to be both small and mobile if they are to survive.

The Soviets have always had a considerable numerical tank superiority over NATO. The modernisation of the T64 and T72 and the active development of the T80 successor, with their greatly increased qualitative capabilities, indicate the continuing importance the Soviets place on tank warfare. This qualitative improvement, which is one of considerable degree, requires a reappraisal not only of NATO's tank and anti-tank capabilities and performance but also of the Alliance's tank and anti-armour concepts and tactics.

In tank evolution, developments in armour have stimulated improvements in fire-power, and vice versa, with mobility a greater or lesser bonus. The armour-*v*.-fire-power confrontation has inevitably been constrained by the two-dimensional, mainly frontal aspect of tank warfare. With terminally-smart weapons, thinking must now be in terms of all-round protection and survivability. Another potentially rewarding area is that of inhibiting mobility – and developments in environmental engineering technology against air-breathing engines could perhaps alter the shape of tomorrow's battlefield. Also, the great potential of the rapidly laid anti-tank mine could be a major factor while the traditional value of static anti-tank obstacles continues to be important.

Then there is the effect that new technology will have on expanding the time and weather aspects of the operation of some weapons systems. As has been mentioned earlier there is the possibility of vehicles using highly accurate navigational aids to extend their all-weather operating capability. Modern imaging devices will further assist this trend, and round-the-clock operations will become possible within human and logistic constraints.

A corollary to the manning problem is that many of the new technology weapons greatly enhance the role of the small unit, and often of the single soldier. Small or specialised units, such as the Soviet Diversionary Brigades, paratroop and helicopter forces, and units like the British Special Air Service, established for specific and elitist tasks, may have an increasingly important role to play. Organisations may need to be tailored to accomplish specialist roles at variance with the standard force groupings of today, such as Combat Teams and Battle Groups, which, in turn, rely on units of a uniform structure like the Battalion. It will also become necessary to think in terms of re-equipping men, with all that this implies in terms of training, tactics, reinforcement and reserve manpower.

The antithesis of the requirement for highly mobile and dispersed forces is NATO's current dependence on complex infrastructure, and in particular that necessary to support aircraft operations. A number of airfield denial weapon systems are already under development in the West and it must be assumed that the Soviets are following a similar line of development. Given the capability of modern delivery systems it is essential that dependence on the airfield complex, as known today, should be reduced. Though the NATO hardened-aircraft-shelter programme is now nearing completion and is a step forward in improving survivability, it is little more than a short-term palliative. Unless there is a move away from long concrete runways, the next air war may be much shorter than presently conceived with many serviceable aircraft remaining unusable on the ground.

It is not the intention of this chapter to develop requirements for the next generation of tactical combat aircraft though, in the light of the previous assertion, it appears axiomatic that this should have an ultra-short field take-off and landing performance, and be capable of operating from rudimentary surfaces. Indeed, serious consideration should be given to providing VSTOL characteristics for all new close-support, offensive and tactical transport aircraft.

AIR

Predominant characteristics of the new generation weapons are their growing self-sufficiency and autonomy. Until fairly recently air-to-ground weapons have been unguided and largely dependent on operator skill. From this it might be concluded that aircraft and the new weapons are mutually competitive.

New generation weapons will not render the aircraft obsolete; rather the two will become complementary. But there must be changes in concepts and tactics if the combined potential of both systems is to be fully realised. It is the ubiquity of 'air power' – and here the reference is to all air transit weapons, and not exclusively the aircraft – with its inherent mobility and speed of response that will underline its value in future conflicts.

With 'intelligence' built into the weapon rather than its parent aircraft, the latter should become the 'lifter' and 'carrier' of missiles and PGMs of increasing stand-off range, as well as being a highly mobile weapons-platform – analogous to the Army's indirect fire forces – for both offensive and defensive operations.

At the strategic level, continued improvements in the range and lift capability of transport aircraft are likely to become increasingly significant. The USA's support of Israel in the Yom Kippur war, and later the Soviet supply of major weapons systems to Ethiopia, and Afghanistan have clearly demonstrated the impact of air mobility on the conduct of future operations. With time at a premium, the importance of the air bridge from North America to Europe for reinforcement forces cannot be overstated. But the associated risks must be recognised, as with aircraft transiting the Atlantic in a wartime or reinforcement situation at three-minute intervals, the air bridge will be a most lucrative target for the stand-off missile whether launched from sub-surface, surface, or attack aircraft.

The role of the maritime patrol aircraft merits special mention. In its sea-surveillance role, operating over considerable distances, it is a most important adjunct to satellite systems. It has a formidable – and continually improving – detection and monitoring capability against submarines and, with new generation stand-off weapons, it will have enormous offensive potential against both surface and sub-surface forces. It will also be possible to give the next generation of maritime aircraft a useful self-protection capability. It is often forgotten that the maritime aircraft in the 1939–45 war sank more submarines than did surface forces. The air mining campaign also sank more surface ships than did Naval forces.

Speed of reaction, together with the ability to strike with weapons of comparable effectiveness to major surface forces, will confer on the increasingly long-range, multi-capability maritime aircraft a most vital role for the future. Whereas in the last war there was an airborne capability gap in mid-ocean, this need no longer be the case.

CHANGING POSTURES

QUALITY *v.* QUANTITY

Many studies have been carried out to determine the relative merits of quality *v.* quantity, but the simple model evolved by Lanchester[1] postulated quality as a linear force effectiveness parameter and quantity as a square factor. Thus a force that is half the size must be four times as effective to sustain victory; a force that is a third the size would need to be nine times as effective. This example vividly illustrates the significant increases in quality that are needed if numerical inferiority is to be offset.

But can the West afford new technology? Given present force asymmetries and the probability that the Warsaw Pact will continue to spare no effort in exploiting the technological opportunities available to them, the West cannot afford to retain out-of-date systems. However, in view of the enormous cost associated with some high technology areas and the pressures on defence budgets, priorities will need to be established and inefficiencies avoided. Difficult balances will have to be struck, not only between quality and quantity, but also between manpower and equipment. In the latter case, there will be areas where the need will be to equip men, and others where the emphasis will be on manning equipment.

THE STRATEGIC AND TACTICAL DILEMMA

Few of the new weapons currently under development conform readily to the accepted definition of strategic or tactical weapons, the cruise missile being a particularly good example. The cruise missile can carry both conventional and nuclear warheads; it has the range to attack both strategic and tactical targets; and it has the accuracy to attack, with a conventional warhead, targets that previously would have required a low-yield nuclear device.

In the air environment, the combination of stand-off weapons and aircraft of increasing range and performance give many of the new generation of offensive aircraft systems a capability at least matching the last generation of strategic bombers. Also, with available options for weapon-tailoring and -selectivity, collateral damage from the new generation of munitions will be greatly reduced. These factors combine to alter the political appreciation of the difference between strategic and tactical weapons while adding to the difficulty of differentiating between the two groups of weapons.

THE OFFENSIVE/DEFENSIVE CONUNDRUM

One of the prevailing beliefs underlying new technology weapons is that they tend to favour the defensive rather than the offensive situation. In a prepared defensive situation a combination of precision guided munitions (PGM) and area weapons will undoubtedly have a most telling effect. Surveillance sensors will provide warning of enemy strengths, dispositions and likely avenues of advance. Given full regard to concealment and deception, defensive positions may therefore be prepared and the full kill-probability of PGMs and area weapons brought to bear on an attacking force. In these circumstances, the advantages of new technology weapons unquestionably favour the defender. But – and the query is an absolutely vital one – are these assumptions valid against all likely contingencies?

The critical factors to be reviewed are the interaction of surprise, pre-emption, and weapon effectiveness. Surprise has always been a decisive factor in battle and its apparent force effectiveness has often been sufficient to overcome both numerically and qualitatively superior forces. But, in the past, surprise has not always been fully complemented by individual weapon characteristics. All too frequently a tactical victory has been achieved, but the strategic objectives have not. The emerging characteristics of high technology weapons alter the importance that should now be attached to these factors.

A compendium of changing military factors, principally the asymmetric military balance and changing weapon characteristics, have led to general acceptance that the minimum warning time of a possible Warsaw Pact offensive has been reduced to approximately forty-eight hours. However, despite all the sensors available through modern technology, only a few hours' warning of impending attack may be available. NATO's ability to sustain a pre-emptive attack by PGMs and area weapons on a wide range of interdiction, counter-air, command and control of air defence or similar high-value targets, and recover sufficiently to mount a cohesive counter-defence, could be reduced to nugatory proportions unless action is taken to minimise the effects of pre-emption.

All this points to the fact that the time for decision-making at the tactical level will be severely reduced. Fortunately developments in weapon system delivery accuracy and attendant reductions in collateral damage may reduce the political restrictions on the use of modern weapons. While currently it is generally acceptable for the delegation of military decision and response to be given at the rifle and bullet level, delegation criteria must be re-examined to reflect the potentialities of conventional PGMs.

CHANGING DIRECTION

One of the greatest paradoxes in the history of warfare is that developments in technology are often slow to be recognised and adopted by the military.

In a stable situation there is a natural reluctance to accept change, since hierarchies and organisations tend to thrive in a non-dynamic environment. A tendency develops to impede reform or, more generally, to channel reform into areas of least resistance. To exacerbate the situation further, new technology weapons rarely fit neatly into the established order of affairs and are hence all too frequently ignored, resisted, misunderstood or simply misused. As Admiral Mahan has noted:

> Changes in tactics have not only taken place after changes in weapons, which is necessarily the case, but the interval between such changes has been unduly long. This doubtless arises from the fact that changes in tactics have to overcome the inertia of a conservative class. It can be remedied only by a candid recognition of each change, by careful study of the power and limitations of the new ship or weapon, and by a consequent adaptation of the method of using it to the qualities it possesses, which constitutes its tactics. History shows that it is vain to hope that military men generally will be at pains to do this,

but that the one who does will go into battle with a great advantage – a lesson in itself of no mean value.[2]

Several of the new weapons becoming available cut tangentally across many of the currently accepted divisions of responsibility between the present grouping of functional services. When considering the use of stand-off weapons in the land battle, for instance, it is largely irrelevant whether they are launched from ground, air, sea or sub-surface platforms.

The danger is that, unless great care is taken to avoid the adoption of too parochial a position, a considerable conflict of single-Service interests could develop which, in turn, could delay, if not deny, the introduction of the new weapons. The Soviets, with their single grouping of forces, such as their strategic rocket forces, have long since recognised this principle. Alliance energies might best be directed towards becoming aim-orientated rather than means-orientated.

The prime characteristics of the new generation weapons are that they are swift, selective and deadly – attributes that have always favoured the pre-emptor. But NATO is a defensive alliance, and if new technology is not to tilt further the already adverse balance of power in Europe, NATO must not shrink from a radical reappraisal of its existing concepts.

In short, how can NATO use new technology to its advantage? Has it got right its balance of investment in manpower and equipment? Given the increasing vulnerability of the Atlantic air and sea bridges, should NATO be looking towards a different force posture with less reliance on reinforcement forces? Are we justified in adhering to traditional methods of aircraft operations, and should all future aircraft have a short take-off/short or vertical landing capability? Encompassing all military considerations is the requirement to get the Command and Control process correct; and there is the need for all-weather, all-arms, round-the-clock operations.

The solution may lie in using the characteristics of new technology systems to offset both numerical inferiority and reduced reaction time. In a peacetime situation, at whatever the prevailing level of tension, the full range of surveillance sensors will be available to give at least some tactical warning. Given the already-stated qualities of new technology weapons, the initial, instant, and automatic response to Soviet aggression would most effectively and economically be made by a combination of area and precision-guided munitions. The attack would thus be countered by a protective curtain of conventional weapons, ideally not subject to political restraint, preserving forces which, having paid full regard to concealment, deception and dispersal, would be free to confront the damaged and delayed aggressor.

The possibility thus exists for accurate target acquisition and identification, instantaneous response, and near-certain destruction of the aggressor. This, in turn, will lead to a requirement for prepared automatic fire programmes; a considerably reduced – and less vulnerable – forward deployment; and delegated responsibility to a much lower level than hitherto.

LESSONS FROM THE FALKLANDS

The military are fond of stating that the only way of testing their equipment and concepts is to have a war. Well they have now had one of sorts, though it is dangerous to draw conclusions which may divert attention from their main scenario in Europe.

The major lesson from the Falklands was that naval forces and shipping are desperately vulnerable to what should be called 'obsolescent' air-, sea- or land-launched missiles, and ordinary iron bombs. The Exocet has a short range of some 30 km or so. Air-launched from the Super-Etendard it was a serious threat to the Task Force. In addition, if the conventional bombs that hit our shipping had all gone off, or one or both of the *Hermes* and *Invincible* had been sunk, there is little doubt that the Argentinians would have won a notable victory, with considerable loss of face for the British. It seems now that ten ships were hit by bombs that did not explode, so sixteen ships might have been sunk instead of six out of a total of twenty-three ships on station at any one time. The full horror of these implications must be studied for the future so that our armed forces are designed to be given at least a fair chance to cope with the wide variety of new technology.

Clearly in most circumstances it is madness to send a naval task force against a well-equipped enemy without, or with limited, air cover, but the problem goes deeper than that. The fact is that large ships providing large radar signals are very vulnerable to a missile force, whichever way it is launched. The latest Soviet missiles have a range of 400 km, and it will not be long before this figure goes up to 1000 km. Regardless of the air support a naval task force may have, it is not going to be able to cope with a well-organised and sustained Soviet attack of regimental proportions. This also applies of course to convoys of merchant ships destined to bring vital supplies to Europe in event of war, considering that the first convoy may not leave the USA until around D + 20 or so. The Atlantic is swiftly taking on the dimensions of a large pond, with the various methods of covering its surface with satellites, radar sweep aircraft, and other means, with all the information gained being gathered into computers and piped instantly to a variety of control centres. These techniques are virtually with us now, and we would do well to bear this in mind when planning future equipment. The Navy must get under the sea as much as possible and as quickly as possible and also recognise that the day of the big ship is over. A case can be made for the use of the big ship in small wars and for showing the flag, but we are not rich enough to devise forces for these roles alone. As regards showing the flag, surely the submarine is the most menacing vehicle and it is a pity that we did not have one or two showing the flag in South American ports before the attack on the Falklands. Anyone who attended the Jubilee naval Review at Spithead must have been impressed by the suggested menace of the nuclear submarine force lying there at anchor.

But it is not just the Navy that must be conscious of the developments in new technology. The Air Force, too, has some thinking to do. The large airfield will be just as juicy a target as the ship at sea, and vulnerable to either missile, bomb or chemical attack. The airfield is also stationary and can be well targeted in peacetime. Long runways can no longer be relied upon – they are likely to be cratered at an early stage of a European war by direct or stand-off missile attack. If the enemy has any sense they will use delayed action weapons, which will make repair of airfield damage a difficult task. It is true that some hardening has been introduced on most NATO airfields, but this is a short-term measure. The airfield complex is vulnerable and this includes aircraft in hardened shelters. One answer to this problem is surely Vertical or Short Take-off and Landing (VSTOL). At last the military are beginning to think seriously about it, though the system has now been with us for some twenty-five years. The delay in embracing the concept has meant that VSTOL has not developed at the speed that it should. Scientists, engineers and designers have not been challenged to move the idea forward to later stages of development. The major problem with VSTOL has been the lack of range in the aircraft using it. There is little doubt that if tackled properly this problem could have been solved. Time, however, is not now on our side – the vulnerability of airfields means that aircraft and missiles must be dispersed and hidden or they will be lost in a first strike. Certainly NATO airfields will be at the top of the Soviet targeting list in any future war.

The tank must also be nearing the end of its life in several roles, due to the accuracy of anti-tank missiles, guns, bombs, rockets and mines. The greater accuracy of precision-guided munitions means that the tank, particularly the tank used in any numbers, has become vulnerable. With good battlefield reconnaissance now available the tank will be seen, and this means a high possibility of destruction. Tanks massing for a concentrated attack will be a fine target. The old adage that the best way to fight a tank is with another tank goes off to the history books. The tank may still, however, have an important role in Third World countries. It is interesting to note that the Soviet seem to be building more and more tanks of greater sophistication and larger and more heavily armed naval ships – this is good news for NATO, because there are now in existence the weapons to destroy such systems. They are also building more and more submarines, conventional and nuclear, and they are getting under the sea in a big way. We could do well to follow their lead.

CONCLUSION

This chapter has attempted to highlight the various aspects of new technology that are bound to affect strategy and tactics. It would be comfortable to say that all aspects of new technology are under discussion in the respective Ministries of Defence, and that a pronounce-ment on an alternative strategy or at least a vote of confidence in the old one will be made soon. Alas, as Admiral Mahan indicated nothing could be further from the truth. The military are slow to change and, to be fair, they are often held back by financial restrictions dictated by the politicians.

Flexible response is an uncomfortable strategy, in that if the Federal Republic of Germany did not insist on being defended on their frontier a more realistic plan could be evolved. But here is a political fact being introduced to military planning, which complicates the issue. If NATO could have an in-depth defence plan the chance of fighting a successful conventional defensive battle against the Soviets would be greatly increased. But Germany has no desire to be destroyed again, though it is doubtful if the present posture will make any difference to this aspect should an attack take place.

There will be much discussion about nuclear free zones and pressure for a declaration that on no account will NATO use nuclear weapons first. The issue of a nuclear free zone is worth discussing, as indeed is any idea that might break the log-jam with the Soviets on nuclear weapons, but in the present circumstances of considerable Soviet conventional superiority it would be madness to pledge NATO forces to 'no first use'. President Reagan has made several very tempting approaches to the Soviets recently on the reduction of nuclear weapons but all have gone unheeded. The main elements in the situation are that NATO is greatly inferior to the Soviets in conventional weapons and there is no guarantee that the Soviets would not use nuclear weapons as a first strike against NATO forces in Europe. The possibility of NATO being the first to use nuclear weapons in Europe in the event of an impending defeat must be a deterrent to the Soviets, and it must remain a part of NATO strategy until there is a fundamental agreement with the Soviet Union on disarmament.

However, the unequivocal support of the USA in the terms of nuclear support for NATO must come under some examination in the light of the Soviets achieving at least equality with the USA in nuclear throw-weight (and possibly superiority). This must change the USA's appreciation of support, as Henry Kissinger has been at pains to point out. The stunning confidence some distinguished UK commentators have that the USA will still be prepared to give NATO full nuclear support in ten years' time is frightening. Who can tell what sort of a world we will have in ten years or even five. Their view that this country can safely get rid of its nuclear capability or greatly reduce it because of this continued support by the USA makes little sense, and many would wish for a better insurance policy than that.

There is at least a reasonable case that can be made for an inflexible response strategy; not on the lines of the old Dulles 'trip-wire' doctrine, but in giving the Soviets a very clear idea of exactly what would happen in certain circumstances. It is said that the Soviet character appreciates the direct answer. This is not put forward as an entirely responsible concept but in certain circumstances the more certain the Soviets are about the NATO approach the better.

Flexible response can mean all things to all men. It was adopted reluctantly by the Europeans on American urging. In a way it makes a mockery of the German insistence of defence on their eastern border. The FGR would be largely destroyed again, but the decision-making is much in the hands of the USA and there is no doubt that they would dictate the time and place of response. It is highly unlikely that the USA would be in a hurry to initiate nuclear war. The chance of NATO being able to hold a surprise Soviet attack by conventional means alone cannot at the moment be great, considering the number of options the Soviets have for offensive action and the number of spoof attacks that they could carry out. The side with the initiative starts with a great advantage. Certainly the USA would wish to see exactly how the attack was going to develop, and a losing situation to a NATO European power would not necessarily have the same significance for the USA. A nasty situation of indecision could develop and a Soviet success and American delay could swiftly turn into a rout. As has been mentioned earlier, NATO is going to rely largely on reinforcements coming from the USA. They are unlikely to get moving much before $D + 20$ and they will have a difficult passage. There is also the possibility that the US could be engaged in some other enterprise in another part of the globe and the reinforcements and other supportive action might not be available when required. There are many ifs and buts about guaranteed support from the USA. The message surely is that NATO Europe must act to make itself more self-reliant while at the same time managing to keep the US involved. This is not exactly an alternative strategy but a revised political appreciation of the facts of the defence situation for the next decade. The danger is that few members of NATO will face the facts of the situation, arguing that to open up a discussion on the subject will drive the Americans out of Europe on the assumption that they are no longer needed. But there is no doubt that war could escalate out of some situation in the Middle East where the US had already deployed the Rapid Deployment Force and were getting into further trouble when the time came to reinforce NATO Europe. They have already indicated that they will have to call on reinforcements from their forces in Europe in the event of their getting embroiled, say, in the Persian Gulf when they decide to launch the Rapid Deployment Force. This could seriously damage the present forward defence plan, with other forces having to cover an even greater area of the Front. There is thus all the more reason why the FGR must be pressed by their allies to reconsider 'defence as far forward as possible'. The political element for Germany still applies, but they must be persuaded that it is the worst posture for a conventional defence, or indeed deterrence. In any case, with the new offensive posture of the Soviets many countries are in the front line, including mainland UK. The Soviet Union now has a very large force of transport and attack helicopters. No doubt their operational plans include a large-scale helicopter operation to get behind SACEUR's forward defence. This could create havoc, particularly if it is done in conjunction with a frontal attack. It would be a perfectly feasible operation, and carried out in bad weather or at night. The defence on the border would be completely outflanked. Chaos and defeat would be the likely result.

The concept of a defence in depth is not put forward lightly as an alternative strategy. Many of the present dispositions would have to be changed – barracks, supply dumps, airfields, and Headquarters. The Germans would have to be encouraged to form a Home Guard throughout the narrow heartland of the FGR. But this new deployment would give SACEUR a chance to deploy his forces sensibly not only against a surprise attack but in order to be able to fight a sensible battle. For the Soviets it would pose a much more involved problem than the one they have now. Rather than getting a fairly early victory on the border they would have to be prepared for a campaign in depth. This would soon take them beyond their surface-to-air guided-weapon air defence screen, which would make the task of allied aircraft a good deal easier. Defence in depth would also be the best operating environment for precision-guided munitions. Certainly if the Soviets were made to fight in depth they would have to use their large tank force, and it would have to be gathered together for attack if it was in any way to be effective. This would quickly be spotted and provide a splendid target. It could be argued that the Soviets might be driven into using nuclear weapons earlier by this change in NATO posture; but the early use of nuclears in an attack has always been their intention if their military writings are to be believed.

It seems that defence in depth coupled with taking the full advantage of the vast amount of new technology that is available must be the way ahead for NATO. The growing Soviet surface fleet will have difficulty in moving on the oceans without being seen and attacked. New technology is giving NATO the means of doing this. The Soviet submarine force is a threat of a different order and as yet there is no real answer to it. (Let NATO planners take note and strengthen their submarine forces.) New thinking and planning will be required on how to get US reinforcements to Europe in wartime. Perhaps pre-stocking in peacetime is the answer, though this can be expensive and difficult for storage and maintenance; but something will have to be done because little reinforcement will get through against even the present capability of the Soviet maritime attack forces. The vulnerability of airfields should also be exercising the minds of NATO planners. Many of them are too far forward for strategic comfort and well within the range of aircraft and missiles. They can be defended by fighters or ground-to-air missiles but the stand-off missile is going to make life very difficult for airfield defence. The hardening of Command and Control facilities also needs attention. There will be a colossal amount of information available for commanders to digest, and though the computer will be a big help the skill will come in knowing what to reject and what to retain. The most fundamental rethink in the 'defence in depth' concept will give the biggest challenge to the army. The acceptance of the allied armies spreading across Germany 'in depth' will have a big political content; and in these days of peace movements it may be a difficult concept to get across, but defence in depth might help a nuclear freeze or similar disarmament possibilities. But given the dynamic capability of the latest anti-tank guns and missiles, and the air-launched possibilities as well, including the air-laid anti-tank mine, armies would have for the first time the chance of developing a defensive (and deterrent) plan that would make an aggressor pause.

These are but a few of the changes that will have to be in the minds and hearts of planners as they attempt to organise our defence effort to cope with the greatly enhanced Soviet capability over the next decade. The fact that the Soviet Union has been spending nearly twice as much on research and development than the West means that they may certainly have some unpleasant surprises in store for us should they decide to attack. The Falklands War and the very close call we had on that occasion must be taken to heart and not used as proving the point that we need a lot more surface naval forces. This would be money badly spent. The thinking must be much more dynamic if we are to face the next decade and beyond with any confidence.

> If the strategy be wrong, the skill of the General on the battlefield, the valour of the soldier, the brilliance of the victory, however otherwise decisive, fail of their effect.
>
> Admiral Mahan, 1660–1783

NOTES

1. Shelford Bidwell, *Modern Warfare* (London: Lane, 1973).
2. Admiral Alfred Thayer Mahan, *The Influence of Sea Power upon History, 1660–1783* (London: Sampson Low, Marston & Co., 1889).

5 Return to a National Strategy

ADMIRAL OF THE FLEET LORD HILL-NORTON

The Defence Policy outlined in the White Papers of 1981 and 1982, and to a large extent restated in that of 1983, is based on several fundamental misconceptions, of which the most dangerous (certainly in the long term) may be briefly summarised as: 'Our front line is in Germany where lies the greatest threat to the United Kingdom; war, if it comes in Europe, will be short, so the Atlantic (never mind more distant seas) hardly matters, and where it does it can be defended by a handful of nuclear submarines and long-range maritime patrol aircraft.' Virtually every word of this is demonstrable rubbish; it flies in the face of history and the NATO assessment of the total threat, and would serve neither our national interests, nor those of the Alliance, best.

For the former, which must always be the primary concern of Her Majesty's Government, nothing but a return to first principles, and there to find the optimum means of defending British interests, will serve as a realistic basis for our foreign and defence policy. Let us, in brief, first be very clear about what we are seeking to defend, and then create the armed forces that can do the job most cost-effectively.

As for the latter, Mr Elliott Richardson has recently shrewdly observed:

> We cannot treat the NATO area as though it were on a separate planet from all the other countries and problem areas of today's world. The degree of interdependence of our societies on imported energy (and raw materials) is such that any threat to the free movement of international commerce and resources would pose as direct a threat to (our common) security and survival as Soviet military aggression in the Atlantic area itself.

It is a welcome sign of readiness to learn that the White Paper on the lessons of the Falklands Campaign (Cmnd 8758) has gone a long way to recognising these stark truths. It is also welcome that the harsh realities of that brilliantly successful campaign have brought home to our government that our defence policy simply must provide sufficient strength, flexibility and versatility in the order of battle of all three Services to meet the unexpected challenge, whether it be to NATO or to national interests. On the other hand it is impossible for any objective practitioner to agree with the conclusion to that White Paper, where it asserts, 'the lessons learned ... do not invalidate the policy we have adopted following last year's defence programme review', for both the campaign itself, and the whole body of the White Paper, do, specifically (and not surprisingly), invalidate that ill-conceived policy. Indeed it was fortunate that the intended consequences of the White Papers of 1981 and 1982 had not had time to work through to the front line of the Royal Navy, or of its support, for had they done so not only would the operation have been doomed to fail if attempted only two years later, but it could never have been mounted at all. And, while this author warmly agrees with the further conclusion that 'The Soviet Union ... continues to pose the main threat to the security of the United Kingdom, and our response to this threat must have the first call on our resources', this chapter will seek to demonstrate that there are better means both of deterring that threat, and disposing of our resources, than the defence policy now adopted.

THE NATIONAL INTEREST

It is a fundamental assumption in this chapter that Britain will remain an independent nation-state. This is a less blinding glimpse of the obvious than it appears, because many people in high places, including Whitehall, are ready to put forward or accept policies eroding our freedom of action to the extent that such independence would be in doubt. As for what independence is, I shall not be drawn into a definition; like the common cold, when you've got it you know it.

I also assume that the nation will retain its democratic institutions and general economic character. This is clearly an important assumption for a host of reasons, of which the most critical is perhaps that it rules out a force-led foreign policy. Such policies are characteristic of totalitarian powers, and indeed of terrorist organisations, but not of democracies.

Given those assumptions, it is fair to underline that the first duty of any government is the defence of the realm. Without this fundamental security the fibres of the country's social structure cannot withstand the strains placed upon them by the demands of freedom of action and speech and independence, which are the basic ingredients of democracy.

But the 'realm' of the United Kingdom is a very special one. All nations are unique, but ours is more unique than most. Two of its vital interests are, of course, in the words of the United Nations Charter, 'territorial integrity and political independence': but there are others, which flow from certain particular national characteristics.

Britain is, first, a medium-sized, densely populated, highly industrialised state whose people expect a high standard of well-being. It depends critically upon trade which, because of its geography and history, is oceanic to an unusual degree. It is a post-imperial power with some specific remaining commitments and considerable ill-defined, if gratifying, world-wide influence. It is a member of the trading, capitalist, democratic West; its links are at present most closely institutionalised for defence in the NATO Alliance, and for economic matters in the European Economic Community. All countries of the latter depend greatly on trade with the rest of the world, but no extension of the Community into the military dimension, with the aim of safeguarding that trade, is realistically in sight despite some no doubt well-meaning attempts to make it so.

This brief catalogue of what we are, points to some further interests which can, for the UK, truly be called vital, and which have fundamental security aspects. They are:

1. good relations with the developed countries of Western Europe, America, Australasia and Japan, and comfortable working relationships with primary producers;
2. maximum lawful and unimpeded access to resources, trade routes and markets;
3. though a less tangible interest – to influence, and to absorb or reject the influence, of others; and to look after those who still require our protection.

THE MAKINGS OF STRATEGY

It follows from all this that British strategy must serve British vital interests. That is the test, and it is a great mistake to use any other, though the temptation is always there. Because for our security we belong to various international organisations, officials particularly are inclined to say that 'what's good for the organisation is good for us', That may be convenient, but it is by no means necessarily true: second-order judgements of this sort must be avoided. No one (not even the same officials) ever expects other nations to take this line; it is always assumed that they will act in support of their own national interest, and so they do.

Even more to be avoided is the temptation to write strategy in order to justify the forces and organisation that exist, or to suppose (as planners too often do) that the politico-economic and thus the strategic future can be regarded as merely an extrapolation of the present. Certainly, because a defence policy is a constant requirement it continues to evolve, and to that extent any proposed changes must take as their baseline existing force structures; moreover, stability is a most important condition for the maintenance of well-motivated fighting services and for consistent defence planning. Nevertheless, if the chosen strategy is seen no longer to serve the national interest in the most effective way, it must not be perpetuated merely to preserve the stability of the military organisation – nor, come to that, the pride or reputation of the responsible Minister. Finally, it is an axiom that defence policy is the servant of foreign policy: but it is less well understood that, simply because of this, defence forces must be flexible enough to respond to the foreign policy changes that are almost bound to arise during their lifetime, which may, for equipments, be thirty years and for organisations even longer. What is required, and has not recently been offered, is an imaginative leap forward in time to assess the future threat as it may exist in the circumstances of ten or fifteen years ahead, and on that basis to formulate a defence policy that will then be able to deter or contain it.

Such a policy must, in practical terms, be based on available resources of money, the country's established industrial base, and the inherent skills and expertise of its people. It must take full account of the effect of the relative difference between the general rate of inflation and the coincident escalating cost of defence expenditure – statistically the latter has always risen faster – to avoid what has been called 'disarmament by inflation'. But a balance must be struck between the investment to be made in national defence assets and in wealth-creating activities. This will remain an important consideration as long as the economy remains weak.

British strategy, then, must serve British vital interests – which, I may reiterate, are to maintain the security and independence of the UK base, to foster good relations with states important to us, to promote stable trading conditions, and to preserve the influence and status of a medium power. It must be within our means, and it must not be so radical as seriously to destabilise either national or international institutions. This would all be quite a tall order against modest threats. But the present threats are far from modest.

THREATS

Given the assumptions already made, Britain must regard the Soviet Union as the most potent threat to its vital interests. The dynamics of Marxism, as practised by the Soviet Union, are such that any weakening of capitalism is always to be regarded as a success; that the movement of history in the direction of the Communist millennium is always to be aided by whatever means are to hand; and that changes in the 'correlation of forces' which are favourable to the Soviet Union are always to be fostered. The Soviet Union may occasionally choose to act like a status quo power for tactical reasons, but it is not such a power. No other nation is so fundamentally inimical to the United Kingdom, nor so capable of hurting it. But concentration on this threat should not obscure the fact that clashes of interest and policy may occur with many lesser states over a wide variety of issues; one need only mention Indonesia, Iceland and Argentina to indicate the diversity of such temporary conflicts over the last twenty years.

Britain's territorial integrity is still to some extent protected by geography. But this does not mean that invasion by a superpower is impossible or even implausible. There are several scenarios that could make invasion an option the Soviet Union would seriously consider. One is a highly volatile political situation in the UK which included a communist attempt to govern the country. Another is a Soviet desire to diminish or deny the value of the UK base both as an unsinkable aircraft carrier and as the main channel for the supply, resupply and reinforcement of NATO in Europe. In neither instance would assault forces necessarily need to attempt full-scale invasion, for if British land, sea and air defences remain as weak as they are today, very damaging attacks on, and the occupation of, key points could be readily achieved by the numerous specially trained Soviet 'diversionary brigades'; the Russians have ample tactical mobility, as witness their eight airborne armoured divisions and two amphibious assault brigades now facing NATO.

The threat of aerial bombardment of the UK, short of general war, must be regarded as rather unlikely. Nevertheless the option of such pre-emptive strikes must be considered to be part of Soviet military thinking, on a similar basis and for the same purpose as that of air- or sea-borne assault, in a period of rising tension. The capability certainly exists in the Soviet Air Force to mount conventional 'iron-bomb' attacks both through NATO air-space, and with much less opposition from the North and West of our islands. Nuclear strikes, which are more likely to be by missiles, can only be prevented by the success of the general deterrent strategy of the Alliance or, should Britain once again stand alone as in 1940, by the deployment of an independent strategic nuclear force under our own control. It is for this reason, with the defence of British interests at the heart of any sound defence policy, that Polaris, Chevaline and later Trident correctly form the very corner-stone of the soundest deployment of our military resources.

The history of both World Wars has highlighted in dramatic fashion the UK's vulnerability to blockade, and brought us close to defeat in both. It is a matter of fact that the threat from the Soviet Fleet (and particularly its attack submarines) by far exceeds that previously posed by Germany, while the Royal Navy has been allowed to shrink in almost direct proportion.

Invasions by the Soviet Union of our neighbour countries are not the likeliest of contingencies, short of general war, resting perhaps on the same sort of scenarios as were described for the UK; but they would, of course, pose great danger for Britain whatever her strategy was. Far more likely, unless NATO's cohesion can be effectively re-kindled, is the growth of Soviet hegemony over countries bordering the present Soviet bloc, aided by both internal subversion and by the menace of Soviet armed forces apparently ready to invade. Such an outcome, in even one or two Western European countries, would be gravely detrimental to our interests.

Turning now to those threats that may stem not only from the Soviet Union but elsewhere, it may be said that they are not confined to threats to the territorial integrity or political independence of this country, but may directly affect the other interests that were identified above as vital. These can conveniently be split into two categories: local unrest, and attempts to establish local hegemony.

Some such threats are quite insensitive to any military counter, in a democracy. For example, serious industrial unrest and subversive action which can be attributed to Soviet sources is probably not amenable to any military response, although it can in general be said that, however constituted and deployed, a country's armed forces can by their discipline and organisation present an important obstacle to many types of unrest and subversion. On the other hand, Soviet-inspired attempts to subvert and eventually gain control of the Oman, and with it the Southern side of the important Strait of Hormuz, were between 1972 and 1975 effectively countered by British military assistance to the Sultan.

When local unrest occurs in a British dependency, both responsibility and reputation require that it should be checked. Military forces have many times proved an effective means of helping to solve such problems before they get out of hand, and we can expect this requirement to continue; the last few of our dependencies are taking an unconscionable time a-dying. But local unrest can affect British interests in countries outside our jurisdiction. It is not easy to trade with a state that is in turmoil, nor are trade relations with newly formed revolutionary governments likely to be favourable or tranquil.

Attempts to establish local hegemonies may, again, affect UK interests in two ways. First, countries with irredentist claims against British dependencies may continue to pose a threat, and such threats are clearly susceptible to military counters, and may indeed be susceptible only to such action or deployments. Non-military moves in the same direction may have more effect on economic interests, and these can include attempts to exert undue degrees of power and jurisdiction in maritime economic zones, the establishment of discriminatory trading practices, and the formation of regional pressure groups with the aim of influencing the policies of other countries. Many of the threats of this last type are not at all amenable to military responses; on the other hand, some may be diverted or damped by their initiators' knowledge that certain countries, against whom threats might be directed, have a military capacity which could conceivably be used if they were pushed too far.

BASIC STRATEGY FOR A MEDIUM POWER

From the catalogue of threats outlined above it must be common ground that Britain cannot secure herself against them all unaided. Her population, industrial and economic base are not strong enough to provide the means of withstanding alone a determined assault by the Soviet Union, whether by sea or air, even if it does not extend to invasion. Nevertheless, as an independent medium-sized power, the UK must look for the ability to initiate, control and sustain coercive actions whose outcome will be the preservation of its vital interests.

This sort of autonomy cannot be complete, of course. Security will depend to some extent, as Britain's security has always depended, on alliances, and because the principal threat is posed by a superpower, Britain's primary alliance must be a superpower alliance; nothing else will do. Nevertheless, the 'ability to initiate, control and sustain' that I have just mentioned is emphatically not a simple falling-in with a more powerful partner, nor is it to be met by providing forces that are merely contributory in nature. It demands attributes of independence in the military as well as in the political field. The nature and extent of that independence, and the way in which it can operate, is the theme of the rest of this chapter.

ALLIANCES

After the Second World War the main threat to Europe was perceived to be that to its physical security, posed by the growing military strength of the Soviet Union and its Eastern Bloc allies. Individual nations, very wary of the escalating cost of providing independent guarantors of territorial integrity, resorted to a collective security in the form of the North Atlantic Alliance. A key factor, probably the key factor, was the engagement of the USA in the defence of Europe. This was achieved by three main means; the stationing of a substantial US force in Western Europe; a solemn obligation in the North Atlantic Treaty of 1949 binding the USA to the proposition, among others, that an attack on one was an attack on all; and the evolution of a complex Allied command structure in which US commanders and staff officers figure prominently.

Britain's contribution to the Alliance was driven largely by historical circumstances. For the European Allies the importance of engaging us in Western Europe's security to some extent paralleled that for the USA: the UK adhered to the treaty, provided numerous commanders and staff officers, and stationed substantial forces on mainland Europe.

Because of current claims that this latter commitment is an inescapable determinant of our Defence Policy, the facts are worth some brief analysis. In Protocol II of the Brussels Treaty, as modified in 1954, maximum force levels are laid down in Article I for all participants, while in Article VI, for the United Kingdom alone, this maximum is also stipulated as a minimum. At that time the figure was four divisions and the second Tactical Air Force. The four divisions were notionally 77 000 men, but this figure was renegotiated down to 55 000 in two stages in 1957–9. The diplomatic formula used was the timehonoured one of acquiescence, that is to say there was no formal amendment of a Protocol. The reason given, and accepted, for the reduction was the burden on our balance of payments, even though at that time it was offset by a German defence contribution of several hundred million pounds a year. This was steadily reduced during the 1960s and 1970s and finally phased out in 1980.

These glimpses of history are important partly because I return to them later in this chapter, and partly because they give a feel for the pace and mode at which the NATO 'machine' operates. It is, as I have every good reason to know, very deliberate and careful, but pragmatic and essentially understanding towards its individual members.

A question often asked (as it always has been, though in these later years it may have become more acute), is whether NATO is really able to move fast enough, either for short-term measures in emergency or in the longer-term context for the formulation of plan and policies. One or two examples come to mind. The NATO Council, the Major NATO Commanders and the Military Committee have many times over the past fifteen years drawn attention the growth of Soviet maritime power and the fact that it is now deployed world-wide. Numerous NATO documents have also discussed the growing use of proxy forces by the Soviet Union in countries such as Angola, Ethiopia and Vietnam. No one pretended that these developments did not gravely threaten the outflanking of the Alliance. Yet no move was made to change the Southern NATO boundary from the Tropic of Cancer in the Atlantic; and it was only after several years of detailed argument that the NATO Council approved, in 1973, the Supreme Allied Commander Atlantic's request that *planning* for out-of-NATO-area operations, with no ear-marking of NATO-declared forces and no commitment, could be carried out at his Norfolk, Virginia headquarters.

Other examples of the failure of NATO to react in real time to real crises can be seen over Czechoslovakia, the Yom Kippur war, Afghanistan and Poland. Press reports in all these cases suggested not so much that NATO was caught on the hop, but that its constituent political 'management' was unable or unwilling to initiate any positive Alliance response. This applied particularly to any possible joint *preventive* action. In such matters it was always individual nations, and not the Alliance as a whole, that did anything effective.

This factual criticism is offered in a spirit of friendship, not of rancour. NATO is the best major alliance Britain has, and particularly in its engagement of the USA it is critical to her security. It can justly claim to have kept the peace in Europe for a generation, but the fact that it is slow-acting, both in the short and long terms, points up most forcefully the need, certainly for its British member, to have a sufficient degree of military autonomy. Such power can have decisive effects on Alliance strategy; if any country regards its interests as special enough, or important enough, to confront a threat by national actions which will or may eventually involve its allies, this can have a catalytic effect. The knowledge that such an effect is possible will undoubtedly help to deter any potential threat.

I would not like it to be thought that NATO is the only alliance useful to the UK, nor that highly structured alliances of the NATO type are the only ones that are worthwhile. There are, in fact, many arrangements around the world, from formal agreements like the Five Power Defence Agreement with Australia, Malaysia, New Zealand and Singapore, and ANZUK, to understandings that are unwritten and scarcely spoken about. All can be of use to the UK if the appropriate need arises, but there is one thing demanded of Britain by each of them: the ability to initiate some convincing military response to a threat. Here again, a strategy that will best serve our needs requires a degree of autonomy.

DETERRENCE

Before drawing together some of these strands into a statement on how I believe British defence policy should develop, and discussing how this could affect our force structures and deployments, it is necessary to say something about the concept of deterrence by which the West has quite rightly set such store since the Second World War.

At its simplest the concept is embodied in the motto of HMS *Excellent*, the erstwhile Gunnery School at Whale Island: *Si vis pacem para bellum* – if you want peace prepare for war. Put in only slightly more sophisticated terms, the aim is to block all the aggressive military options of any rational opponent by persuading him that they will be unprofitable. One of the most important words in that statement is 'all'. Deterrence, to be successful, must operate at all levels and in all military fields. Nor is it all military: economic and diplomatic pressures are available in support. It is certainly not all national: allies are essential to the deterrent structure even if they are not expected to take an active part at the early stages of every confrontation. It is, emphatically, not all nuclear: a potential aggressor must be faced by credible counter-actions at any level of force, though the chain leading to eventual nuclear options must be credible too. Thus the only rational deterrent posture is one providing flexibility and an appropriate degree of national autonomy; and above all the military component must be backed by a manifest political will to use it, and (which is much more difficult) to do so in good time.

ALTERNATIVE DEFENCE POLICY

The UK's top priority is the country's territorial integrity, its political independence and its economic viability. These must be defended, if necessary to the death. The present-day economic situation requires the absolute essentials of the country's defensive needs to be identified. A 'first principles' approach leads to the conclusion that, while NATO remains fundamental to the UK's security, the country's Alliance contribution to this or any other alliance must be dictated first and foremost by national interests. Britain must therefore maintain a capacity to initiate action at appropriate levels, outside the NATO area as well as in it, if potential aggressors are to be convinced that interference with her vital interests will be met with military power, enough either to thwart them or to draw in Britain's allies. Such allies will not always be NATO nations, and, while it is to be hoped that they will wish to co-operate in constabulary tasks, they should not be counted upon to do so and Britain must preserve an independent capacity for such action.

This is not at all to diminish the need to maintain alliances with European nations and the USA, for it is quite essential for the defence of our interests that they should continue. Moreover they are to the mutual benefit of all parties, in that properly nourished they suppress any tendency to either European continentalism or American isolationism. But the overwhelming military, industrial and financial powers of the USA must not be allowed to dominate European powers, and the latter should remain resolved to preserve a degree of autonomy not only in the military field but – as they have already clearly shown that they wish to do – in political and economic matters too. The Europeans, in return, must show a greater readiness to support their most powerful ally, where it is to the benefit of all, than they have done in the last decade.

The purely military burdens of the Alliance will undoubtedly be most effectively shared if members contribute as they are best able, taking appropriate account of relevant national circumstances such as historical precedents, financial resources, established industrial capability, geographical considerations, and perhaps above all, aptitude. It is, in this important context, much to be lamented that continental European governments are quite unable to comprehend the nature of maritime power. Our nearest allies, hypnotised by the historic cockpit of Europe, retain a child-like faith in the safe and timely arrival there of seaborne trade in peace, and of reinforcements and re-supply in tension or war. Even in the UK, centuries of bitter experience of the vulnerability of sea communications have not driven home, either to our present government or to the general public, the harsh fact that maritime power must be created and nourished in peace if it is to withstand the shock of war. Navies may or may not be able to win wars, but they can certainly lose them. It is this lesson that should be at the heart of future arrangements for sharing the allied burdens of deterrence, as well as of a strategy which serves our national needs best.

SOME IMPLICATIONS OF THE POLICY

The threat to the UK base is one which national forces must be seen to be adequate to deter. I have already suggested scenarios in which invasion or air bombardment might occur, and that very heavy conventional bombardment or nuclear bombardment are only likely in general war which Allied or national strategic nuclear forces have failed to deter. Attempts to block maritime approaches are much more likely, and may well precede overt land/air offensive action.

In these circumstances, the maintenance of the national strategic nuclear deterrent provides the ultimate signal to the Soviets that any attempt to isolate and then wage war against the UK itself would not be worth the certain and appalling consequences. It also ensures a continuing measure of military independence from the USA. In any superpower confrontation it also gives the Soviets another flank, and another centre of decision, to worry about; and it may, in times of doubt in the Alliance, provide a crucial stiffening of NATO resolve against any attempt at nuclear blackmail. To be credible in all these important respects however, Britain must dispose of adequate conventional forces linked to her nuclear power. These forces must be seen to be able to act as the first and crucial stages of deterrence, and if that fails, to defend against conventional forces attacking the UK base. This demands, above all, aircraft and surface-to-air missiles to counter the conventional air threat, maritime forces to counter the submarine, surface ship and mining threat, and land forces to contain and then mop up incursions by sea or air.

Our economic viability as a trading nation and security responsibilities for the remaining dependencies, indeed all our interests outside the country, must equally be safeguarded. Very many of the raw materials we need for trading purposes are found in countries whose recently achieved independence is the target of Soviet expansionism and subversion, often by proxy, or which suffer from inherent instabilities. The very sources of the commodities forming the essential ingredients of our trading interests are thus put at risk. As we have already seen, NATO's arbitrary maritime boundary no longer remotely fits the global threat, and so there is no help to be found in meeting this threat from the NATO Alliance as such. The USA is creating its Rapid Deployment Force and this, together with her naval forces, may sometimes be available, if the Americans identify their interests as the same as our own; but even when that is so, they will surely be grateful for British support. All the more so will other nations, such as Australia and Japan, who see their maritime interests threatened. There must be a visible and sufficient presence in the vital sea lines of communications upon which these trading commodities must pass, to deter any potential aggressor from adventurism.

Third World countries are being armed with increasingly sophisticated weapon systems, and the threat they pose becomes more and more serious as they continue to scramble for regional positions of influence to be found in the void left by the Western colonial powers. The temptation for such nations to resort to bullying tactics can best be deterred, and Soviet expansionism countered, by maritime power. Such power, in the form of policing patrols, operations with allies and a clearly demonstrated capability to intervene on land, or in the air as well, if the situation requires it, are the essential ingredients of a constabulary task in support of the UK's overseas interests. The lack of overseas bases requires intervention forces to be flexible and highly mobile: such a capability, out to the limits of our economic sphere of interest, requires a sea- and air-portable 'all arms' force, including naval, marine, army and air elements, at about reinforced-brigade-group strength with appropriate logistic support.

Such a constabulary task is indispensable in that it provides a visible presence, a cross-section of flexible deterrent capability, and a clear indication of political intent. Operations of this nature may well have to be undertaken independently, and a sufficient capability to do so must be made available. I have said often enough elsewhere that such a maritime constabulary task is analogous to that of the policeman on the beat, whose presence on the spot is now widely accepted to be far more effective in deterring crime than the policeman available at some distance in his panda-car.

Diplomacy, aid, military training teams and joint exercises are also important elements in maintaining friendships and cementing under-standings. British ability to tread lightly in these matters, learned over many decades of dealings with all sorts of nations at all stages of development, is widely appreciated. British efforts in this field are more likely to be complementary to those of the USA than supplementary to them.

MEETING THESE REQUIREMENTS

Having established forces for these tasks in support of the highest priority national interests, remaining resources can then be committed in direct support of NATO. Any such contributions would signal the great importance of our political commitment to a mainly military Alliance. The right blend of the UK's maritime and continental strategies and foreign-policy objectives, undoubtedly requires land forces with supporting air elements to be permanently stationed in Europe, but the size of these deployments should flow from what can be made available after first priority has been given to the creation of forces of the right size and shape to serve the national interest, and not to obligations entered into thirty years ago when all the surrounding political, military, and economic circumstances were different, and the total Soviet threat hardly included a maritime element. Reservists would form an important part of a reinforcement effort and, given that adequate warning-time is anticipated, mobility of these forces will form an important element of this reinforcement strategy. Only if total resources permit, should our politically significant land/air forces in Central Europe be boosted to a more militarily important presence.

The size and shape of our maritime forces must allow the UK, in support of the Alliance, to contribute at about the present level to the defence of the Eastern Atlantic, Norwegian Sea and Channel areas. These tasks include support of the strike fleets operating in compliance with NATO's strategy of forward defence, and the protection of reinforcement and resupply shipping without which no successful land/air campaign on the continent of Europe can be realistically contemplated.

The forces mentioned above as necessary to maintain a useful overseas intervention capability in support of national tasks, would of course be available to NATO to reinforce the European flanks, most notably as the earliest which could arrive in Norway. As a well-trained and well-equipped, highly mobile, 'all-arms' force this would give considerable political as well as military significance to Britain's commitment to stand with her allies in a time of crisis.

THE FORCE STRUCTURES REQUIRED

The independent strategic nuclear deterrent force must be maintained at a level that will convince an aggressor that he faces the certainty of unacceptable damage if he compels its use. Given this criterion, it is entirely right to accept the present government's arguments for acquiring the Trident D-5 system. The acquisition costs are high, but the running costs are small, and if the figures in the 1982 Defence Estimates are correct, and are held, the project is certainly manageable, provided that the rest of our strategy is kept within the bounds I have suggested. In order to give our allies, as well as our own people, a true picture of what this involves in terms of total defence resources, it should be unambiguously funded quite separately from the conventional sea, land and air forces.

Maritime forces need to be capable of world-wide independent operations, up to quite high levels of conventional conflict, sustained over a period of perhaps weeks. They must also be strong enough to re-enter the campaign after a reverse, otherwise their ability to deter will be in doubt. A halt to the present mistaken trend of policy away from surface ships, including amphibious shipping, and a return to the provision of balanced forces at sea is obviously necessary in relation to the perceived threats; but this must not be to the exclusion of submarines, which are excellent vessels not only for NATO operations but for deterring escalation world-wide. Organic air power, including air surveillance, is an essential element, but the success of the Harrier concept, and the potential for development of anti-ship and anti-air missiles, makes a return to the large fixed-wing carrier concept unnecessary, and out of scale with the task for Britain. The constabulary task underlines the need for some new medium-sized surface ships, much simpler and cheaper than current designs, if their numbers are to be maintained at the minimum necessary strength, which is barely adequate today, and would fall to a quite inadequate level under present plans. In the search for making the most effective use of the resources allocated to defence, *how* you spend your money is at least as important as *how much* you spend. Tactical quality rather than high technology should be dominant in the design and development of all military hardware, and the Naval Staff particularly must be made to recognise that acceptance of less-than-perfect weapons systems is not only meritorious for these reasons, but makes a great deal of money available for more of them.

Air forces must be capable of defending the UK base, of making a significant contribution in Europe, and of helping to counter the maritime threat in the Eastern Atlantic area. The main elements, therefore, should be air defence and strike/attack aircraft and long-range patrol aircraft, including some airborne early-warning and anti-submarine units. The shift in emphasis towards national tasks would make it necessary to reduce the size of RAF Germany, probably by between one-third and one-half. This would not, of course, cause a pro rata reduction in the effectiveness of RAF support for the Central Front in the case of a European war nor indeed in its deterrent value; for the added security of bases further back would actually improve Tornado availability for operations such as airfield interdiction.

Land forces would have to undergo the most radical restructuring. Concentration on the national tasks implies increased emphasis on mobile, relatively lightly equipped forces with a high proportion of infantry. Armour and armoured personnel carrier holdings would be progressively reduced as anti-tank and anti-air capability is increased. Air and sea mobility must be held at least at their present levels, and more reliable and carefully pre-planned means for charter and taking up both ships and aircraft from trade made more quickly available. Training must move quite sharply away from the formation-related battle tactics of the North German Plain to emphasise individual, major-unit skills. All these developments would, of course, help to alleviate such inefficient situations as exist at present where troops from BAOR have to undergo lengthy retraining before and after a Northern Ireland deployment. The peacetime size of BAOR would certainly have to be reduced, in order to provide stronger and more flexible forces in the UK. A suitable permanently deployed Corps in Germany would be of the order of two armoured divisions, with equipment for a third stockpiled, and the appropriate level of artillery, engineer and supporting arms and services. It could be brought up to battle strength, as now, in seventy-two hours.

EFFECTS ON NATO

Any sharp shift in major policy of this sort – and indeed far more timid changes of direction – have been doggedly and consistently resisted by the official and military Establishment, often most fiercely by those who have served with or in contact with NATO. Having done some NATO time myself, at the very top of the military tree, I feel competent to comment on these arguments, which are on two grounds: spirit, and letter.

It is suggested that the will, particularly of the weaker and more reluctant members of NATO, would be broken by what they would see as a British defection from the core task of the Alliance, the defence of Central Europe. This raises, first, the interesting question of how robust an Alliance it is that could be unravelled by the departure of well under 5 per cent of its ready front-line troops. Fortunately, in my experience, NATO is much more solid than that. It has faced and coped with far more radical moves by France and Greece; it accepts the great military disadvantages that flow from national sensitivies in the Nordic countries, for example, without rancour; and the wiser NATO officials are very conscious of the slow-moving character of the Alliance and the need for occasional radical moves by its members. Moreover it has always accepted that national forces are provided for national tasks and subsequently assigned to NATO, and the North Atlantic Council has expressed frequent and real concern about the way events are moving outside its area, most recently and clearly at the Heads of State and Government meeting in June 1982, when the communique declared:

> Noting that developments beyond the NATO area may threaten our vital interests [agreed that] steps which may be taken by individual Allies to facilitate possible military deployments beyond the NATO area can represent an important contribution to Western security.

At present, of the ready forces available to NATO, the UK provides in the Eastern Atlantic 70 per cent, at a cost of something like 26 per cent of its defence budget; and on the Central Front under 10 per cent, at a cost of about 40 per cent of its defence budget. There is an evident mismatch here, which is much better appreciated by our Allies now than it was ten years ago, and, more important, they are well aware that if we lay down this maritime burden there is no one else, not even the Americans, who can pick it up. But when to this is added due consideration of the quite unique and recently proved British aptitude in sea-power matters, the logic of a shift in the distribution of the burden to give the maximum cost-effectiveness is overwhelming. After some predictable initial outcry had died down, it is my view that NATO would accept the change I recommend in British policy with sympathy, and would even come grudgingly to welcome it as a move in the long-term interest of world security. The notion that the Alliance is so brittle that such changes would cause it to unravel is as false as it is hysterical.

As to the 'letter', legalistic arguments are often advanced against the reduction of BAOR from a level 'sacrosanct by Treaty' of 55 000, even though this figure was negotiated down from 77 000 in the late 1950s without real or lasting difficulty. Nor is the front to be defended by British forces, at present 65 kilometres, any more sacrosanct; this figure occurs only in military planning documents and Defence White Papers, but not in the relevant Treaties.

Finally, the North Atlantic Council declared as long ago as 1974 that 'the circumstances affecting their common defence have profoundly changed' and 'the nature of the danger to which they are exposed has changed'. The main change, of course, has been the growth of Soviet maritime power – about which Britain, and only Britain, can do something positive. Without going as far as Prince Bismarck, who declared in 1898 that 'Treaties are only valid as long as they are useful to the nations that sign them', there is a good old rule concerning treaties called *rebus sic stantibus*, which means that if the circumstances surrounding a treaty change, revision of the treaty may be sought. Even the most vociferous supporters of the status quo must concede that all the circumstances have dramatically changed since our unnatural commitment to maintain large standing forces in Europe was undertaken.

THE EFFECT ON RESOURCES

In spite of the attempts in recent Defence White Papers to keep the public informed of the shape of current defence spending, it is difficult for anyone not in the know to discuss how changes in strategy would affect the spending pattern in the future. That pattern is closely guarded; the public has no access to the long-term costings.

One can of course derive a broad picture from the government's 'Way Forward' paper of 1981 and the 1982 Statement on the Defence Estimates. It is, for example, luminously clear that the proportions of the defence budget – itself rising at 3 per cent a year in real terms – allocated to naval general purpose forces, to their repair facilities and support services, are all planned to fall; while the proportions allocated to the nuclear strategic force, the ground and air forces, and reserve formations will rise. Allocations for other categories will absorb much the same proportion of the defence budget as they do now.

It will be seen that the alternative strategy I have proposed would change these trends. Naval general purpose forces would maintain, perhaps slightly increase, their present proportion. The nuclear strategic forces allocation would rise sure enough, but it would be seen as a central system and not as a naval allocation. So far as ground and air forces were concerned, their proportion of the defence budget would fall somewhat, mainly because of the reductions in heavy and sophisticated equipment flowing from redeployment towards the UK base rather than because of reductions in uniformed manpower. These changes, too, would almost certainly cause a downward movement in the Research and Development allocation – at present very high, at 12 per cent of the defence budget, and a much higher proportion than any other European country. Training costs would certainly have to rise, as would those for reserve and auxiliary formations.

This necessarily brief analysis of resource costs reveals that a change in strategy of the kind I have proposed is containable within the defence budget at its predicted future levels. It would, moreover, be cheaper in hard-currency foreign exchange; this is not a burning consideration at this moment, but economic pundits have predicted renewed problems in the next few years, even allowing for the bonus of North Sea oil. Once that starts to fall off, the continued stationing of large forces and their huge and expensive 'tail' on the continent becomes scarcely conceivable in foreign exchange terms. In this connection, the suggestion that because transferring troops from Germany to the UK would save no money immediately it cannot be countenanced is, to anyone who has experience of defence financing, ludicrous. I may remark in passing that the sophistry with which some civil servant briefed his master on that subject is quite staggering. Long-term economies almost always involve increased short-term spending, but that has never stopped politicians deciding upon them in the past, partly because short-term economies are almost always bound to be very damaging operationally.

CONCLUSIONS

Since the Brussels and North Atlantic Treaties were signed, and more particularly since the middle 1960s, Britain has been at extreme pains to prove herself the best of European and Atlantic Allies. She has done her national interests considerable damage in the process, and no small damage to Alliance interests to boot, especially since 1981. It is now time to re-establish our autonomy as a medium power, to provide forces – as do our Allies – which most effectively safeguard the national interest, and then to assign and use them in Alliance interests wherever appropriate.

Our chief Alliance must still be NATO, as a necessary means of engaging the USA and Western Europe, as the surest means of deterring Soviet aggression, and as the lynch-pin of collective security. We should, in parallel, foster and maintain associations and understandings with all those like-minded powers which perceive a common threat in global areas beyond the arbitrary NATO boundary. In all alliance matters the capacity of British forces for independent operation, up to a fairly high conventional level, will be an important element in engaging the commitment of allies. Potentially decisive influence will powerfully help deterrence at all levels.

British forces must obviously be restructured to support the new strategy. The priorities that should be followed are:

1. Trident and associated forces;
2. Limited air and maritime forces in defence of the UK base to provide convincing linkage to the independent strategic nuclear deterrent, and sufficient infantry and supporting arms to ensure the security of the home-land against all threats short of general war;
3. Naval forces for the defence of merchant shipping on a constabulary basis, in concert where possible with friendly powers, to the limit of our economic sphere of interest;
4. Aid, training, visits and a highly trained mobile intervention capability to assure friendly states and our few remaining dependencies of British support. Such forces could contribute to American efforts in this field, or that of a more broadly based Rapid Deployment Force, where and when appropriate;

5. Militarily significant maritime forces in the Eastern Atlantic, Channel and Norwegian Sea areas;
6. Somewhat reduced, but still militarily important, land and air forces to remain in place on mainland Europe as an indicator of political resolve, rapidly reinforceable by substantial reserves from the UK.

It was Palmerston who said – 'Britain has no permanent Allies, only permanent interests.' However unfashionable a doctrine, even harsh, this may seem today, it is certainly a much sounder basis for our defence and foreign policies than any other. To those who share this view, an alternative strategy on the lines outlined above must seem not only logical but positively essential.

6 Flexibility, Mobility and Involvement

MICHAEL CHICHESTER and JOHN WILKINSON MP

The Soviet Union – its policies and its military capabilities continue to pose the main threat to the security of the United Kingdom and our response to this threat must have the first call on our resources . . . In allocating these [more defence resources] we shall be taking measures which will strengthen our general defence capability by increasing the flexibility, mobility, and readiness of all three Services for operations in support of NATO and elsewhere.[1]

THE THREAT TODAY

In military terms Britain is still the most powerful European member of NATO, and her contribution to the collective security system for the defence of Western Europe and its sea approaches which NATO provides now largely determines the shape and size of her armed forces. To the extent that the threat to the security of the NATO 'area' posed by Soviet and Warsaw Pact forces deployed in and around the European theatre also represents a threat to the security of the United Kingdom itself this assignment of the majority of its armed forces to NATO enables the British government to fulfil at least in part its obligation to defend the realm.

However, the threat is now also the long-term campaign waged by Soviet Russia and her satellites and surrogates to advance the cause of international Communism worldwide by political means backed by massive military strength on land, sea, and in the air. Two objectives of this campaign are to gain control of sources of energy and raw materials essential to the economies of the West in peace and to the ability of

NATO to fight in war, and of key ocean chokepoints through which Alliance shipping must pass to Europe and North America with its cargoes of these resources. So now the threat extends beyond the defensive circle of the original NATO area with less risk of escalating the level of conflict and with equal if not greater chances of strategic success than would result from an assault on Western Europe. The military threat to NATO Europe still exists and Warsaw Pact forces now enjoy an overall superiority over NATO forces deployed along the European front. But it is now only one source of the global threat and it has become essential for the West to strike a new balance in defence resource allocation between the historic NATO area and vital interests further afield.

Just as the nature of the threat to NATO has changed during the past thirty years so have the status and economic circumstances of Britain, now no more than a middle-rank European power with an economy in apparent industrial decline despite the possession of North Sea energy resources. In the lifetime of NATO, national military service has been abolished, a military withdrawal from East of Suez completed (in the process creating a power-vacuum in many areas of strategic importance to NATO), and the British armed forces more than halved in size.

In 1983 the 55 000 men of Britain's Rhine Army represent no less than 35 per cent of the whole British army (just over 14 per cent in 1957), and RAF Germany over 10 per cent of the Royal Air Force (4 per cent in 1957). But the Royal Navy has borne by far the greatest proportion of the reductions in other defence resource allocations which a combination of escalating defence costs and budgetary restraint have made necessary in order to maintain the 'Brussels Treaty commitment' of three divisions and a tactical air force in West Germany. However, at long last the Defence White Paper on the lessons of the Falklands campaign[2] does seem to infer that for the time being at any rate this process of cutting the Royal Navy has been halted if not reversed.

BRITAIN AND NATO

Where NATO and national interests coincide a British contribution to the defence of that interest or asset is also a contribution to national security. For example, the defence of the UK also provides defences for an offshore island base of major importance to NATO in war, the loss of which would seriously endanger the capacity of the Alliance to fight a conventional war in Europe for more than a few days.

The march of events since NATO was founded has reduced the situations in which this helpful coincidence of national and NATO interests can be found. The Soviet strategic threat to the West has been extended geographically and is no longer confined to Western Europe and the North Atlantic. Yet NATO remains a defensive alliance responsible only for the defence of the Treaty's area (the central front in Europe, its northern and southern flanks, the Mediterranean Sea, and the North Atlantic ocean north of the Tropic of Cancer). Its writ does not extend beyond this area, nor does it have any responsibilities for the defence of the vital interests or territories of any of its members which exist outside this area and which are now also threatened by Soviet strategic advances.

With the exception of France, Britain has more interests and residual territorial responsibilities to defend outside the NATO area than any other NATO European country. The 1982 Falklands campaign was an example of the need to deploy military force to defend one such territory. Britain is not self-sufficient in natural resources and cannot survive without importing. Over 95 per cent of its import–export trade is carried by sea on voyages that extend well beyond the artificial confines of the NATO area. The Soviet navy is now capable of mounting an offensive campaign against Western shipping throughout the whole Atlantic ocean and in the Indian ocean as well. Among the NATO European countries Britain would be the principal sufferer from such a campaign.

As the Falklands campaign showed, the defence of British or Alliance interests outside the NATO area requires flexible and mobile forces, principally naval and air forces, land forces capable of rapid deployment by sea or by air, and long-range air transport forces backed by in-flight refuelling tankers. Although their inherent qualities enable them to be switched rapidly between the NATO area and other more distant areas as the situation demands or a threat emerges, forces of this type are less suitable for meeting one of Britain's binding obligations to NATO, namely to maintain an army of 55 000 men and a tactical air force permanently in Western Europe in peacetime until 1992.

Here is a most serious case of growing divergence of British and NATO strategic interests. A British political initiative is urgently necessary to obtain NATO agreement to a recasting of the British roles in future NATO plans for the defence of the NATO area, in ways that will permit greater use of Britain's increasingly flexible and mobile forces and allow the basically inflexible and strategically immobile armoured units in Rhine Army to be substantially reduced.

In its post-Falklands defence White Paper,[3] while reiterating its policy of giving priority in its defence effort to the four main roles of the British armed forces in their contribution to the defence of the NATO area,[4] the British government effectively admitted that the reductions in the surface fleet, particularly the virtual abolition of its amphibious capability represented by the assault ships *Fearless* and *Intrepid*, proposed in the 1981 Defence Review,[5] had been too sweeping, and that the provision of flexible and mobile forces 'well suited to respond to unforeseen challenges arising outside Europe'[6] (as well as being capable of performing useful roles within the NATO area) must now receive a higher priority in the allocation of defence resources than it had done in the recent past. As *The Times* put it:

> Throughout the White Paper the wording makes it clear that British forces must now be maintained, equipped, and trained to operate not just in the NATO area, where the main threat is presumed to lie, but in the 'out of Area' role in which the Falklands for all its distinctive political characteristics, was militarily not so unique.[7]

The need for a review of Britain's role in NATO is matched by the equally pressing requirement for a modernisation of NATO's plans for the defence of the NATO front in Europe. NATO has to adapt to the political, strategic, economic, and technological environment of the 1980s which is almost totally different to that which it faced at its inauguration over thirty years ago. The nature of the Soviet threat to the Atlantic Alliance has changed fundamentally, the defence of Western Europe demands a fresh appraisal, and the contributions of the individual European members to the collective defence system that NATO provides require rearrangement.

This is particularly true of the present British continental contribution in peacetime, which a combination of reduced economic circumstances and escalating defence costs will soon render unsustainable. The additional resources to be injected into the British defence budget over the next few years to pay for the Falklands campaign and for the replacement of its losses, and to maintain the garrison of those remote and windswept islands, may have delayed but will certainly not prevent a new crisis in British defence spending, leading inevitably to yet another defence 'review' in the mid-1980s.[8]

Why will this crisis be different from its many predecessors of the past two decades? Primarily because it will be impossible for the British government to continue to state as fact what is fast becoming fiction, namely that Britain can afford to maintain at their present levels (in some cases already cut to the bone and barely viable in any case) the contributions that it makes to the four components of its NATO role, and at the same time make adequate provision for the defence of its own realm and of its national interests throughout the world.

The recasting of NATO's defensive strategy for Western Europe must, therefore, incorporate a new role for Britain in which greater priority is given to those areas where national and alliance interests coincide, and which is based on a realistic assessment of what Britain can afford to contribute to the Alliance over the rest of the 1980s.

GROWING PRESSURES ON LIMITED UK DEFENCE BUDGET

The Falkland Islands war fortuitously ensured that extra funds were made available by the government not just to make good the losses sustained during the conflict in the South Atlantic but also to provide a garrison on the islands and a rapid reinforcement capability within the UK.

Although the strategic priorities of the June 1981 Defence White Paper (Cmnd 8288) were maintained, the capabilities necessary for swift intervention overseas at extreme range by sea and air which were at the heart of the defence improvements announced to Parliament in December 1982 gave Britain's post-Falklands armed forces a composition and balance more akin to those proposed in *The Uncertain Ally*[9] than those proposed in Cmnd 8288, with the sole significant exception that the UK's commitment of 55 000 men and a tactical air force to the continent of Europe in peacetime remained sacrosanct.

Nevertheless, the pressures on Britain's defence budget, which had been contained in the pre-General Election period thanks largely to the extra allocations to defence following the Falklands Islands war, are bound to pose serious problems to the new government. The coincidence of major equipment programmes in the mid-1980s, as well as the inherent budgetary problems that have always beset the management of UK defence in recent years, will ensure that another defence review is necessary within the first two years of office of the incoming administration.

The relative price effect whereby sophisticated weapons systems escalate in cost at a significantly higher rate than the level of inflation, will be accentuated with the procurement of the new generation of equipment. The armed forces will still have to attract from a competitive employment market the highly technically qualified personnel they need. The remuneration of the armed services will remain correspondingly high, to which must be added pension, health, housing, education and other support costs which the Treasury will unfortunately not permit to be excluded from the Defence Budget.

The cost of Trident will start to impinge on the defence budget in a significant way just when important new items of equipment are in the most expensive state of the procurement process. Among these will be the AV8B (Harrier 2) and Agile Combat Aircraft for the Royal Air Force, AMRAAM guided weapons, the Sea Eagle anti-ship missile, defence suppression missiles for the Tornado, the Tornado F2 itself, the Type 23 Frigate for the Royal Navy, the EH101 helicopter Sea King replacement (SKR), the Stingray lightweight Torpedo and the new heavyweight Torpedo, the lightweight Seawolf anti-missile missile, presumably more Challenger tanks for the Army, and new Armoured fighting vehicles.

As so often in the past, the review will have to match the overextended roles and capabilities of the British armed forces to resources which at the time of writing have not been decided beyond 1985–6. Until then, adherence to the target set in the 1981 Defence Review of an annual 3 per cent increase in real terms in the defence budget, in addition to the extra Falkland Island-related expenditure, will have prevented a crisis over defence spending, but the respite can only be temporary. The defence options for the incoming government are starkly unattractive unless bold steps are taken to revise the UK's strategic priorities and the manpower policies of the armed forces.

One possibility would be to abandon the modernisation of the UK independent nuclear deterrent and to forgo procurement of the Trident submarine-launched ballistic missile system. Theoretically the total saving to the defence budget over a ten to fifteen year period would be of the order of at the very least £7 billion, excluding cancellation charges and the cost of any alternative system such as cruise missiles. However, Trident is so much the most capable ultimate strategic deterrent system that to abandon it would be a sorry reflection upon the nation's will to contribute to the deterrence of war and to the sovereign independence of the United Kingdom. The procurement of Trident will, in the words of Sir John Nott, enable us to 'retain that vital, and purely European, second centre of decision-making that adds so significantly to the uncertainties faced by any aggressor contemplating an attack on Europe'.[10]

Further weapon cuts could be pursued but some of the most

superficially attractive cancellations would have a devastating effect upon British industry and would so degrade the capabilities of the armed forces that alternative systems would have to be procured from overseas. The Agile Combat Aircraft (ACA) must be vulnerable to cancellation but without it the British Aerospace Corporation's main military aircraft complex at Warton and Preston in Lancashire might ultimately have to close. Likewise the AV8B (Harrier 2) is important if British Aerospace is to continue to have an interest in the joint development with the McDonnell Douglas Corporation of a supersonic variant of the Harrier. The EH101 (SKR) has a relatively limited numerical market with the navies of the UK and Italy but again industrially it is a critically important programme for Westland Helicopters and Agusta respectively. Even so, the technical advances in helicopter design and the attractions of licence construction of an American aircraft must make the EH101 vulnerable.

New armoured fighting vehicles (AFVs) and guided weapons could also be bought from the USA, but the industrial and political arguments against such a step are very strong. In short, wielding the axe to the equipment sector will not solve a budgetary problem. In the long term it can only be resolved by relying much more on cheaper Reservist manpower, and on the total defence inherent in converting civilian assets in addition to a burden-sharing initiative with our allies, which relieves the UK of much of the cost of its static inflexible continental commitment of the British Army of the Rhine in Germany.

In the equipment field much innovative thinking is required if worthwhile budgetary savings are to be achieved. First of all a new government ought to remove the cost of the Trident programme completely from the Navy budget, thus making possible a significant enhancement of the conventional capability of the Fleet. Unfortunately it is unrealistic to expect the cost of the modernisation of the strategic deterrent to be removed entirely from the defence budget, but at least if it came from all three Service votes equally its impact would distort the individual Services' capabilities less.

There will have to be a major drive to achieve much more standardisation of equipment within the Alliance as a whole. An Atlantic-wide market for armaments must be the objective, and within it the establishment of more collaborative programmes both to spread more widely research and development costs and also to achieve lower unit costs through longer production runs.

Undoubtedly, new tactical doctrines involving the deployment of more mobile and better-equipped forces, especially on the Central

Front, to offset the armoured preponderance of the Warsaw Pact will favour this process. The new air–land battle concept, relying for its effectiveness against tanks upon more intelligent precision munitions allied to airpower and greater reliance on stand-off weapons to interdict the battlefield from Warsaw Pact second-echelon sources of supply and reinforcement, will require numerous new NATO equipment pro-grammes. These should be the first candidate for an augmented collaborative approach on an Atlantic-wide basis. Similarly, advances in electronic warfare, communications, command and control, es-pecially in the new AWACS environment that will dominate future air operations, will necessitate substantial new procurement, preferably on a collaborative basis.

However, the trouble with British defence reviews in the past is that they have stemmed from unilateral budgetary cuts in defence spending as a direct consequence of British economic difficulties, rather than from strategic analysis. They have been foisted as *fait accomplis* upon our reluctant allies, who have been required to make consequent adjust-ments to their defence plans. The British Secretary of State for Defence should make a virtue of the necessity for a further defence review by obtaining, through prior consultation, the agreement of our allies to new divisions of responsibility in NATO.

THE NEED FOR A STRATEGIC SUMMIT CONFERENCE

By making the choice of strategic priorities which it did in 1981 entirely on national economic considerations and without any prior con-sultation with its NATO allies, the British government gave fresh support to a NATO strategy that was already in need of modernisation. Thereby was lost the opportunity, which the need for further British defence economies had created, of initiating a major strategic review within the Alliance designed to look forward and to reform NATO doctrine rather than to maintain the status quo.

Such a review is urgent. The development of the Soviet global threat to the interests of the Atlantic Alliance, the need for a reallocation of total allied defence resources between the defence of the historic NATO area and of other areas of vital interest to all the NATO allies, and the problem of how best to share the military burdens of a global grand strategy for the West, require political discussion at the highest levels of Alliance management by means of a strategic summit conference of all the NATO allies, including France. The object of such a conference would be to reach agreement on a broad division of strategic responsibilities between the USA as the superpower of the West and its NATO European allies, and on the military roles of each of the latter in the context of a global defence plan.[11] At this conference the British government should seek to obtain the agreement of the NATO allies to a new military role for Britain in such a plan. What this role should be is described below, but first, a brief review of the political, economic, and technological factors that must be taken into account in any strategic reappraisal, will be useful.

THE ALLOCATION OF RESOURCES

With their economies exposed to a lengthening world recession, unemployment at unacceptably high levels, and welfare and social costs rising in consequence, the NATO European countries will find it both politically and economically difficult to reach a target of a 4 per cent annual increase in real terms in their defence budgets until 1988. SACEUR considers such an increase to be necessary merely to meet the force goals required to match the expected level of Warsaw Pact forces in the European theatre.

Yet it is not too much to say that the future of the Atlantic Alliance depends crucially on the extent to which NATO Europe meets this target for increased defence spending. Its achievement will weaken even if it does not totally destroy the case of those in the USA who now press for a partial or in some cases a total US withdrawal from Europe, and it will mean that NATO Europe is itself providing the increased resources that are needed for the defence of its own territory.

This will allow the USA to allocate the bulk of the increase in its own defence spending planned for the next few years to the defence of Western interests outside the historic NATO area while maintaining its peacetime deployment in Europe at its present level but no higher. By this change of emphasis in the division of strategic responsibilities between the USA and its NATO European allies a basis for sharing the burdens of a global defence and strategic plan for the West will be established.

During this period of transition the British role in NATO should be redesigned so that her own substantial rapid deployment and intervention capabilities, particularly her maritime forces, form a larger proportion of her contribution to NATO than is the case today. The suitability of such forces for operations both within the NATO area and also in the defence of Western and purely national interests in other parts of the world, makes them a particularly cost-effective contribution to a global strategic plan.

THE DEFENCE OF THE NATO AREA

An essential component of any such plan will be a new assessment of how to defend the NATO area during the forthcoming period of rapid change. This has become a three-dimensional problem, the defence of territory along the NATO front in Europe, the defence of air space against both bomber and missile attacks (351 Soviet SS-20 triple-headed missiles now threaten the whole of Western Europe and the UK), and the defence of the Atlantic reinforcement route and the sea approaches to Europe. Deciding on the most effective allocation of NATO Europe's total defence resources in resolving this three-dimensional problem, and how best to employ future weapons and new military technology in the conventional defence of Western Europe's territory and air space, are the two most important issues when preparing a new defence plan for the NATO area.

The concepts of forward defence and flexible response, which have formed the basis of NATO defence plans for over twenty years, need to be replaced by tactical doctrines that will raise the nuclear threshold in Europe. Among other measures, they will replace battlefield nuclear weapons with precision ('Smart') munitions of various kinds, and will incorporate advanced C3, surveillance, and intelligence-gathering systems to increase warning of enemy attack and to improve the identification of targets well within enemy territory. This will facilitate the transition to a more economical deployment of 'in-place' forces within Europe in peacetime.

An overall objective of a new NATO defence plan for Europe should be to share the military burdens among the European allies in the most logical and cost-effective manner and on the assumption that the size of the US contribution will not be increased. It will, however, be realistic to assume that French forces will quickly join with the allies in the event of an attack on Europe. The defence of the Central Front and of the flanks against a Soviet offensive by land and air forces will become the prime responsibility of those NATO members whose territories are situated within the confines of the European mainland. This task will be a priority in their defence budgets.

Within NATO, discussion on future strategic and tactical doctrines for the defence of Europe has already begun. At their meeting in Brussels in December 1982 defence ministers ordered an investigation into means whereby new defence technologies could strengthen Alliance conventional forces with particular reference to the key areas of surveillance, precision-guided munitions, communications, and electronic warfare. The USA has suggested that any new build-up of conventional forces in Europe must be accompanied by new tactical doctrines embodying greater manoeuverability and flexibility, and tighter co-ordination of land and air forces to facilitate offensive defence, which would include the destruction of Warsaw Pact forces and reinforcements inside enemy territory instead of waiting for them to penetrate into West Germany.

There is no doubt that the introduction of third-generation guided weapons, fire-and-forget stand-off missiles for aircraft, and the further development of the armed helicopter, will swing the battlefield balance more towards effective defence, particularly against the offensive use of traditional armour. In December 1982 General Delaunay, the French chief of the army staff, announced that France would establish airborne and heliborne units for rapid intervention in Europe, endowed with a strong anti-tank capacity.

Britain will need to follow these developments closely since they should dramatically affect her own military policies. The present emphasis on armoured units in the British Army of the Rhine and the relative lack of helicopters to provide tactical mobility will require re-examination. By the end of this decade Britain should have begun the conversion of most of her armoured regiments into more flexible and mobile units with substantial helicopter support. Such forces will also be able to operate outside the NATO area, which armoured forces are unable easily to do. The primary British antidote to Warsaw Pact armour will be airpower.

BRITAIN'S ROLE IN NATO

In NATO's new plans for the defence of its area Britain's roles will have to be redesigned. They must take account of her unique geo-strategic position as an offshore island base and energy-supplier of major importance to the Alliance in war, of her maritime capabilities and expertise, and of her responsibility for the defence of the ocean approaches to Europe (a responsibility that no other NATO European country can easily assume), and of her possession of air mobile and amphibious intervention forces which can be used throughout Western

Europe or outside the NATO area if needed either by NATO or to defend national interests.

The British government should obtain the agreement of NATO to this more flexible and mobile British role in NATO war plans. To do so they will have to point out that in the face of escalating defence costs and budget limitations, the rigid maintenance of the Brussels Treaty commitment by the UK to maintain three divisions and a tactical air force permanently in Western Europe in peacetime until 1992 is now creating an unacceptable degree of imbalance in the structure of the British armed forces. A re-negotiation of this commitment has become a matter of urgency.

In such a re-negotiation, while maintaining a firm commitment to reinforce the northern flank and also the central front in an emergency or war, Britain would undertake to maintain in West Germany in peacetime a Regular army force of not more than two divisions, together with a tactical air force, both of which would be based west of the Rhine. These forces would have minimum civilian support. They would be augmented by Royal Auxiliary Air Force squadrons and Territorial Army units in time of emergency or war. These Reserve units would also deploy to West Germany regularly in peacetime for training.

THE IMPORTANCE OF TOTAL DEFENCE

The importance to our security of being able to mobilise the industrial, logistical and skilled manpower resources of the nation rapidly was fully demonstrated during the Falkland Islands War. This lesson must not be forgotten. In the words of the post-Falklands Campaign White Paper:

> The Campaign brought home to us the significant contribution which civil resources can make to the nation's strength in a crisis ... Our intention to review the use of national logistic and manpower resources in this way has now been given even greater impetus. The smooth and rapid implementation of existing contingency plans to use merchant shipping in support of the Services was a major success of the Campaign. Some 45 ships were taken up from trade, from passenger liners to trawlers. They provided vital support across the entire logistic spectrum ... Civil air carriers supplemented the efforts of the RAF Air Transport Force and between April and June transported more than 350 tons of freight including helicopters to Ascension Island.[12]

There is already evidence of a growing awareness in official and informed quarters of the importance of Reserve Forces to Britain's defences. Mrs Thatcher's government raised the long-term recruiting ceiling of the Territorial Army to 86 000 men and women, increased the number of Royal Auxiliary Air Force Regiment squadrons from three to six, and ordered new minesweepers for the Royal Naval Reserve. Important innovations were initiated under Sir John Nott's stewardship as Secretary of State for Defence. First, the raising of a Home Service Force of 4500 to protect key points in the UK was announced. Second, studies were put in hand to restore a flying role for the Royal Auxiliary Air Force by equipping a squadron with Wessex-5 helicopters, and a Royal Auxiliary Air Force Movements Unit was created at RAF Brize Norton.

Meanwhile, a former Chief of Defence Staff, Admiral of the Fleet, Lord Hill-Norton, and others have been rightly compaigning for the creation of a large Home Defence Force of volunteers which, exploiting local knowledge and civilian skills, would counter the growing menace to the UK home base from Soviet diversionary brigades and other hostile infiltrators and saboteurs, a threat acknowledged by Mr Nott in his speech to Parliament on the post-Falklands White Paper.[13]

Nevertheless, except for the Territorial Army, the Volunteer Reserves are inadequate. Both the Royal Auxiliary Air Force and the Royal Naval Reserve should be greatly strengthened. In the case of the Royal Auxiliary Air Force, flying squadrons should be recreated on the lines of the highly successful United States Air National Guard. In the case of the Royal Navy Reserve, there is a great need for much enhanced Coastal Forces, which would constitute an ideal role for Reservists. Furthermore, the Regular Reservists of all three Services should receive periodic training, and the call-out of Reserves generally should be facilitated by new legislation.

All in all, the former US Army Secretary's quip about the British Army – 'all generals and bands' – is too true for comfort. There is an inflation in the rank structure of all three Regular Services, and as a proportion of the country's manpower far fewer men and women are in the Regular Forces or Reserves in the UK than in France, Germany, or Italy. The proposals set out in *The Uncertain Ally* for involving more people in Britain in national defence and on future manpower policy for the armed forces should be implemented.[14] Regular manpower, particularly in the Army, could be cut, thus saving excessive personnel and support costs, while extra funds would, as a result, be made available both to broaden the base of British defence in society as a whole with extra Reservists, and also to procure more equipment thus improving the firepower of the armed forces.

SHARING THE BURDEN OF DEFENCE IN NATO

In conclusion, there is little doubt from the research of David Greenwood of The Centre for Defence Studies, Aberdeen University, and others, that on current projections, even allowing for the extra budgetary allocations to defence to meet the cost of the conflict in the South Atlantic, 'defence could cost 10% more than planned by 1984/85 while the underfunding could amount to 16% by 1986/87 if the cost of maintaining the Falkland Islands is included'.[15] Controlling inflation will be critically necessary to keep overspending on defence to a minimum.

The new government ought to make a virtue of the imminent necessity of another defence review, both to harmonise the UK's defence roles and capabilities with its economic resources, and to match our country's budgetary provisions to defence more closely to those of France and Germany. Both these countries spend a smaller proportion of their gross national product on defence than does the UK. Perhaps a Christian Democratic Union Government in Bonn might ultimately wish to build up the Federal German Republic's military capabilities on land and in the air in line with its economic power and growing political influence. Such a West German military build up would greatly enhance the security of the Western Alliance.

Ideally, NATO nations in western Europe should spend more on defence to meet the target set by SACEUR, General Rogers, of a 4 per cent increase in defence expenditure in real terms per year in order to be able to match the conventional capabilities of the Warsaw Pact by 1988. However, more efficient use could be made now of NATO's joint provisions for defence through more equitable burden-sharing and a more rational allocation of national roles and responsibilities within the Alliance.

France's independent nuclear deterrent is already a valuable specialist contribution to the defence of the Western Alliance. For the UK, its position as the island link with North America should logically entail an enhanced British role at sea and in the air in order to keep the lines of transatlantic reinforcement open. The mobility and flexibility inherent in sea- and air-power are also indispensable to meet the Soviet Union's growing political and economic challenge to the interests of the Western

Alliance worldwide, a challenge very effectively underpinned by the awesome capability of global military power projection by the Soviet Union – a capability that it has shown itself all too ready to exploit.

Highly versatile primarily naval, amphibious and airmobile intervention forces, together with a formidable national nuclear deterrent allied to augmented Reservist manpower support, should provide the core elements of Britain's contribution to NATO. Pressure for US troop withdrawals from Europe will grow, unless those West European countries who can do so, notably Britain and France, share some of the burdens of global peacekeeping with the Americans.

Although the security of continental Western Europe is vital to the UK, Britain as a trading nation cannot afford to ignore the course of events in the wider world or deny herself the military means of influencing them. As a defensive Alliance, NATO must adapt to new challenges and threats if its members' collective security is to be assured. In the last analysis, NATO's ability to mount effective military operations at all levels of conflict is the best deterrent to war. In the interests of the Western Alliance as a whole the peacetime convenience of politicians and their more narrow national susceptibilities have to be rigorously subordinated to the building of a war-winning capacity if the peace is to be preserved.

NOTES

1. *The Falklands Campaign: The Lessons*, Cmnd 8758, December 1982.
2. Ibid.
3. Ibid.
4. These roles are:
   (a) The provision of an independent element of strategic and theatre nuclear forces committed to the Alliance;
   (b) The defence of the United Kingdom homeland;
   (c) Deployment of a major maritime capability in the eastern Atlantic and Channel;
   (d) Provision of a major land and air contribution to the European mainland.
5. *The Way Forward*, Cmnd 8288.
6. Cmnd 8758, para. 304.
7. *The Times*, leading article, 15 December 1982.
8. In December 1982 the costs of the Falklands campaign were estimated as:
   (a) Replacement of assets, about £900 million over three years;
   (b) Cost of the conflict, £700 million;
   (c) 1983–4 cost of Falklands garrison, £424 million.

9. M. Chichester and J. Wilkinson, *The Uncertain Ally – British Defence Policy 1960–1990* (Aldershot: Gower, 1982).

10. Rt Hon. John Nott, MP, Secretary of State for Defence, to the North Atlantic Assembly, London, November 1982.

11. For a detailed discussion of military burden-sharing and how a global strategic plan could be prepared by the Western Alliance, see Chichester and Wilkinson, *The Uncertain Ally*.

12. Cmnd 8758, p. 26.

13. House of Commons Official Report (*Hansard*) 21 December 1982, col. 853.

14. Chichester and Wilkinson, *The Uncertain Ally*, pp. 177–203.

15. *The Financial Times*, 21 December 1982, p. 6.

7 Strategy and Conscription

KEN BOOTH

Britain obviously has a defence policy, but it is debatable whether the country has a rational strategy, if by 'strategy' we mean that marriage of weapons and doctrines that promises to maximise our chances of surviving, and surviving passably well, in war as well as peace. Since the Sandys' era the British people have relied upon a desperate form of deterrence theory, which will survive everything except being tested, and a conventional military posture determined more by the accountant's mentality of successive governments than by the strategic inspiration of Clausewitz. This should not be allowed to continue, for in strategy no sin is punished more implacably than a refusal to change.

It has frequently been observed that Britain has lacked a tradition of strategic theorising.[1] Its island position, its great navy, and the possession of the traditional elements of national power gave Britain a luxury denied to the continental powers. For the latter, military preparedness, in both mind and machines, could make all the difference between whether they directed the course of a war, or suffered it. With enemies just the other side of a river or a mountain range or even a field, the first battle might count for all. The British, on the other hand, secure behind their moat and their warships, lapsed into a military habit that tended to produce victories in default of preparedness and strategic theory. We had the luxury – though like all luxuries it was costly – of being able to lose every battle but the last. Victory in war excuses many things, though it should not, and in Britain's case the long tradition of final success encouraged an over-relaxed attitude towards bearing defence burdens in peacetime. National unpreparedness was even rationalised into the 'strategy of the long haul'.

Since 1945 British national power has declined and the strategic environment has changed dramatically. The outcome has been a retreat from empire and the concentration of military effort in Europe, where the strategic framework has been set by two heavily armed alliances eyeball-to-eyeball in the valley of the shadow of nuclear deterrence. As a result of this, even the British now live on the next battlefield. 'We are all Berliners', John Kennedy said, though obviously some of our allies have their noses pushed harder against the wall. As a result of these historical developments British security, like that of the rest of Europe, now depends above all upon deterring war, and then upon limiting its damage in the event it occurs. Not surprisingly, in the last twenty-five years, British defence policy has put much more emphasis on the former than the latter, although history suggests that it is foolhardy to believe that any deterrent will always work. A rational national strategy should be concerned with presenting potential adversaries with an image of a robust defensive capability for deterrent purposes, and preferably one that will maximise the chances of survival in war. In peace our priority should be to maximise national security rather than to seek further trivial increments in prosperity: and in war our priority should be the integrity of the British cultural infrastructure rather than seeking a 'victory' in the traditional sense. In order to be a continuation of politics, war must first permit the continuation of civilised society.

Since its inception NATO's posture has been heavily pro-nuclear. Because of the deep horror of war in Europe, NATO members have placed an almost absolute reliance on the nuclear deterrent doing its job. Partly as a result of this, there has been something of a mental blockage when it has come to thinking about what to do if deterrence fails. NATO's wartime 'strategy' has therefore been determined by the weapons and attitudes that have shaped and that have been shaped by a generation of belief in successful nuclear deterrence. Unfortunately, as many people would admit – including nuclear-deterrers – such weapons and attitudes do not necessarily form the basis for a sensible war-fighting strategy.

If the worst came to the worst, and nuclear war began, West Germany would be in the most exposed position of all; but Britain would not be far behind, in view of its military significance, relative smallness, and densely populated character. West Germany's immediate threat in war would be from a Warsaw Pact blitzkrieg and the mutual use of battlefield nuclear weapons. Britain's immediate fear would be of a devastating nuclear strike against its high-value targets.[2] To meet this possibility, successive British governments have supported a policy of independent nuclear deterrence based upon a willingness, in some circumstances, to commit quasi-national suicide as a result of inflicting quasi-genocide on the enemy. This anti-strategy is one that increasing numbers of the British community have come to believe is neither right nor prudent.[3] Our recent military posture – it does not deserve to be dignified by the name 'strategy' – is calculated to achieve the long-term security of Britain by threatening in the last resort to destroy the nation in order to save it.

Until the late 1970s it was relatively easy to avoid thinking about these matters. The British people as a whole had come to live with the relatively low costs and apparent utility of their nuclear weapons. Like a course of valium, nuclear weapons made it easier to face the complex world in which we found ourselves; they seemed to relieve us of both mental and physical burdens. Matters began to change at the end of the 1970s, when a conjunction of developments provoked a more intense interest in British defence policy than had been seen for twenty years. It has far from run its course, and this book is one manifestation of it. An 'agonising reappraisal' is taking place, and for once Dulles's phrase is not being devalued. The issues involved in the Polaris replacement question, the role of cruise and Pershing II missiles in NATO strategy, and the future of conventional defence have arisen against a background of economic depression in Britain and what many people believe to be profound and dangerous trends in the international situation. There is a new sense of uncertainty and unpredictability, and a fear that a nuclear war is becoming more 'thinkable'. These fears are justified, for objective and subjective trends in world affairs promise to make crises more likely and more dangerous than in the 1970s, and in these crises edgy and dogmatic superpowers will be determined not to be outdone in displaying interest and resolve. Furthermore, if miscalculations are made and shooting begins, the superpowers will find it easier to slip into a nuclear war.[4] Nuclear weapons obviously remain an impressive deterrent, but major war, including nuclear war, is again on people's minds, and it is this which has given such a sense of urgency to the activities of the peace movement. The members of the latter, with their many different attitudes and levels of expertise, share a fully justified belief that the rationale supporting an 'independent nuclear deterrent' for Britain has never seemed weaker.

As if there were not already enough issues provoking, complicating, and confusing the increasingly lively debate about the future of British defence policy, in 1982 the British government allowed itself to fall into a war with Argentina over the Falkland Islands – an episode that cast doubt on the government's strategic flair, if not its resolution. The fight over these remote islands[5] distracted the nation's attention for three months, as it promises to distract thinking about British defence for much longer. The outbreak and course of the war revealed some major miscalculations on the part of the British government. Subsequently, however, the government seems to have calculated the long-term implications of the episode rather more deeply than it calculated its response to original Argentinian challenge: the White Paper of December 1982, *The Falklands Campaign: The Lessons*, showed that the government would not be moved from its overwhelming commitment to the defence of Western Europe, though it inevitably had to accept that it must provide a respectable defence of the Falklands for a respectable time to come.

Against the background of such a concatenation of issues and developments in the strategic arena, the need for the British community to engage in a sophisticated discussion of its defence options was never more urgent. This discussion should also include, because of the intimate relationship that exists between defence and foreign policy, a full examination of Britain's proper place in world affairs. Strategically, should Britain be simply a European power, or should it have some capability to act elsewhere? Within NATO, should Britain become more closely identified with its EEC partners rather than trying to maintain whatever remains of its 'special relationship' with the USA? Technologically, should Britain stay in the first division of powers when it comes to possessing the 'best' (or at least the most destructive) weaponry, or should it adjust its efforts in the direction of less-ambitious 'middle powers'? Militarily, should Britain remain a pro-nuclear power or should it shift its defence energies in a non-nuclear direction? In the long term, should Britain remain a member of NATO, or should it strike a posture of armed (or unarmed) independence? If Britain remains a nuclear power, what should it target? Without doubt, the defence and foreign policy issues confronting the interested British public are numerous, and so are the answers that are being offered. But the debate was never more important, for we are at a crossroads. Whatever we decide, we will have to live with our answers for a long time; or we may have to suffer through them; and some of us, perhaps many of us, may even die by them.

As a result of the circumstances in which we presently find ourselves, those who think about strategy in Britain – a group that is not entirely conterminous with those who talk about it – have been giving increased and worried attention to such problems as: what makes 'deterrence' work? what is the proper role of conventional forces in a pro-nuclear defence policy? and what should be our military and political response if deterrence breaks down and war begins in Europe? The discussion of these questions over the past couple of years has led to a new and growing attention being given to the importance of conventional forces, which in turn has led to discussions about the appropriate size and character of such forces. Out of these discussions has emerged, for the first time in a quarter of a century, the glimmerings of a debate about the possible value of national service.[6] This is a subject that is much too hot for any of the political parties to handle, but it is a subject that should be faced; and it is the purpose of this chapter to carry the debate forward by suggesting that the reintroduction of national service in Britain would represent a sound basis for a rational defence strategy. Furthermore, the case for national service will be argued whether or not Britain retains its own nuclear weapons, though it should be made clear at the outset that this chapter is based on a belief that on both security and ethical grounds a non-nuclear strategy is the appropriate course for a physically small and densely populated middle power, with a complex and vulnerable cultural infrastructure.

To date, those who have contributed to the recent discussion about national service have invariably concentrated on the social and political advantages and disadvantages of such a step, and the problem of economic costs. Strangely, this discussion has largely skirted around the strategic aspects of the question, although these are surely the most important of all. Liberal democracies can hardly justify conscripting their youth, and disrupting their 'normal' lives, unless there exists a real military need. A major exception to this general neglect of the military dimension is the attention given by Michael Chichester and John Wilkinson in their book *The Uncertain Ally. British Defence Policy 1960–1990.*[7] But even here there are more ideas concerning the character and costs of such a reform than of the military reasons why it should be considered. Nevertheless, these authors should be congratulated for facing up to the issue, while a generation of others have ignored it. The reasons for this neglect are not difficult to find, for in Britain compulsory military training has never been thought to be justifiable unless there was a major national emergency, and obviously the latter has not been the nation's assessment of its position in the last twenty-five years. However, increasing numbers of people do believe that Britain is facing an emergency of sorts, and a handful of us consider that the unpopular measure of national service is part of an answer to some of our problems.

The overriding issue of our time – political, strategic, and moral – is that of nuclear war and how it is best avoided. National service can play a part. It is a step by which Britain can meet some of the weaknesses in its present defence posture, and at the same time contribute to a more rational strategy in future. The case for the reintroduction of national service on strategic grounds is powerful, and rests on its potential usefulness in dealing with six major problems:

1. THE PROBLEM OF THE LOW NUCLEAR THRESHOLD

Raising the nuclear threshold is one of NATO's most pressing problems. Indeed, to those who believe that nuclear war is our worst nightmare, it is the most urgent problem of all. And for once it is a problem about which we can do something, for all agree that the problem can be eased by providing the Alliance with greater conventional power, including manpower. What Britain could contribute to the latter by means of conscription will be discussed in more detail later.

Most defence analysts, including those committed to a pro-nuclear strategy, concede that the nuclear threshold in Central Europe is uncomfortably low.[8] In 1969 the British Defence Secretary, Denis Healey, said that the pause between a Soviet attack and the need for escalation would be a matter of days, not weeks.[9] The dozen or so years since that comment was made do not appear to have changed anybody's opinion. The reason for the expectation of such an early nuclear release is in part the result of a belief in NATO's conventional weaknesses, though it is increasingly accepted by all but NATO's alarmists that the Alliance's conventional forces are in a stronger relative position than has been commonly thought in recent years.[10] But there are also other factors lowering the nuclear threshold, some of which are psychological and some which are related to the physical aspects of NATO's pro-nuclear posture.

Since the mid-1950s NATO strategy has involved the growth of a heavy concentration on theatre nuclear weapons, including the forward deployment of shorter-range 'battlefield' weapons. Unfortunately the latter risk being overrun at the very outset of any Warsaw Pact attack, and so commanders will face considerable pressure to use them before they lose them. This pro-nuclear battlefield posture, which grew out of three powerful drives – the desire for an overwhelming deterrent threat, the political need for a 'forward defence' in Germany, and the desire for the cheapest possible defence policy – has gained the approval of the majority of the British public, because it has seemed to work. On the other hand, an ever-increasing number of people in recent years have become concerned lest the deterrent element fails, because they know that the strategy planned would then precipitate a nightmare. If and when the deterrent fails on the central front, as Field-Marshal Lord

Carver has argued so effectively, nuclear weapons will then not prove to be a sensible way of trying to redress existing conventional weaknesses.[11] Furthermore, NATO planning is also based on dangerous psychological rigidities, arising from NATO's present combination of perceived conventional weakness and pro-nuclear doctrine; these are likely to have a self-fulfilling and self-annihilating character in the event of war, for there would surely be a strong inclination, if a local or general collapse seemed imminent, to begin the process of nuclear escalation before it proved 'too late'. Whether or not it was objectively 'too late', the subjective pressures for an early nuclear release would ensure that it was in practice.

In an era of rapid warfare, coalitions cannot change strategic doctrines in mid-stream. Even in the Second World War the RAF could not escape the mind-set produced by its pre-war technology, doctrine, and commitment to strategic bombing. Such problems will be even greater in the next war. In an era of 'go as you are' warfare, therefore, having adequate and appropriate forces in readiness should be a priority in defence thinking. Unfortunately, as earlier comments made clear, this goes against British traditions, and perhaps even the British temperament. But uncomfortable facts must be faced, and one is that more men are needed now, to fill gaps that presently exist, and so add to the Alliance's strength and flexibility. Under existing doctrines and attitudes, it would be likely that NATO would begin using nuclear weapons at an early stage in a war, even if the Warsaw Pact forces did not begin their attack with selective nuclear strikes or, as is less likely, a mass nuclear attack. It should therefore be obvious that the longer NATO forces are able to contain a Soviet attack by conventional means, the longer decision-makers will have to bring about that settlement – be it surrender, compromise, or whatever – which would make all the difference between a bloody mess in the centre of Europe and the destruction of civilised society in most of the northern hemisphere. Stronger conventional forces on NATO's part, permanently in place, promise to postpone the decision to fire nuclear weapons. Is any strategic reform more important?

2. THE PROBLEM OF LIMITED ATTACKS

If war occurs in Central Europe it obviously might take several forms. A massive premeditated Warsaw Pact attack is only one. Other possibilities include: probes by Soviet forces against specific targets to test

Western resolve; miscalculations on the part of the Soviet leaders which lead them to believe that their forces could attack and occupy parts of Western Europe at an acceptable risk; and war 'by accident' in the sense of a clash of arms arising out of uncontrolled escalation in a crisis, and a resulting war that 'nobody wanted'. Limited Soviet action to clear away specific threats – analogous with the announced Israeli 'cordon sanitaire' of 40 km in southern Lebanon in 1982 – might expand, like the Israeli advance, by either force of circumstance or design. Crises are moments of opportunity, as well as threat.

Crisis scenarios are manifold, but we cannot accurately foretell which ones will spill over into war. We can only be wary, for the way wars begin is a sad confirmation of Brecht's cynical line: 'War is like love, it always finds a way.' Increased manpower is one of the reforms that would help improve NATO's ability to deal with limited Warsaw Pact attacks without having to face the prospect of a relatively early escalation to nuclear war. As matters stand, NATO's present pro-nuclear strategy, like the Schlieffen Plan before 1914, threatens to turn even limited conflicts into general European war. A stronger conventional capability on NATO's part is the only means by which flexibility can be restored. Were a Warsaw Pact attack to take place, NATO's existing posture does not promise to offer the Soviet leaders enough time to discover whether or not they have made a 'mistake'. Once war has broken out negotiations will be extraordinarily difficult, amidst all the fog and fury of battle, but they are surely preferable to the deadly alternative of pressing on.

3. THE PROBLEM OF 'WARNING-TIME'

The idea of 'warning-time', political and military, is built into much NATO thinking, either explicitly or implicitly.[12] But this is always a dangerous dependency. An effective reaction should not have to depend to any decisive degree on what could be achieved in the days or weeks offered by warning-time. First, if the decision-makers concerned are not completely confident about what they are seeing – and this will be the normal position – they will be unwilling to respond positively, for fear of provoking a real crisis out of what might be a false one. In addition, decision-makers (especially in democracies) will be reluctant to mobilise their forces and raise the international temperature for fear that they will be exposed for having made a costly error. Second, ambiguous signals might be misread or simply ignored, as has happened so often in the history of intelligence. The Japanese attack on Pearl Harbour in 1941, the German attack on the Soviet Union in 1941, the Soviet missile emplacement on Cuba in 1962, and the Egyptian attack across the Suez Canal in 1973 all illustrate the ways in which one nation can take another by surprise, even when there was information available that suggested an attack.

NATO in general and Britain in particular can have no confidence that they will be immune from such avoidable errors. The Argentinian invasion of the Falklands Islands in 1982 was not an encouraging lesson. The British Cabinet either failed to see the accumulating signs of hostile capability and intent, or, if it did, it was unwilling for whatever reason to act quickly. There was some warning-time, but it was not utilised. As a result, the enemy stole a march, and Britain was taken by tactical surprise. The British government thereby compounded its failure to provide a credible deterrent with a failure to take advantage of whatever warning-time was available. Since Britain also lacked local forces in adequate strength, having allowed them to run down in the belief that the worst would never happen, the situation could only be retrieved at a staggering cost. This episode confirmed yet again the old lesson that a heavy price has always to be paid to rectify strategic errors. And when the errors are avoidable, the price is always excessive, however limited the war.

These remarks are clearly pertinent to the more important situation we face in Central Europe. If war breaks out, it will almost certainly come by surprise, no matter how much political 'warning' we are given. As the period of peace stretches out, our leaders will find it even more difficult to accept and piece together the signs indicating that a great catastrophe is about to happen. After years of believing that war in Central Europe is remote, there will be a natural tendency to filter out discrepant information, in order to keep alive the psychologically comfortable belief that the worst cannot happen. Furthermore, if the Soviet leaders decide on war, their tactics will naturally be keen to encourage such disbelief. Their plans will place a premium on achieving tactical surprise. And the configuration of their forces since the early 1970s has been such that they will be able to attack almost from a standing start, or at least have their offensive evolve out of manoeuvres. Their forward echelons are not heavily reliant on prior reinforcement, and so will not require a prolonged and substantial build-up of the sort that will offer unambiguous warning to the defenders. The contingency of an unreinforced attack became widely accepted among Western defence planners in the late 1970s.[13] Without strengthening NATO's in-place conventional forces, to meet the Warsaw Pact's in-place threat, Western political leaders will continue to face in full the dilemmas and dangers exposed by a reliance on 'warning-time'.

When confronted by uncertain signs – or certain signs that are interpreted with uncertainty – the natural tendency for democratic leaders will be one of 'wait and see'. In such circumstances it will be easier for a British government to raise the readiness-status of forces which are already sizeable and in place than to start the costly and possibly provocative business of moving troops from Britain into Germany. The more manpower NATO has deployed in readiness, the more circumspect the Soviet leaders will be. This again suggests that NATO should have larger numbers of men permanently in place. Such a capability will give NATO more confidence in a crisis, and, even if things do go wrong and an attack begins, stronger forces in-being will help meet the challenge and help postpone the nuclear decision.

4. THE PROBLEM OF MILITARY RESERVES

Whatever the character of the next war in Europe, almost all defence observers are agreed that NATO should improve its staying power.[14] And almost all writers about British defence policy stress the value of greater numbers of reserves. The Alliance needs an enhanced capability to keep fighting, day and night, until the issue is resolved. Modern war is an extraordinarily greedy tyrant.

The attrition rates in a European war would be enormous, even if it were to remain conventional. In order to improve NATO's staying power a bundle of reforms are conceivable – in weaponry, deployment patterns, logistical practices, and tactics. As far as Britain's potential contribution is concerned, national service would not only provide many more men in place or readily available, but over the years would create a large body of trained reserves. The latter is a capability that British defence specialists have regularly been recommending, as the overall knowledge of military skills within the community has declined.[15] As it is, every year 'some 20 000 men leave the services with a liability for reserve service of which little use is made'.[16]

Reserves, it is generally agreed, are not as capable as professionals, but they can be well trained and can perform a variety of important military roles. In war, reservists and national servicemen could release the regulars from various chores, and so allow the professionals to undertake more specialised and difficult tasks. Some could be trained to fight alongside regulars, especially in the defence-in-depth ground-holding formations on the central front. Loaded up with a variety of anti-tank weaponry, and trained for a narrow task, they could help channel enemy advances, and try to wear them down. And we should not be dismissive of the fighting capabilities of reservists. It is the opinion of one knowledgeable commentator, for example, that the 30 000 Territorials sent to Allied Command Europe for exercises in 1980 'showed up better than most allied regulars'.[17] Numbers count, as well as skill: both are essential for military strength. And as T. E. Lawrence and Liddell Hart have both stressed, the key to a successful defence is the ratio of force to space.[18] The greater the density of force, the greater the prospects for a successful defence.

The denser the anti-tank defence that NATO forces can put in the path of the Warsaw Pact's mechanised divisions, the greater will be the requirement for the Warsaw Pact to provide infantry and artillery to suppress this defence. Alternatively the Soviet leaders might decide to meet the problem by means of nuclear weapons. In the light of Soviet military doctrine the latter possibility could not be unexpected, but the Soviet Union's political leaders would be reluctant to take such a step, since they apparently believe, as do most Western observers (and leaders), that once nuclear weapons have been used in any number, escalation to general war is likely. If the Soviet leaders decided against a disabling nuclear strike on the central front, they would have to meet a denser NATO defence by sending infantry and artillery forward to accompany the tanks as the cutting edge of their attack. Inevitably this would mean that the prospects for any rapid advance would decrease. Rather than the German blitzkreig into France in 1940, they would have to face the prospect of something similar to the slogging Israeli counter-attack against Egypt in 1973.

As the prospects for a successful lightning strike decrease, so should the confidence of the Soviet leaders in a short and successful war as a whole. Significantly, Soviet military doubts in this respect have already been growing in recent years.[19] Furthermore, expert Western observers have noted that the Warsaw Pact forces of the 'northern tier' – Poland, Czechoslovakia, and East Germany – will prove less reliable the longer any war proceeds.[20] Since the role of non-Soviet forces in an offensive is greater than is commonly thought, this is another reason why it is important for NATO to show an ability to blunt the first attack and be able to fight a long war. And foreign policy should be the handmaiden of defence policy in this area, by avoiding positions that tend to push the Eastern European countries into the Soviet fold. Clearly it is important for NATO to do whatever possible – by improving its foreign policy, weaponry, deployment patterns, logistical practices, tactics, strategy, and manpower policies – to discourage any Soviet confidence in an early success. In the late twentieth century aggressors will not opt for protracted wars. Defensive alliances must therefore do all they can to rule out the option of rapid victories.

5. THE PROBLEM OF TERRITORIAL DEFENCE

Although it seems unlikely, the possibility of a Warsaw Pact invasion of Britain has to be faced. Strategists must consider worst cases, and the threat of occupation falls not far behind that of a nuclear attack on the British homeland – some misguided patriots would even put it ahead. At present there is some capability for the local defence of the British homeland against the threat of invasion, but it could obviously be improved. An efficient system of territorial defence will help this. More important still, such a system should help to deter invasion in the first place, by promising to make the costs of occupation too great. The more the NATO allies can persuade the Soviet Union, individually as well as collectively, that they are ready, willing, and able to fight to defend their patches of territory, the greater will be the disincentives for a fateful Soviet move westwards.

Territorial defence is a system of defence-in-depth in one's own territory.[21] It aims to harrass the invader by means of a well-organised and trained body of troops – the more the better. Such an approach is exemplified by Sweden, Switzerland, and Yugoslavia, each of whose defence posture is served by some form of conscription. As is the case in these countries, a system of compulsory military service in Britain would, over the years, provide a body of trained men who could form the core of locally based military forces. If such a system was to be seriously put into operation, and if signals were to be directed to the adversary and his allies, then it would represent an important increment to deterrence. Particularly after the experience of Afghanistan, Soviet military and political leaders will not be blasé about the prospect of trying to subdue a hostile nation in arms, where most men and some women will be organised, where the citizens will have access to rifles (and possibly worse), and will know how and when to use them.

Such a system of defence will make any potential aggressor wonder more than twice about whether the costs of invasion and occupation could ever justify the benefits. Furthermore, a nation in arms, if it has the right reputation, can be a formidable diplomatic asset in its own right, as is evident from Soviet relations with Yugoslavia and Poland. In the decision process that led to the rejection of a Soviet intervention in Yugoslavia in the late 1940s and Poland more recently, the worries placed in Soviet minds by the image of united nations willing to fight ferociously for their national territory cannot have been insignificant. The contrast with the Soviet perception of Czechoslovakia in 1968 is telling. The British could project a similar image to that of the Yugoslavs. We are a nation with a long and proud military history, and our martial spirit and professional military skill has recently been burnished by the campaign for the Falklands. These points should not be allowed to be lost upon the Soviet forces and leadership. It should be evident that a reputation for being a fierce and skilled nation in arms is a 'capability' upon which all British statesmen should be able to call: if we lack it, our leaders go naked into the conference chamber.

Apart from dealing with the Soviet threat, an infrastructure of military training will help the country to meet some of the problems of an unpredictable and difficult world. These include varieties of natural disaster and civil disorder, though obviously calling in the militia should only be a last resort when it comes to matters like strikes. In addition, a degree of military training would also help with civil defence. This is a controversial subject, but one that should be less controversial in a non-nuclear Britain. Passive defence measures are widely opposed at present because some people believe that a combination of civil defence and a pro-nuclear strategy will send the wrong signals to the adversary, while possibly helping to delude our own decision-makers into thinking that nuclear war might be a survivable option.[22]

6. THE PROBLEM OF POLITICAL SIGNALS

It is well understood by strategists that armies, navies, and air forces are most useful when they contribute to the advancement of policy without having to be used. In this sense the use of brute force must be seen as the breakdown of a country's military power.[23] This means that nations must attempt to demonstrate an appropriate military capability, and also the will to use it. At the same time their governments must attempt through their foreign and foreign economic policies to create the conditions in which their interests can be furthered by non-violent means. If a deterrent is used, by definition it has failed.

In this light, Britain's Falklands campaign of 1982 should be understood, first and foremost, as a breakdown of British military power. The government sent the wrong military and political signals to Argentina, and so had to be rescued by the professionalism and sacrifice of its fighting services. As a result, British strategy for the defence of the islands oscillated within months from sub-minimal deterrence to one of 'Fortress Falklands'. Such a mistake and turnabout cannot be contemplated in Europe. Deterrence has to be got right first time. Consequently, the reintroduction of national service will utimately be vindicated only if it results in a strengthening of deterrence through the sending of effective signals to Britain's allies and adversaries. Like increased nuclear forces – cruise missiles and Pershing IIs, for example – increased conventional forces must primarily be regarded as a politico-military signal. Unlike increased nuclear forces, however, stronger conventional forces can be employed in a direct and rational manner in the event of war breaking out.

It is one of the major contentions of this chapter that the reintroduction of national service would be a powerful signal of British intentions. To our allies it would signal a stronger commitment to the defence of Western Europe, as a result of the new costs and obligations it would involve for the British community. To Britain's potential adversaries the reintroduction of national service should signal a stronger national will and an improved military capability. These signals should automatically strengthen deterrence. By helping to strengthen the Western Alliance – and in a relatively unprovocative way – Britain should be helping not only to reduce the risks of war in Europe, but should also be helping to limit the prospects for the 'Finlandisation' of the West. A healthy NATO also offers the opportunity for a continued role for the USA in Europe (though not necessarily the same as the one to which we have become accustomed) and a collectivist rather than an independent role for West Germany. NATO clarifies. It contributes not only to the defence of the allies, but it also helps establish a framework within which detente might develop.

The comments above refer to the possibility of strengthening the Alliance by making a bigger conventional and manpower contribution to the Central Front. Some defence commentators in Britain have argued for a different emphasis – a maritime one – while others have pointed out that economic imperatives are likely to chip away at the country's long-standing commitment to defence on the Rhine. Both these alternatives should be resisted, since they would send exactly the opposite signals to those that the reintroduction of national service would be designed to transmit. A run-down of Britain's conventional contribution to the Alliance, notably the British Army on the Rhine (BAOR), would have a far-reaching effect on the perceptions of our allies regarding the depth and character of Britain's overall commitment to the defence of Western Europe. As a result, it would have the most serious political and military consequences.

Any run-down of Britain's conventional contribution to the defence of Western Europe could be expected to have consequences for the future of NATO which would probably be more serious than any decision to renounce Trident. On the question of the commitment of troops to Germany, a Senator in the Belgian Parliament, General Robert Close, recently declared: 'If the British go, the Belgians go.'[24] He was referring to the strong pressure being exerted on his government at the time to withdraw Belgium's own troops from Germany; and he added that if Britain reduced its forces in Germany by anything like the 50 per cent being recommended by *The Times* at the end of 1982, it would make the pressures on the Belgian government irresistible. One might expect similar attitudes to be displayed by Britain's other Western European allies. One would not expect such an outcome if Britain scrapped Trident, but at the same time strengthened its conventional forces through conscription.

In addition to the adverse effects of a run-down of BAOR on Britain's European allies, there would also be the prospect of a backlash on the part of the USA. The ground is already politically fertile, as is evident by the worry of NATO supporters about the campaign of Senator Ted Stevens to cut the expenditure on both US hardware and manpower in Europe. At a time when President Reagan was wanting to increase US forces by 37 600 men, Stevens attempted to trim the commitment by 20 000 men. The balance of political forces within the USA may be such that a favourable decision will fall in Stevens's direction; to some commentators his prospects already appear more hopeful than did Senator Mansefield's a dozen years earlier, although Stevens is by no means as well known.[25] In such circumstances, it only requires a 'show of reluctance' on the part of the Europeans to meet their commitments – especially by major allies like Britain – and the US Administration might find the pressures for reduction irresistible.[26] In an America where devils, heroes, and scapegoats are all in demand, resentment against Europeans for 'free riding' could have a profound political effect. It could set NATO on a very slippery slope. Britain's attitude to its conventional commitment is therefore critical to the future of the Alliance.

In addition to the possible political consequences of a run-down of

Britain's conventional commitment to NATO, there would also be major military implications. At the beginning of December 1982 General Bernard Rogers, the Supreme Allied Commander Europe, said that British forces were critical to the balance of his forces in the central region.[27] They were deployed in an important sector of the central front – indeed one of the obvious avenues of a Warsaw Pact attack. And if an attack were to occur, Rogers stated that allied forces were already outnumbered by two to one, and the attacker would have the further advantage of surprise and concentration. He noted: 'Our flexible response strategy for a forward defence requires troops deployed in strength well forward. I need BAOR forces at the general defensive position and not in reserve.' Provided the units now stationed in Belgium, the Netherlands, and the UK in peacetime were rapidly deployed, he believed that the forces available would be marginally adequate for the initial defence. More would obviously help.

NATO is in a serious situation – everybody agrees that 1983 will be a crucial year[28] – and the way Britain acts will play a part in whether the Alliance emerges from its discussions intact or in shreads. It should therefore be evident from the earlier comments that Britain's top priority, for a mixture of political and military reasons, should be to avoid a run-down of its present contribution to the defence of the central front. Such a move, whether taken for economic reasons or as part of a new strategic orientation towards the open seas, would undermine the Alliance politically, would weaken NATO's initial defensive strength, and would lower the nuclear threshold. It would thereby contribute to a perceptible increase in the likelihood of nuclear war. The corollary of these arguments is that a new and enhanced conventional commitment to Western Europe defence would inject new strength into the Alliance, in both its military and political dimensions. The reintroduction of national service, if it were to be accompanied by appropriate diplomatic and military signals, would strengthen strategic stability in Europe – our overriding policy objective. By demonstrating in a practical way that the British are willing and able to fight for and defend their allies, we might hope never to have to face the terrible choice between 'red' or 'dead'.

National service can therefore be regarded as part of the price the British community should be prepared to pay if it is serious about wanting to raise the nuclear threshold, reduce its unstrategic over-reliance on nuclear weapons in the event of war, strengthen stability in Europe, and generally improve the health of the Western Alliance. Although in some sections of the British community national service will not be popular – this includes parts of the armed forces as well as those who might be called 'peace artists' – the benefits should be recognised by almost all responsible opinion. It should be apparent that national service offers important advantages to both a Britain with an independent nuclear deterrent, and one that is set along the path of nuclear renunciation. It meets the political signalling requirements of both these postures, and provides the wherewithal for a more rational strategy in the event of war. Not only would national service help plug gaps in the existing position, it would also provide a basis for the future reform of British defence strategy. Set against the benefits national service offers, the social and economic costs involved and the political difficulties its reintroduction might encounter, should all be seen in better perspective.

To achieve the stated objectives, Britain's shift to national service must have military validity. If it does not have this, it will fail to transmit the right (strong) signals. Obviously the creation of a robust conventional force would be costly, but it is by no means impossible, for although there are disagreements among specialists regarding the trends in conventional warfare – as there always will be in such a complex and dynamic business – a consensus has emerged which believes that technology has been working in favour of the defensive.[29] Building a satisfactory non-nuclear posture would not be a cheap or easy alternative to reliance on nuclear weapons. Many problems would have to be overcome in matters of tactical doctrine and weapons procurement, as well as cost; and these problems must be directly confronted by such groupings as the Labour Party and CND. Money and effort will have to be found, to the detriment of other needs that are both more pleasant to think about and more popular with the electorate.

Supporters of a non-nuclear strategy must also contemplate other unpleasant implications of their choice, notably the horror of even 'conventional' warfare in Europe. The only consolation one can find in contemplating such a war is the possibility that it would be somewhat less indiscriminately destructive than the nightmare of nuclear war. But in this horror lies the strategic utility of a robust non-nuclear defence. For if the potential aggressor comes to believe that no attack could be carried through quickly or cheaply, then the stronger conventional forces will have done their job. Ultimately, stronger conventional forces are to be valued by the extent to which they work as an effective deterrent to war. Like all forms of military power, they will have failed if they ever have to be used.

The British contribution to the Alliance following the reintroduction of national service could be significant. France, with a population slightly smaller than Britain's, has 200 000 national servicemen in its Army alone. The potential infantry force which Britain could deploy in Germany would therefore become substantial. In the light of what is possible as a result of the decentralisation of firepower today, an additional contribution by Britain of 20 000 Land Rovers, armoured personnel carriers, and light-tracked vehicles, each containing a handful of men and a full complement of ATGWs or surface-to-air missiles, or mines and minelets, could make a decisive contribution to NATO's conventional strategy. This is all the more likely in view of the growing evidence that the conventional military balance in Europe is not as bad as many have hitherto supposed.[30] By reintroducing national service, Britain could make an enormous boost to the Alliance's efforts in a non-nuclear direction, as was highlighted by General Bernard Rogers in September 1982.[31] Supporters of a greater or exclusive non-nuclear emphasis in defence should therefore press on with confidence, for as one former US 'insider' has recently argued, a conventional defence of Europe is feasible, but even if it ultimately proves unattainable, 'what better alternative do we have but to try'.[32]

If a strategy is to work over a long period it must have the support of the country's population and, if that country is in an alliance, the support of its allies as well. It is in relation to the former problem where the reintroduction of national service in Britain is likely to confront its major problem. It is unlikely that any of Britain's allies would object to such a step, but considerable opposition might be expected at home, though it is difficult to estimate how much in advance. Even if national service is thought to make strategic sense, is it politically and economically practicable?

When the issue of the reintroduction of national service in Britain is raised, the discussion invariably focuses on its social and economic advantages or disadvantages rather than on its military rationale. And on the whole the disadvantages have appeared to be too heavy to encourage many politicians to contemplate such a step. Naturally, the disadvantages will loom larger at a time when a general election is in the air. Even so, if proper leadership is provided, there could well be a bigger political constituency for the idea than might at first be expected. As was suggested earlier, national service could even be an issue on which both sides of the nuclear debate might come together, since almost everybody accepts the importance of trying to raise the nuclear threshold. Stronger conventional forces are a logical component of all strategies that seek to put the nuclear genie back in the bottle, without leaving us defenceless. Furthermore, there is a solid pro-defence body of opinion in Britain,[33] while the boost in the prestige of the forces as a result of the Falklands War is a useful foundation on which any conscription-minded government could build.

Regardless of the strategic rationales for national service discussed earlier, any forthcoming debate about the issue will almost certainly concentrate on its social, economic, and moral dimensions. The British public is still generally happy to leave military matters to the experts, despite the famous warning of Clemenceau and the further experience of six troubled decades.[34] In the future, as in the past, we can expect any defence debate to become a matter of domestic politics writ large, especially if conscription is the issue. Typically we can expect that the majority will be inclined to design a defence policy on the basis of what they want to afford, rather than on the basis of what can be afforded.

It is unlikely, to say the least, that any political party in the immediate future will include national service on its election platform. But this does not mean that consideration of the issue is futile. First, by arguing about what constitutes a rational defence posture we might better come to appreciate the gap between the feasible and the desirable. And second, the reintroduction of national service, by its nature, is the sort of step that a government would take as a result of a display of strong leadership once in power, rather than as part of the fulfilment of a ballot-box mandate. In this respect it should not be forgotten that the British people tend to be responsive to strong leadership, a feature of national life that was again confirmed by the Falklands War. So, the possible 'unpopularity' of reintroducing national service, on the basis of opinion polls or letters to the press, should not be given undue weight. Public opinion in a democracy sometimes leads and sometimes is led: the reintroduction of national service is one of those issues on which the public will have to be led.

The arguments that would be deployed in any forthcoming debate will have been heard many times, and they are easily identifiable in a set of quite distinct 'for' and 'against' positions. For the most part these arguments are based on quite different assumptions about man and society, the nature of democracy, and the 'realities' of international politics. This can be seen from Table 7.1 below, which attempts to summarise the main debating positions. Some of the arguments overlap; others are contradictory; and others are not exactly commensurate. Nevertheless, it is hoped that this tabulation will help to reveal the likely spectrum, nuances, and tone of any debate.

From Table 7.1 it is evident that it will be extraordinarily difficult to tip the balance either way on social, moral, or economic grounds: the differences of outlook are mainly conducive to continuing debate and, practically, to continuing stalemate. This suggests that those who want progress on the matter should shift the emphasis of the debate on to the overriding strategic rationale for national service, while attempting to meet the various objections of the critics by adopting a type of national service that, while militarily valid, is both flexible and imaginative. In a liberal democracy conscription should only be adopted to meet a military need, and never simply to provide an element of youth control.

The issue of costs will undoubtedly figure prominently. This is unavoidable and proper, but it is imperative that 'costs' are considered in the widest possible terms. We should therefore consider not only direct costs in monetary terms, but also the possible strategic and political costs of *not* undertaking such an effort. Since the monetary costs will be immediate and tangible, and the costs of *not* having conscription will be long-term and intangible – unless and until war breaks out – it is likely that accountants rather than neo-Clausewitzians will talk loudest. But to any who would assert that national service is 'impossible' and prohibitively costly we should look for empirical evidence among our allies. Then we would better appreciate that national service is a familiar institution which is maintained by all our European partners. Once the general public has a better understanding of the way our allies cope, national service will not appear to be the impossible burden it might now seem. Rather than national service being seen as an aberration, the British will see that they made themselves the European odd-man-out when they ended the 'call-up' a generation ago, during a period of 'you have never had it so good'.

How costly national service will actually be cannot at present be answered; and since the subject has been closed over the past generation, the studies have not been done on which accurate assessments can be made. However, there are some rules of thumb, and these can be seen if we examine the characteristics of the military systems of those European allies that are nearest to Britain in size and economic power (see Table 7.2). This is then followed by Table 7.3, which reveals the characteristics of three 'unilateralist' countries, which are sometimes seen as models that Britain might follow.[35] In both cases the results are not discouraging for proponents of national service.

Tables 7.2 and 7.3 reveal several striking features. First, that national service is 'affordable' for a country of Britain's size and resources. Second, that it is possible to be both richer than Britain and have

TABLE 7.1   *Major themes in the debate about conscription in Britain*

Critical positions	Favourable positions
1. The armed services do not see it as part of their responsibility to provide training for the unemployed, the immature, and the discontented. The armed services should not be responsible for 'youth control'.	1. 'A few years in the armed services will make a man of you.' Such an experience instils a sense of national consciousness and discipline. This is particularly important at a time of large-scale unemployment, periodic street violence, and widespread hooliganism.
2. National service is boring and a waste of time. It is a means by which governments try to acquire cheap labour. It should not be considered as a palliative for unemployment.	2. In a period of heavy unemployment, the youth of the country could profitably spend a short time developing skills and learning about the world while they are deciding what they want to get out of life.
3. The armed forces have a shortage of training resources, space, and competent instructors for a massive influx of conscripts.	3. All our Western European allies run conscription schemes, and Britain has in the past. Where there is a will there is a way.
4. The costs are prohibitive: conscripts need to be equipped and housed, as well as trained.	4. Conscripts are paid less than regulars, and cuts can be made in some of the high-cost technology presently being considered. But the main point is that we can 'afford' such a scheme if we want to: we remain the only large European country without such a system.
5. The direct costs are more than Whitehall could consider.	5. The benefits of national service may be indirect as well as direct, and may include better work discipline, a stronger sense of national unity, etc. In addition, direct benefits would include the creation of a reservoir of practical skills.
6. Professionals do a much better job than conscripts: we do not need large forces. In any case, recruiting is satisfactory at present and is likely to remain so.	6. Britain alone of its European allies relies on the market place to ensure that the country has an adequate defence capability.

TABLE 7.1 – *continued*

Critical positions	Favourable positions
7. Increased manpower would weaken the armed forces by distracting large numbers of regulars into training unwilling conscripts who soon leave and lose whatever skills they acquired.	7. Increased manpower would strengthen our armed forces. The military consequences of the ending of conscription have been obscured by the relative security which has existed in Europe for the last twenty-five years, our overriding faith in nuclear weapons, and the pull-back from east of Suez.
8. Our armed forces are proud of their professionalism, and this would be diluted by a massive influx of conscripts. Elitism would continue to exist; the possibility of a coup is so remote as not to be included in the argument.	8. National service 'civilianise' the armed forces; it curbs elitism and militarism; and it reduces the chance of a military coup.
9. The period of any conscription scheme would be too short for the participants to learn to handle the latest weaponry.	9. Modern technology is complicated to make and maintain, but relatively easy to operate.
10. Nobody should be compelled to learn to fight and kill.	10. Taking up arms in defence of one's country, in peace as well as war, should be a democratic duty.
11. Conscription is morally objectionable in a liberal democratic society.	11. The vast majority of people are not pacifists, but it is axiomatic in a liberal democracy that individuals should be allowed to opt out of national military service on grounds of conscience.
12. Future wars will be short and probably nuclear. There is no requirement for a mass army. In any case, the forces themselves would not be happy to admit very large numbers of conscripts, since their attitudes and lack of skills would degrade the efficient machines which have been built up.	12. War has always proved to be unpredictable, and many wars which were expected to be short turned out to be prolonged. In a prolonged war it is useful to have a large body of trained reserves, as well as ready manpower. In an inherently unsafe world it is essential for a country to have large ready forces and trained manpower for the many unexpected contingencies which can arise.

TABLE 7.1 – *continued*

Critical positions	Favourable positions
13. It is best to leave a country's defence to a relatively small group of specialists.	13. The best, most credible, deterrent to invasion is a whole nation with the training and determination to defend itself.
14. In practice the armed forces are class-ridden. There is a rigid division between 'officers' and 'men'. The dirty work will continue to be done by the children of unskilled workers, blacks, etc. Regular officers will have no real interest in the welfare of conscripts in general and non-officer conscripts in particular.	14. People today put too much emphasis on their rights rather than their duties to their national community. The experience of national service will improve every citizen's appreciation of the importance of responsibilities and duties, as well as rights, and will strengthen their sense of service to their local and national community. The experience will enable those from all walks of life to meet a cross-section of people. It is a common experience which will cement society. Fewer and fewer people have any direct contact with the services, and an unhealthy division has grown up between the people as a whole and the 'professional' servicemen.
15. National service is spent in pointless activity. The prevailing aim is to dodge work and try to make the time pass as quickly as possible.	15. The experience of national service inculcates a sense of comradeship and discipline in most of those who undergo it. People should be given the opportunity to serve their country.
16. It is enough that people support defence through paying taxes.	16. National service touches every family, and is a reminder that national defence needs the support of every citizen. It increases public awareness about defence issues.
17. Such a step needs public consent, and at present the idea of service is popular with the old rather than the young. Among the latter, conscription would only increase the tensions between the advantaged and disadvantaged.	17. If they were given 'proper' leadership the youth of this country would respond to the call. They always have, and national service, after all, is 'normal' throughout Europe.

TABLE 7.2 *The defence profiles of selected Western European allies (1982–3)*

	Britain	France	Italy	West Germany
Population	55 965 000	53 874 000	57 300 000	61 665 000
Military service	Voluntary	12 months (18 for overseas)	Army and Air Force, 12 months, Navy 18 months)	15 months (to be 18)
Total regular forces	327 600	237 850	128 000	266 000
Total conscripts	–	255 000	242 000	229 000
Total armed forces	327 600	492 850*	370 000	495 000
Total reserves	281 700	457 000	799 000	750 000
Army: regulars	163 100	116 200	67 000	155 500
conscripts	–	198 000	190 000	180 000
Navy: regular	73 000	50 000	10 300	25 400
conscripts	–	18 000	23 700	11 000
Air Force: regular	91 500	61 900	30 700	67 900
conscripts	–	38 500	28 300	38 000
GDP (in dollars 1981)	$449.85 bn	$570.51 bn	$350.154 bn	$687.12 bn
Total Defence expenditure (1982–3)	$25.4 bn	$19.295 bn	$7.711 bn	$18.44 bn
Defence as % of GNP (1981)	5.4	4.1	2.5	4.3
Per capita defence spending (1981)	$443	$437	$153	$471

* Includes 10 250 on inter-service staff.
Source: *The Military Balance 1982–1983* (London: The IISS, 1982).

conscription. Third, that it is possible to be smaller than Britain and yet be able to mobilise greater military reserves. Four, that the period thought necessary for training, fifteen months on average, is not likely to be an unbearable social burden. And five, what is notably different between Britain and the other countries is the voluntary service and nuclear character of Britain's defence posture, and at the same time its relatively heavy defence outlay in both absolute terms and as a percentage of GNP.

It is possible that France, Italy, West Germany, Switzerland, and Sweden have badly underestimated the effort that they should spend on defence. Alternatively, it may be that they have correctly assessed the threat to themselves and have developed an appropriate defence posture. It is the contention of this chapter that the latter is true, and that, in contrast, Britain's pro-nuclear and all-volunteer forces are not appropriate for the country's power or the strategic predicament in which it finds itself. Heavy savings could be made on the pay and pensions of the voluntary forces, and on the research and development involved in maintaining a nuclear capability. As Tables 7.2 and 7.3 show, nuclear weapons are not a cheap form of defence when tied with all-volunteer forces: in contrast, conscripted manpower is relatively cheap. Although the opponents of national service would stress the costs involved, the comparison with other countries shows that these need not be overwhelming, though it should be pointed out that there are various hidden costs in conscription (job dislocation, social costs, etc.) which cannot be shown in a table.[36] On the other hand, the proponents of national service would argue that there are hidden advantages to the system, such as a higher level of technical training in the country.

A nation can always spend more than it wants to afford. So against those who might complain about the undue costs likely to be involved, it is instructive to remember Neville Chamberlain's contribution to British defence during his period as Chancellor of the Exchequer in the mid-1930s. In 1934 the Defence Requirements Committee requested more funding, but Chamberlain 'pre-judged the issue', to use Stephen Roskill's words.[37] Rather than seeing whether the money requested to repair Britain's defences could be found, Chamberlain merely reacted with the words, 'to put it bluntly we are presented with proposals impossible to carry out'. But obviously the proposals were not 'impossible to carry out', for again as Roskill has explained, the money requested was only about one-tenth of the sum that the government had to find, and found, only three years later. The defence improvements were 'impossible' psychologically rather than objectively. And it hardly needs pointing out that three years' extra preparedness would have been very beneficial to Britain's forces at the start of the war which eventually did break out. Furthermore, it is even conceivable that extra preparedness would have given the British government additional confidence to have stood up to Hitler; this, in turn, would have gathered a stronger anti-Hitler coalition among the nations of Europe. Britain can afford national service, and we should let our minds be dominated by the potential benefits of such a step rather than the unstrategic priorities of accountants.

Whether we as a national community want to afford national service will, in part, depend upon the characteristics of the actual system chosen. Discussion of such matters as the precise level of manpower needed, or the length of an individual's commitment, go far beyond the confines of an essay seeking merely to open up a debate in the light of what has been argued is the overriding strategic rationale for such a step. It suffices simply to lay down two propositions. First, on the question of size, there is much to commend the suggestion of Chichester and Wilkinson that we need at least half-a-million men-at-arms.[38] This figure could be split very roughly 50:50 between regulars and conscripts, though the ratios would vary between the three services. It should give an extra 100 000 men to the Army. As it happens, the overall size proposed is similar to that of our major Western European allies, France and West Germany. Second, for social and political reasons, it is desirable that *national* service must be universal, but that *military* service is not obligatory. For this reason 'national service' should be much broader than a commitment to the fighting forces, though the latter should have first call on willing and able-bodied manpower (and womanpower). It is also important that proper account be taken of conscientious objection. As a result, a three-tier system of national service should be conceived, which will cater for all – men and women, the fit and the unfit, and the pacifist and non-pacifist. Its profile is shown in Figure 7.1.

Such a three-tier system would be difficult to organise and it would require flexibility, imagination, and commitment to put into operation – not least from trade unions and local government officials – but such a system would clearly be both national and a service. It would provide training and a common experience which over time could manufacture a more mature, involved, and unified national community. One year to fifteen months is proposed as the length of an individual's commitment. This should be enough time to develop the basic military skills and fitness, as long as the maximum use is made of the time available. The

TABLE 7.3 *The defence profiles of selected European non-aligned countries*

	Britain (for comparison)	Sweden	Switzerland	Yugoslavia
Population	55 965 000	8 323 000	6 370 000	22 650 000
Military service	Voluntary	Army and Navy 7½–15 months, Air Force, 8–12 months	17 weeks recruit training followed by refresher training, 3 weeks– 1 week†	15 months
Total regular forces	327 600	17 400	1 500	96 500
Total conscripts	–	47 100	18 500	154 000
Total armed forces	327 600	64 500*	605 000	500 000
Total reserves	281 700	735 000	580 000 on mobilisation	50 000
Army: regulars	163 100	9 000		140 000
conscripts	–	36 000		
Navy: regulars	73 000	3 400	–	9 500
conscripts	–	6 600		6 000
Air Force: regulars	91 500	5 000	45 000 on mobilisation	37 000
conscripts	–	4 500		8 000
GDP (in dollars 1981)	$449.88 bn	$110.9 bn	$110.03 bn	$69.867 bn (1980)

Total defence expenditure (1982–3)	$25.4 bn	$3.22 bn	$1.78 bn	$2.87 bn (1981)
Defence as % of GNP	5.4	3.1	1.8	4.6
Per capita defence spending (1981)	$443	$412	$281	$126

* There are normally approximately 95 500 more conscripts (70 000 Army, 4 500 Navy, and 6 000 Air Force) plus 15 000 officer and NCO reservists doing 11–40 days refresher training at some time in the year.

† 3 weeks for 8 out of 12 years between age 20–32; 2 weeks for 3 years age 33–42; 1 week for 2 years between age 43–50. Some 400 000 reservists a year do refresher training.

Source: *The Military Balance 1982–1983* (London: The IISS, 1982).

FIGURE 7.1 Britain's three-tier national service

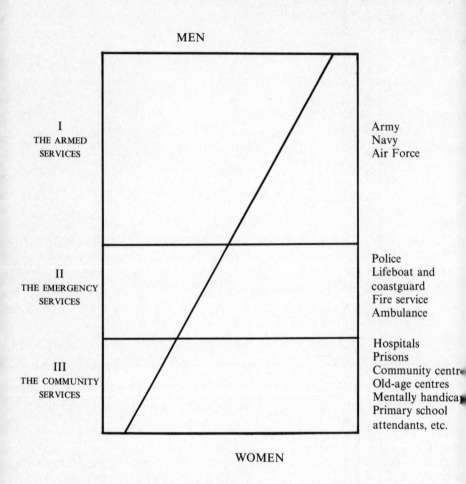

MEN

I
THE ARMED
SERVICES

Army
Navy
Air Force

II
THE EMERGENCY
SERVICES

Police
Lifeboat and
coastguard
Fire service
Ambulance

III
THE COMMUNITY
SERVICES

Hospitals
Prisons
Community centre
Old-age centres
Mentally handica
Primary school
attendants, etc.

WOMEN

latter is particularly important, in any case, in order to avoid conscripts feeling bored. The term of training should be so organised that nobody will have time to brood. It should be more Outward Bound than 'Dad's Army'. Furthermore, although modern weapons are complex, the average recruit should be able to handle those necessary for his own narrow role within a short time. The battle for Westphalia may well be won in the Atari-dominated living rooms of England.

It may be that national service is 'hardly a starter', as General Sir John Hackett has recently put it, even though such a step would be 'so desirable in many ways'.[39] Hackett recognised, as do other observers of the British defence scene, that the country makes inadequate use of its manpower potential. Lord Carver, for example, has expressed his lack of faith in the willingness of governments to allow desirable increases in resources to conventional forces; consequently he sees little alternative to proposing a better use of reserves.[40] This is also the view of Chichester and Wilkinson, who favour a major expansion of the volunteer reserve forces.[41] However, while an expansion of the reserves would do something to meet some of the needs of the situation, it would fail to meet the wide range of objectives that national service proper might hope to fulfil.

The time to reintroduce national service will never be 'right', so it is as well that it be done as quickly as is practicable. Since one cannot be confident that Britain will be able to avoid another period of financial difficulty in the near future – our economic prospects in recent years have never been so bad that they cannot get worse – it is important that this major step be taken before more immediate economic distractions again come to dominate national thinking, as they so often have. In an uncertain world, strategy should never be kept waiting.

But national service on its own is not enough. It should be seen as but one of the steps towards creating a more rational defence strategy for Britain, that is, a military posture and associated doctrine of employment which offers us the best promise of deterring and if necessary combating our most likely military challenges, within the capabilities of the British economy, and having due regard to some of the geographical advantages and particular vulnerabilities of the country. This rational posture may be described as one of 'conventional continental defence based on a strategy of expedients'.[42]

This strategy has four elements: (i) a shift from a pro-nuclear to a conventional defence for Western Europe; (ii) the maintenance of the NATO framework; (iii) the allocation of greater resources in Britain to conventional forces, including national service; and (iv) the replacement of the escalatory strategy of flexible response with a doctrine based upon a 'strategy of expedients'.[43] Some of these proposals are bound to be more controversial than others, but what is thought controversial will depend upon what part of the political spectrum the reader stands. Some might agree that the proposed package takes the most sensible elements from the prescriptions of several sides of the current debate; it can therefore be seen as representing a conjunction of the desirable and the feasible for British defence policy for the difficult years ahead.

The individual elements of the proposed strategy have been discussed at length over the past few years, and some have been referred to in this chapter. The value of NATO, the advantages of a conventional rather than a pro-nuclear strategy, the dangers of flexible response – all these have had their proponents and critics in the defence debate which has been forced upon a normally reticent establishment by an abnormally loud and increasingly knowledgeable peace movement. But there is one particular aspect of the proposed posture that does require an additional few words, especially in the light of the unnecessary attention being given to a so-called 'maritime strategy' for Britain in the wake of the Falklands War.[44]

The success of British arms in 1982 has led some to recommend changing the emphasis of the wholly sensible trend of British policy in the last twenty years, namely the concentration on Europe. This proposed change of emphasis is misconceived, for the 'realities' of our position should be quite clear: Britain is a European power; our allies value the commitment we make on the ground and elsewhere, and would be concerned if this commitment declined; we do not have the power to take up arms independently elsewhere; the Falklands affair was a one-off episode which should not be repeated, especially since we are becoming increasingly aware of the extent to which it was a close-run thing; the Soviet 'strategic momentum' in the Third World has been vastly exaggerated by the crude Sovietology of the Reagan and Thatcher governments; and Britain's overriding defence objective – without which nothing else makes sense – is the stability of Europe, where Soviet military power, if fully and immediately unleashed, could put an end to our history during breakfast time. As has been the case throughout the twentieth century, our security ultimately rests on a continental military commitment to European stability. Consequently, BAOR should be increased in size: reduction ought to be thought unthinkable.[45]

Having accepted that the continental commitment must remain paramount, it must also be accepted that Britain obviously has wider interests, and a concern for stability in other parts of the world. For this purpose a very modest capability should be maintained to assist local associates and the USA when we consider it to be in our interests. In this respect our main concern for the next few decades will be with the supply of oil from the Gulf, a region where it is difficult to see what decisive military contribution Britain could make, even if we devoted extreme efforts to the task. If the USA has some doubts about its ability to intervene and maintain the flow of oil, those of the High Tory school of British strategy, whose ideas received a shot in the arm as a result of the Falklands War, should be appropriately chastened. In any case, many of the security problems we face are not amenable to military quick-fixes: for this reason we must be more conscious than ever of the wider meaning of 'national security', and should seek to contribute to those mechanisms that help stability, development, and interdependence. In this respect recent British governments have a poor record. Sadly, the government's strategic failure at the start of 1982, which led to the invasion of the Falklands, was matched at the end of the year by its failure to sign the UN Convention on the Law of the Sea.

British security is obviously dependent on developments outside the NATO area, and sometimes the use of military force may be necessary. But it is difficult to imagine circumstances in which Britain could act independently of the USA. If this is the case, Britain should be in a position to offer some military support on those occasions when the USA is proposing to act in such a way as to advance our common interests. On such occasions, warships are particularly useful for demonstrating the internationality of an effort. But at the same time, the most solid help we can offer consists of showing our allies that we are willing and able to plug any gaps that might be left by the Americans in Europe. We are not 'all Falklanders', as *The Times* asserted in its famous leader on 5 April 1982: nor can we be. We are a middle-rank country off the north-west coast of Europe, and our strategy must be determined by our power and interests, not by exaggerated opinions about our capability or anachronistic emotions.

The Falklands War has given a new intensity to the debate about British defence priorities, a debate that had already been under way for several years as a result of converging nuclear questions. In a strictly military sense – in terms of missile development, the vulnerability of ships and so on – the campaign in the South Atlantic produced some useful albeit fatally costly lessons. But in a political sense the effect of this 'splendid little war' has been to distract attention from our overriding concern with the peace and security of Europe, and instead to give a boost to an outdated High Tory approach to strategy. Strategically there were only three 'lessons' from the episode. First, it is cheaper to signal one's determination to defend one's patch of territory in peacetime than it is to try to recover the situation following an invasion. Second, an adequate deterrent and defence force cannot be acquired cheaply: and if we want the ends of deterrence we must be willing to pay for the means. And third, success in war ultimately depends on being able to occupy ground. Translated into the European military confrontation, to which Britain is tied by the iron laws of geography and technology, these lessons again underline the value of national service.

National service is an urgent issue, despite the lack of attention being devoted to it, because in peacetime it requires a prolonged period before becoming operational. Realistically, we must think in terms of it requiring a couple of years rather than months. And even after being put into operation it will take several more years before the benefits can be seen. The obstacles are obviously formidable in a democratic country where most people believe themselves to be reasonably secure and have become used to having their 'defence' on the cheap (socially, if not financially). However, this chapter has suggested that if a system of national service was to be introduced with flexibility and imagination, and if it was to be made broader than merely military service, then its political and moral acceptability to the community at large would be greatly increased. Nor should we underestimate the potential support for it which might presently exist. If properly packaged, national service could quickly become accepted as a proper democratic duty, with the aim of freeing us somewhat from the terrible threat of nuclear war, and helping us to deal with the uncertainties of an unstable world. Most opposition to the reintroduction of national service is likely to come from the young and the political left: but if critics of existing policies are not willing to undertake burdens in order to give Britain an appropriate strategy, can they complain if others, who believe they know better, assert that we should rest our defence for the next thirty years on battlefield and theatre nuclear weapons, and Trident?

For all the reasons mentioned, national service should be reintroduced quickly and in a positive fashion. It should be regarded as a democratic duty, as well as a military necessity: the theme should be 'one man (or woman), one vote, one ATGW'. Citizens should be willing to contribute more to their nation's security than passively allowing tax to be regularly docked off their pay-packets. After all, there is nothing revolutionary in such a step: Britain remains the only major European country whose citizens do not accept such a duty. If we focus on the benefits of such a step, especially its anti-nuclear dimension, we should begin to appreciate its direct costs in a new light. Minimising the risk of nuclear war is the prize we are all seeking – unilateralists and multilateralists alike, left and right, internationalists and little Englanders. Similarly, we all share an interest in raising the nuclear threshold in the event of war. This chapter has shown that larger conventional forces have an important role in both strengthening the credibility of deterrence and in raising the nuclear threshold. If all sides of the political debate keep in mind that the potential prize consists of reducing the risks of nuclear annihilation, we might better appreciate that the cost of *not* introducing national service could well be the heaviest that the British nation will ever have to face.

NOTES

1. See, for example, John C. Garnett, 'British strategic thought', pp. 156–73 in John Baylis (ed.), *British Defence Policy in a Changing World* (London: Croom Helm, 1977).
2. How many bombs would fall, and where, is a matter of lively speculation among the critics of Britain's pro-nuclear posture, if not – apparently – among the proponents of existing policies. One estimate postulates the use of about seventy Soviet nuclear warheads in a 'limited counterforce attack' against thirty-three prime military targets in Britain, plus a number of 'secret' installations which Soviet planners are likely to believe are critical for command and control or the storage of weapons. A 'large-scale attack', which might consist of about 140 Soviet warheads, would attack a mix of about 114 targets – military and industrial centres, energy supply systems, centres of business and administration, and systems of transport and communications. Since many of the targets lie within areas of dense population, 'the future existence of civilisation in Britain would be seriously in question'. Peter Goodwin, *Nuclear War. The Facts* (London: Macmillan, 1982) pp. 68–71.
3. The 'peace movement' presently consists of over thirty major organisations. The largest, CND, is said to have about 250 000 members. A Gallup poll at the end of 1982 found that 58 per cent of the public believed that US cruise missiles should not be deployed in Britain and 56 per cent believed that Trident should be cancelled. The figures for women were 64 per cent and 60 per cent respectively. Judy Foreman, 'The nuclear disarmers', *The Times*, 26 November 1982. Significantly, the opponents of British nuclear weapons now include some who do not fit the former cranky left-wing image of the peace movement. Field-Marshal Lord Carver, former Chief of the Defence Staff, is the most conspicuous example.
4. These matters are discussed in Ken Booth, 'Unilateralism: A Clausewitzian Reform?', ch. 3 in Nigel Blake and Kay Pole (eds), *Dangers of Deterrence: Philosophers on Nuclear Weapons* (London: Routledge & Kegan Paul, forthcoming).
5. Because there is only sea between Britain and the Falklands, our imagination foreshortens the remoteness of the islands. A pair of dividers reveals the surprising fact that, as the crow flies, London is much nearer to Hong Kong than to Port Stanley.
6. Among the published contributions, see 'Your country needs you', *The Times*, editorial, 27 February 1982; Henry Stanhope, 'National Service: should we get fell in?', *The Times*, 2 March 1982; Martin Walker, 'Where

citizens supplant professionals', *Guardian*, 14 August 1982; Michael Chichester and John Wilkinson, *The Uncertain Ally. British Defence Policy 1960–1990* (Aldershot: Gower, 1982).

7. Chichester and Wilkinson, *The Uncertain Ally*, ch. 17.
8. See Kenneth Hunt, 'Alternative conventional force postures', pp. 133–48 in Kenneth A. Myers (ed.), *NATO: The Next Thirty Years: the changing political, economic, and military setting* (Boulder: Westview, 1980).
9. See John C. Garnett, 'Limited "conventional" war in the nuclear age', p. 91, in Michael Howard (ed.), *Restraints on War* (Oxford University Press, 1979).
10. On the relatively small exertions needed to overcome whatever conventional weaknesses exist, note the comments of Robert McNamara, former US Secretary of Defense, and General Bernard Rogers, the present SACEUR: in *The Listener*, 10 June 1982, and the *Guardian*, 29 September 1982.
11. Field-Marshal Lord Carver, *A Policy For Peace* (London: Faber & Faber, 1982).
12. Note its importance, for example, in the contingencies discussed by John J. Mearsheimer, 'Why the Soviets can't win quickly in Central Europe', *International Security*, vol. 7 (1), Summer 1982, pp. 3–39.
13. Note the references in US posture statements, 1978–9, quoted by A. Ross Johnson *et al.*, *East European Military Establishments: The Warsaw Pact Northern Tier* (New York: Crane Russak, 1982) pp. 1–2.
14. See, for example, Hunt, 'Alternative conventional force postures'.
15. Ibid; see also Chichester and Wilkinson, *The Uncertain Ally*, pp. 193–203.
16. General Sir John Hackett, 'More, much more, for defence', *The Sunday Times*, 20 June 1982.
17. Ibid.
18. Captain B. H. Liddell Hart, 'The ratio of troops to space', *RUSI Journal*, vol. CV, no. 618, May 1960, pp. 201–12.
19. Mearsheimer, 'Why the Soviets can't win quickly', pp. 32–6 and notes 75 and 79.
20. Johnson, *East European Military Establishments*, esp. pp. 54–7, 98–102, 137–9, 148–9.
21. The following points are based on Adam Roberts, *Nation in Arms: The Theory and Practice of Territorial Defence* (London: Chatto & Windus, 1976) p. 34.
22. Fortunately, however, Britain has apparently not produced any equivalent to the 'nuke-niks' who give some of the sustenance to the defence thinking of the Reagan administration: see Robert Scheer, *With Enough Shovels: Reagan, Bush and Nuclear War* (New York: Random House, 1982); and the review by Solly Zuckerman, 'Nuclear sense and nonsense', *The New York Review*, 16 December 1982.
23. In the literature of the nuclear strategists, this argument was put most cogently by Thomas C. Schelling, *Arms and Influence* (New Haven: Yale University Press, 1966) esp. ch. 1.
24. Quoted by Frederick Bonnart, 'Troops are needed to maintain credibility', *The Times*, 14 December 1982.
25. David Watt, 'Why the Yanks may start going home', *The Times*, 26 November 1982.

26. Bonnart, 'Troops are needed'.
27. Frederick Bonnart, 'Rhine Army "vital for balance of forces" ', *The Times*, 13 December 1982.
28. See, for example, Ian Murray, 'NATO fears 1983 will be its worst year', *The Times*, 10 December 1982.
29. For a comprehensive and intelligent introduction to the state of the art in conventional warfare see Kenneth Hunt, 'The development of concepts for conventional warfare in the 1970s and 1980s', ch. 12 in Robert O'Neill and D. M. Horner (eds), *New Directions In Strategic Thinking* (London: George Allen & Unwin, 1981). Of basic importance has been the progress in precision-guided weapons: see James Digby, *Precision Guided Weapons*, Adelphi Papers No. 118 (London: IISS, 1975). According to Liddell Hart, 'The ratio of troops, the growing domination of the defensive – if properly conceived – has been a trend in war since the time of Napoleon.' For an important criticism of Liddell Hart's thesis, see Neville Brown, 'The changing face of non-nuclear war', *Survival*, vol. XXIV (5), September/October 1982, pp. 211–19. For sceptical assessments of the prospects for a non-nuclear defence against a nuclear adversary, see 'Do you sincerely want to be non-nuclear?', *The Economist*, 31 July 1982; and Edward Spiers, 'Conventional defence: no alternative to Trident', *RUSI Journal*, vol. 127 (3), September 1982, pp. 21–7.
30. Note, for example, the comments of ex-Secretary of Defense, Robert McNamara, in conversation with Laurence Martin, printed in *The Listener*, 10 June 1982; and Rogers's comments in David Fairhall, 'Non-nuclear defence plan for Europe', *Guardian*, 29 September 1982; and William Rademaekers, 'General Rogers' lonely crusade', *Time*, 25 October 1982. Even *The Economist*'s survey (note 29 above) found the military balance 'surprisingly cheerful'. McNamara's views were further elaborated in a conversation with Robert Scheer, 'The declining strength of the Soviets', *Guardian*, 9 August 1982. By no means everybody in NATO was happy with the non-nuclear emphasis being given by Rogers. See John Palmer, 'Reagan sticks to missile base plan despite NATO proposal', *Guardian*, 19 October 1982; and David Fairhall, 'NATO firm on nuclear deterrent', *Guardian*, 2 December 1982.
31. *Guardian*, 29 September 1982.
32. Robert Komer, 'Is conventional defense of Europe feasible?', *Naval War College Review*, September–October 1982, p. 90. Between 1979–81 Komer was Under Secretary of Defense for Policy.
33. According to one German opinion poll, 62 per cent of English respondents indicated a willingness to fight for the country in the event of war; 11 per cent were undecided: Elisabeth Noelle-Neumann, 'Who needs a flag?', *Encounter*, January 1983, p. 78. In the event of war, the familiar habit of 'rallying around the flag' might be expected, even among the undecided and hostile.
34. Clemenceau said that war was too serious to be left to the generals. It should also be evident that strategy is too serious to be left to the strategists: see Ken Booth, *Strategy and Ethnocentrism* (London: Croom Helm, 1979) pp. 166–7. Although the British public is generally apathetic about defence, the peace movement in recent years has had a very beneficial effect on British

strategic policy, by forcing the strategic community to raise the level of debate on nuclear issues. The appointment of Michael Heseltine as Defence Minister in January 1983 was widely interpreted as showing that the Cabinet was aware of the problem of having to deal with increasingly knowledgeable and forceful critics.

35. See Walker, 'Where citizens supplant professionals'; Adam Roberts, 'The alternative, non-nuclear way to defend ourselves', *New Society*, 4 February 1982, pp. 175–7.

36. We, the British, often forget these hidden costs, which do not show up in calculations of 'defence budget as a percentage of the GNP', when we complain that we make more of a defence 'effort' than our European allies who do have a system of compulsory military service.

37. Stephen W. Roskill, *Naval Policy between the Wars. I. The Period of Anglo–American Antagonism 1919–1928* (London: Collins, 1968) pp. 171–2.

38. Chichester and Wilkinson, *The Uncertain Ally*, p. 185.

39. Hackett, 'More, much more, for defence'.

40. Carver, *Policy for Peace*, pp. 109–10.

41. Chichester and Wilkinson, *The Uncertain Ally*, pp. 193–203.

42. See Booth, 'Unilateralism: A Clausewitzian reform?'.

43. This is explained in Booth, ibid. The 'strategy of expedients' would be a modern application of the inspiration of the Elder Moltke. He believed that strategy should not be the execution of a premeditated plan, but a system of '*ad hoc* expedients' in accordance with an original idea. Large-scale war in Europe today would be so chaotic that military and political expediency is the only rational strategic posture. Unfortunately NATO's existing 'Flexible Response' strategy is Newspeak: in practice it should be translated as 'Programmed Escalation'.

44. See, for example, the series of leaders in *The Times*, 'No end of a lesson', 2, 3, 4, 5 November 1982; and Ian Murray, 'Admiral spells out lessons of the Falklands war', *The Times*, 7 December 1982.

45. Fortunately, Mrs Thatcher's government has apparently not been swayed by the 'maritime' arguments. While acknowledging that resources would have to be diverted to the South Atlantic, John Nott reassured Britain's NATO allies at the end of 1982 that the direction of British defence policy would remain unchanged over the next decade: David Cross, 'Nott explains Falklands lessons to NATO', *The Times*, 19 November 1982.

8 Britain and Non-Nuclear Defence

ADAM ROBERTS

In the United Kingdom, defence has come to be seen, rightly or wrongly, as a largely nuclear business. Not only do we share with our allies in NATO a reliance on possible first use of nuclear weapons in the event of a major conflict in Europe, but in many respects the United Kingdom is actually more dependent on nuclear weapons than other countries. No other country in the world has a defence policy involving all of the following three elements of reliance on nuclear weapons: (i) formal military alliance with a nuclear power (the NATO alliance with the USA); (ii) nuclear bases and facilities of an allied state (USA) situated on its territory; and (iii) possession of its own nuclear weapons and delivery systems of various types. We thus have three types of eggs in the increasingly questioned basket of nuclear deterrence.

This heavy involvement in the business of nuclear strategy has contributed to (though it has not alone created) a situation in which the UK would be at extreme risk in the event of a nuclear war. If all efforts at nuclear deterrence failed, and if there were to be a war between the NATO and Warsaw Pact states involving the use of nuclear weapons, then the UK would be very vulnerable. Its relatively small and crowded territory contains a large number of targets of a type that an adversary would be likely to want to destroy in a war: not only conventional military targets, but also nuclear weapons bases, and the communications systems and command headquarters that go with them. Many of these targets are near cities, the inhabitants of which would be likely to suffer catastrophically in any nuclear attack, even if that attack was more discriminate than the spasm war which is widely feared. It is not surprising, in these circumstances, that many people see our defence system as a potential source of danger. This is the first, though not by

191

any means the only, ground of criticism of current British nuclear weapons policy.

The question is, what else can we do? Clearly no policy can offer complete security. But there is a need for discussion of how, either on our own or in conjunction with other countries, we can tackle some major sources of danger; reduce our reliance on nuclear weapons; and reduce our extreme vulnerability to these weapons. This chapter examines the most common prescriptions in the nuclear debate – namely those for multilateral and for unilateral disarmament – and indicates that both have serious defects. It goes on to suggest that we need to think about defence as much as about disarmament, and that a fundamental change in defence strategy is needed.

Above all, this chapter urges the need to get away from the dismal level of debate in which 'unilateral' and 'multilateral' are presumed to be the main, or even the only, alternatives; in which 'deterrence' is so often equated exclusively with nuclear deterrence; in which the word 'strategic' is applied to nuclear weapons of long range, as if the only strategy now is that of airborne genocide; and in which simplistic moralistic assertions are a substitute for careful consideration of the actual defence options available to states in the nuclear age.

EXISTING NUCLEAR POLICY, AND CRITICISMS OF IT

The UK's triple reliance on nuclear weaponry, as outlined above, is by no means new. It dates back thirty years. The reasons why this policy emerged in the late 1940s and early 1950s, and has continued ever since, are many and serious. They should not be lightly dismissed simply as the outdated legacy of the Cold War. They include a concern about the Soviet Union's role in Eastern Europe, and about the risk that it might be tempted to expand its sphere of influence further West; a belief that security is better organised collectively than on an exclusively national basis; the determination of a whole generation of political leaders not to repeat the appeasement policies of the 1930s; a sense that any conventional war in Europe could be calamitous, and must be deterred; an awareness of Britain's geographical situation, making it a relatively secure base for aircraft and submarines, as well as a staging-post for the US military presence in Western Europe; and a desire to obtain an effective defence at a relatively low cost.[1]

However, the extent of British reliance on nuclear weapons has always been open to criticism. It has never been self-evident that Britain's situation is so serious, its security responsibilities so extensive, its capacity for conventional defence so limited, or its possibilities for credibly threatening to use nuclear weapons so considerable, as to explain such a heavily nuclear emphasis in defence. In the actual wars in which Britain has got involved since the Second World War, admittedly against non-nuclear opponents, nuclear weapons and threats have played little or no role, so that the utility of such weapons has not been obvious: in the 1982 Falklands War, the spectacle of ageing nuclear V-bombers and their pilots being hastily converted for a last conventional fling at Stanley was one indication that the emphasis placed on nuclear weapons may have been exaggerated. Moreover, since Britain's defence expenditure, expressed as a percentage of Gross National Product, has been exceptionally high in comparison with most European NATO members, the idea that nuclear weapons offer an inexpensive form of defence has never been completely persuasive. Nuclear weapons have not proved to be a means of drastically reducing the burden of conventional arms, and with the advent of Trident they threaten to be a rival for the same scarce resources. On civil defence, the pathetic compromise adopted by most post-war British governments – of maintaining a warning and protection system, but a patently inadequate one – has suggested a lack of seriousness in Britain's nuclear policy.

In addition to the above, there have been persistent doubts in Britain both about the morality of relying on the threat of nuclear retaliation, and about the stability – or rather lack of it – of the whole edifice of nuclear deterrence. In the early 1960s, and again now in the early 1980s, the unilateralist movement has been the most evident manifestation of these doubts. In both periods, the unilateralist upsurge took place against an ominous background: an awareness of growing Soviet military power; a relatively low degree of confidence that weapons developments can be effectively restrained by arms control agreements; and an apparent instability in weapons systems and associated strategies.

In the early 1980s, all three elements of British reliance on nuclear weapons are raising problems. Specifically:

(1) The alliance with the USA is undergoing acute strain because of divergent American and West European perceptions, and indeed interests, on a wide variety of issues; because of American impatience with what is perceived as European parochialism; and because of European concern, arising from Vietnam and fortified by events in the Carter and Reagan years, that the conduct of US foreign and defence policy has often been inconsistent and amateurish. The various

American statements in the first two years of the Reagan presidency on the subject of limited nuclear war in Europe inevitably caused alarm. These statements contributed to a situation in which nuclear issues overshadowed all the other sources of strain in Atlantic relations.

(2) The presence of US nuclear bases on UK territory is increasingly questioned not only because of the familiar argument that all such bases risk attracting a Soviet nuclear attack, with consequent large risk to the civilian population, but also because of the absence of any clear and convincing system of British control. Whatever the secret Anglo–American agreement governing the use of US nuclear weapons based in this country says, the apparent absence of a physical dual-key or safety-catch arrangement is bound to increase the concern that Britain might get dragged into a war against its own interests. The fact that there was such an arrangement for the Thor missiles deployed in the UK from 1959 to 1963, in accord with the US–UK exchange of notes of 22 February 1958, only highlights the curious lack of a convincing physical equivalent today.

(3) The British nuclear force is running into very heavy criticism partly because of problems of credibility: despite all the transatlantic troubles, it is hard to envisage conditions in which the UK would use its nuclear weapons and the USA would not; partly because of the high financial cost of remaining a nuclear weapons state; and partly because the off-the-shelf Trident D-5 system, with more destructive power than the military planners had required, seemed an apt illustration of the self-perpetuating character of the arms race.

Apart from these problems affecting each of the three elements of Britain's reliance on nuclear weapons, the whole of British nuclear weapons policy has been characterised by a high degree of secrecy. Time and again, major decisions have been reached without any public discussion or parliamentary debate. From the original decision in the 1940s to make the bomb, to the decision in the 1970s to proceed with the Chevaline warhead improvement project, the public has been kept in the dark. The habit persists. In 1982 it was symptomatic that the information about the plans for transferring US command headquarters from Germany to the UK had to be ferreted out by a journalist – and in Washington DC, not London.[2]

Overall, the record of the UK as a nuclear power is not very impressive, and it may even be sufficiently negative to act as a disincentive to nuclear proliferation. As a nuclear power, Britain has experienced a period of relative economic decline, apparently unending internal trouble in Northern Ireland, acute and continuing public controversy about nuclear defence, and in the Falklands in 1982 an open foreign attack on territory directly held and administered by it. It has no direct part in the most sensitive East–West nuclear arms control negotiations. The spectacle of Britannia clutching Trident D-5 to her bosom while struggling to control the waves of economic recession is not the best possible advertisement for the benefits of nuclear weapons.

At the same time, there has been a lack of intellectual coherence in the UK's policy on nuclear proliferation: on the one hand, the repeated insistence that nuclear weapons are the foundation of our security; and on the other hand, the attempt to discourage other states from developing a nuclear weapons capability. It is not surprising that this approach – like alcoholics preaching abstinence – has run into the banal and tedious criticism that double standards are involved.

It is not at all surprising that, especially in recent years, many have come to see the East–West nuclear arms competition, and Britain's participation in it, as part of a process that is irrational and potentially disastrous. Even if every individual arms procurement decision can be defended on rational grounds, the process as a whole is not easily justified. Moreover, as soon as a nuclear war begins to seem in any way possible, then the whole rationale of defence and deterrence crumbles away: the costs of a nuclear war seem out of proportion to the issues at stake.

The question as to whether any kind of nuclear war is actually at all likely is very hard indeed to discuss, let alone answer; and it is a matter on which the layman's hunch may be quite as good as the conclusions of supposed experts. My own view is that nuclear deterrence, while far from being the only factor keeping the peace between East and West, has at times helped make the major powers somewhat more cautious in their mutual relations. However, the continuing technological arms race, the lacklustre achievements of arms control, the determination of both sides to demonstrate their toughness and resolve, the prevalence on both sides of simplistic and even Manichaean views of the world, the ease with which each side perceives the other's nuclear forces as an offensive threat – all these factors suggest that nuclear deterrence is proving less stable than many of its proponents hoped. Clearly the explosion of nuclear weapons by accident or in anger is not impossible. I would not be surprised to see it in my lifetime.[3]

Paradoxically, at the same time as concern that we may be drifting to some kind of nuclear disaster has grown, so too has a concern that the heavy British and NATO reliance on nuclear weapons is lacking in credibility. This may indeed be the most important line of criticism of current Western defence thinking. Any idea that NATO countries might resort to nuclear weapons first – an idea that is implicit in the NATO strategy of 'flexible response' – is increasingly fanciful. The Soviet Union's potential for nuclear retaliation against Western Europe is so clear, and Western Europe is so crowded and vulnerable, that the NATO threat of first use has become a source of weakness rather than of strength. The Soviet Union's achievement of a massive nuclear capability creates a situation fundamentally different from that of the 1950s, when Britain's heavy reliance on nuclear strategy began: and it necessitates some basic re-thinking of that nuclear reliance.

The all-too-predictable response of most NATO governments and strategists to this situation has been to try to restore the credibility of using nuclear weapons, not to explore possible alternatives. Hence the frenetic attempts to introduce new weapons, new weapons deployments, and new nuclear doctrines. In the USA, the tragi-comic attempts to find a home for the MX missile – the first major weapons project in history with nowhere to go – was illustrative of the absurdity of this approach.[4] The controversies over the neutron bomb, over the stationing of cruise missiles and Pershing II in NATO's member states, and over the ideas of limited nuclear war, all pointed to the same conclusion: that efforts to restore the credibility of nuclear use, and especially first use, seem to be doomed to back-fire. One should add that in any actual crisis or war, any decision to use nuclear weapons first would be very likely to undermine NATO's unity, which is its principal asset on which all else is based. In short, in Britain as well as in the other NATO states there is a need to explore alternatives to our present extreme reliance on nuclear weapons.

THE DISARMAMENT IDEA IN THE DEFENCE DEBATE

The alternatives most commonly considered in the contemporary debate focus on the idea of disarmament – or getting rid of weapons. Indeed, anyone following the debate on nuclear weapons in the past four years or so – not just in Britain, but in many other countries – could be forgiven for thinking that the issue boiled down simply to unilateralism *v.* multilateralism. There have been many interesting variations on this theme, not least the European Nuclear Disarmament vision of a reciprocating series of unilateral and regional moves towards the eventual goal of general European nuclear disarmament. But basically disarmament is widely taken as the agreed goal, and 'uni' *v.* 'multi' sets the terms of much of the public debate.

Calls for disarmament are not new. In face of the evident dangers and expense of reliance on armaments, there has throughout this century been a large and influential body of thought advocating this approach; and the development of nuclear weapons has added urgency to calls for disarmament. However, apart from a few very modest international agreements, little in the way of disarmament by states has been achieved. It may be that the relative failure of disarmament ideas up to now is due to certain inherent limitations in those ideas – limitations that may point to the need for alternative approaches to the whole problem of defence.

The two main approaches to disarmament – the multilateralist and the unilateralist – have many features in common. Both focus essentially on getting rid of particular classes of weapons. They thus tend to draw attention to what is opposed, rather than to what is proposed. True, a great many calls for disarmament have been accompanied by more-or-less detailed suggestions as to how security may be maintained, or states or other human groups protect themselves, in a very insecure world: but the starting point of all approaches to disarmament tends to be the idea that certain weapons should, by one means or another, be discarded.

Formal acts of disarmament are not the only possible means by which the goal of a more sensibly ordered world may be approached. For one thing, some states may pursue non-provocative military policies, and may decide against acquiring weapons of mass destruction, for simple prudential reasons, and without explicitly calling their policy one of disarmament. Moreover, in time of conflict or war, some states, even if they possess them, may avoid the use of their most indiscriminate weapons: they may do so for any of a wide variety of reasons, including a belief that certain weapons of mass destruction are inappropriate in a particular crisis; a fear of various kinds of adverse consequences if they are used; an awareness (in particular instances) that their use would be contrary to the laws and customs of war; or any combination of these. Such approaches deserve to be taken seriously, but on their own they do not all offer a prospect of bringing the arms race firmly and finally under control: hence the continuing attraction of the idea of disarmament.

LIMITS OF THE MULTILATERALIST APPROACH

The idea of disarmament by agreement is indeed attractive; and has been formally endorsed by every British government since the Second World War. This approach offers the prospect that all states may get rid of their major weapons; or at least that all countries possessing nuclear weapons may reduce or even eliminate their stocks of nuclear weapons and delivery systems. In all such cases reductions would be phased and balanced, so that sudden changes or military imbalances, such as might threaten international stability, are avoided. It is a persuasive vision, and the fact that certain (admittedly limited) multilateral measures of arms limitation have been successfully negotiated adds to the plausibility of the approach.

However, throughout this century negotiations for agreed disarmament have yielded only very modest results. Discussion of this matter at the First and Second Hague Peace Conferences, in 1899 and 1907 respectively, was abortive, though these conferences were productive in other ways. After the catastrophic experience of the First World War, many committees and conferences were set up to negotiate disarmament, mainly under League of Nations auspices; and great hopes were held out for these efforts. However, the only significant multilateral disarmament agreements of the inter-war years were the naval treaties concluded in Washington (1922) and London (1930). Since the Second World War there has been a continuous stream of negotiations about disarmament, mainly under United Nations auspices at Geneva. But only one agreement has been concluded that involves a significant measure of disarmament – the 1972 Biological Weapons Convention, which entered into force in 1975.

Negotiations on more limited measures of arms control or arms limitation have been somewhat more successful than those for disarmament. Many important measures have been agreed, including the 1963 Partial Test Ban Treaty, the 1968 Non-Proliferation Treaty, and the 1972 SALT-1 accords. However, these and similar agreements can be criticised on many grounds, and they have plainly neither been a guarantee of good relations between the superpowers, nor an adequate brake on the momentum of the arms race. By the beginning of 1982, with the SALT-2 Treaty in difficulties, and with other negotiations on nuclear and conventional arms control apparently becalmed, some of the hopes held out for arms control a decade or two earlier seemed to have been disappointed.

Negotiated measures of arms control will continue to play an important role in restraining some aspects of the arms race, in reducing its costs, or in contributing to international stability. The new East–West nuclear negotiations in Geneva – whether those on nuclear weapons in Europe, or the START Strategic Arms Reduction Talks – may yet, despite unpromising beginnings, contribute to these goals. However, in view of the past record and the inherent limitations of the approach, it would be unwise to expect too much from arms control.

As for more ambitious measures of disarmament, the continuous failure of all negotiations on this subject throughout this century has not been accidental. It is often assumed that talks on this subject have failed because of the existence of certain 'obstacles' to disarmament, such as pressure from the armed forces, from military industries, or from governmental bureaucracies. However, the problem is not just one of external obstacles to disarmament, but of inherent inadequacies in the approach.

To take, for example, the idea of General and Complete Disarmament (GCD – the 'General' referring to all countries, and the 'Complete' referring to all classes of weapons), there are many genuinely difficult and not-yet-solved problems, namely:

(a) *Military Equivalence during Disarmament.* Virtually all negotiations on GCD, and many negotiations on arms control, have been bedevilled by the very difficult problem of agreeing on some standard of military equivalence between states during any process of agreed disarmament or arms restraint. Are states to reduce their forces by an agreed percentage of their overall forces, or by an agreed percentage of their military budget? Or are they to reduce their forces to exactly equal levels? Each method yields very different results. Added to that is the difficulty that the security problems of different states are very different, not just because states have different shapes, sizes and positions, but also because, on the basis of different historical experiences, they fear different kinds of adversary and different types of attack.

(b) *Verification.* Ensuring, through a variety of means, that a process of disarmament is indeed being faithfully carried out by the parties to an agreement is inherently difficult, and this may be why arms control agreements have tackled only large and conspicuous items of military hardware, such as battleships and fixed-site intercontinental ballistic missiles. While some nuclear delivery systems are relatively easy to inspect by satellite photography and other means, nuclear weapons as such are more difficult. In 1962, a United Kingdom paper prepared in connection with the Geneva disarmament negotiations indicated that it might be possible for a state to conceal from an inspection organisation up to 20 per cent of its nuclear weapons stocks.[5] Even if this particular figure, which was only an estimate, might be called into question, the awkward conclusion seems hard to avoid: nuclear weapons, so enormous in their effects, are fairly easy to conceal. The invention of nuclear weapons has not only made disarmament more necessary, but has also made it more difficult to achieve.

(c) *Control.* If violations of a disarmament agreement occur, how are they dealt with? The late Philip Noel-Baker suggested that the sanction in such an instance must be that the other states involved in an agreement would 'forthwith cease to disarm' and also take collective economic measures against the offending state.[6] Such a sanction seems to make any disarmament agreement very fragile. Not surprisingly, others have suggested that a world government would be needed to repress breaches of a disarmament agreement. Whatever solution or combination of solutions is adopted, the difficulties of controlling disarmament are likely to be considerable.

(d) *The Management of Conflict After Disarmament.* Conflict in some form – whether violent or non-violent, and whether taking place inside or outside some constitutional framework or set of rules – seems basic to human societies. The question of how conflicts within and between states are to be waged or managed after disarmament is often ignored or addressed inadequately: it needs to be tackled more directly than it has been.

(e) *Reliance of Many Governments on Force Internally.* Although virtually all proposals for GCD speak of the reduction of armaments to a level consistent with the maintenance of internal order within states, that level varies very greatly from one state to another. It is very improbable that certain governments, which rely on substantial armed force for the maintenance of internal order or of their own power position, would agree to GCD.

Problems such as these are not necessarily insoluble; and they do not mean that all disarmament is impossible. But they do help to explain why the idea of General and Complete Disarmament, as it is conventionally conceived and presented, has not so far been implemented by governments, and why it is not particularly likely to be implemented in the future.

It is possible to make a more far-reaching criticism of the whole multilateralist approach to disarmament. Although governments and their representatives may be quite sincere about General and Complete Disarmament (or about some other measure of multilateral disarmament), the whole multilateralist approach often operates in practice as an almost perfect device whereby governments can claim to be trying to achieve some real control over the arms race, while at the same time arming very heavily. The multilateralist approach may in some instances lead to three negative sets of consequences: (1) Some governments claim that they are arming in order to achieve or maintain a place in disarmament negotiations, or in order to enable them to bargain effectively in such negotiations; for example by building a weapons system as a 'bargaining chip'. In all these ways the prospect of negotiations is used as a reason, or pretext, for arming. (2) Parties to disarmament negotiations frequently put all the blame for failure to achieve disarmament on the other parties: in this way, disarmament negotiations themselves become a part of political warfare, and the lack of progress in them is used as a pretext for acquiring more weaponry. (3) The whole process of engaging in international negotiations about disarmament and arms limitation has a strong tendency to focus attention on numerical equivalence in at least the more important or obvious categories of armaments: with the regrettable result that states may become obsessively concerned with the maintenance of an exact numerical balance of weaponry with a potential adversary, even in cases where such a balance is very hard to calculate, or has very little practical military significance.

In short, due to all these consequences, the notion of multilateral disarmament can serve (quite unintentionally) as a kind of fig-leaf cover for the arms race. However, not all negotiations have had all these negative effects, and the fact that the idea of disarmament can lead to such strange and unforeseen consequences does not necessarily mean that the idea should be rejected. What it does mean is that the idea needs to be viewed critically; and that other approaches to the problem of armaments should be considered seriously, not least by the multilateralists themselves.

To some extent, proposals for revised defence systems may serve as a substitute for the proposals for multilateral disarmament which have been so strikingly unsuccessful in the past. If it is possible for a state, or a group of states, to move to a more rational defence system unilaterally, then at least in theory multilateral disarmament might decline in importance as a goal.

In practice, however, there may not be a complete dichotomy between proposals for changes in defence systems, and proposals for multilateral disarmament or arms control. For one thing, the evidence is clear that states that do have non-nuclear and manifestly defensive military postures have been vitally interested in international negotiations for disarmament and arms control; and some improvements in security can indeed be best achieved by such negotiations. Moreover, it may be that proposals for defence systems not based on offensive armaments or on massive retaliation, but rather on the inherent defensive capacity of a society, may actually complement some proposals for multilateral disarmament. The problems of the multilateralist approach outlined above mean that during any process of multilateral disarmament any genuinely disarming country would be likely to be deeply concerned about defence. To the extent that it has at least *some* defence system to fall back on, and some alternative conception of how to resist possible military threats, a country may be better able to implement the terms of a disarmament agreement. Whether such a process is called 'disarmament', 'transarmament', or something else, it may indicate how ideas about multilateral disarmament, and ideas about alternatives to existing nuclear defence policies, may in practice not be totally incompatible.

British policy in the field of arms control and disarmament does appear at present to be in a state of confusion. At a time when US indirection and inconsistency in this field is at its greatest, there is a particular need for clarity of purpose in British policy. Yet the UK, which in the past has played an important role in negotiations over nuclear test bans, non-proliferation, etc., seems to be hoist on its own nuclear petard. Having built up its nuclear forces partly on the excuse of staying at the negotiating table, it is now reluctant to bring them into any negotiations. Attributing its own security above all to nuclear deterrence, it at the same time preaches non-proliferation to others. It is no wonder that there is some national and international scepticism about a policy so riddled with paradox, and so lacking in a coherent vision of how to move towards a more stable world.

LIMITS OF THE UNILATERALIST APPROACH

Proposals for unilateral disarmament, or at least for unilateral nuclear disarmament, have featured very large in the British defence debate, and they do have certain strengths. If it is true that the record of negotiations for multilateral disarmament is poor, and if it is agreed that the failure to achieve results is due to certain defects in the whole approach, then there would appear to be a strong case for a different and unilateral approach to disarmament. Moreover, since states, by and large, arm unilaterally, there is a certain logic in suggesting that they should also disarm unilaterally. And if, as many believe, the arms race between East and West is increasing the risk of nuclear war, then drastic action to stop the drift to such a catastrophic war is obviously justified.

Despite the undeniable strengths of the unilateralist approach, it has always been intellectually vulnerable. It lacks a comprehensive theoretical foundation. The many criticisms made of unilateral disarmament must be honestly faced, not dodged.

The criticisms sometimes derive from a degree of complacency about nuclear deterrence: a belief that there is little danger of these weapons being used in anger. While such a faith may be justified in the short term, the dynamism of weapons developments, the instability of relations between the great powers, and the prospect of further nuclear weapons proliferation, all give cause for doubt as to whether mankind can indefinitely rely on threats of genocide as a means of maintaining the peace.

The most serious criticisms of the unilateralist approach derive not from a misplaced confidence in the infallibility of nuclear deterrence, but rather from real doubts as to whether unilateral disarmament would actually help matters. If a country that had unilaterally disarmed were then to become weak and insecure, would that in fact help peace, stability, disarmament, or anything else? The question must be faced, because there have been many cases in which lightly-armed and/or neutral countries have been attacked by well-armed ones, and such cases are justifiably cited as evidence that there is no quick escape route from the perils of a grotesquely over-armed world. For a country with various international commitments – to NATO, and to overseas dependencies – such a question is even more difficult.

There are many genuine questions about the international impact of unilateral disarmament. Clearly, unilateralists seek to have some impact on the other nuclear powers, including the superpowers. Unilateralists often describe themselves as 'multilateralists who mean it', by which they clearly imply that unilateral disarmament by one country is intended to spur other countries, including the USA and USSR, into negotiating seriously about disarmament. There is undeniably some evidence to support this view of the effects of unilateralism. For one thing, unilateral initiatives and gestures have played an important part in many international negotiations in the past, including those for arms control. Moreover, it seems clear that in 1981 the various anti-nuclear movements in Western Europe, which were by and large unilateralist in character, spurred the US government into participation in talks in Geneva about intermediate-range nuclear forces in Europe; and also, for better or for worse, led President Reagan to advocate his so-called 'zero option' proposal in those talks. Thus it is not to be excluded that in specific instances unilateralism can act as a spur to multilateralism, at least so far as negotiations for limited measures of arms control are concerned. However, none of this indicates very definitely that un-ilateralism is likely to lead to any very substantial measures of actual disarmament. The weaknesses of the multilateralist position are not likely to disappear quickly. One may, therefore, have some doubts as to whether unilateral disarmament by one state is really likely to lead to general (multilateral) disarmament being negotiated by others.

Unilateralists often urge that unilateral disarmament will have a significant effect in stopping the further spread of nuclear weapons. However, one may have doubts as to the likely effect of, say, a British renunciation of nuclear weapons on any of those countries which seem most likely to acquire nuclear weapons in the next few decades. Such countries have security problems which they believe to be very different from the UK's. A British renunciation of nuclear weapons would certainly have some consequences abroad, and might well encourage anti-nuclear opinion elsewhere. But it would not necessarily have more effect in stopping the emergence of new nuclear forces than did the decisions of many countries in the past (for example, Canada, Switzer-land, Sweden and others) not to make nuclear weapons, even though they had the undoubted capacity to do so.

The issue of nuclear blackmail also poses some problems for unilateralists. True, events since 1945 have shown that the problem of blackmail has not arisen in practice to the extent that might have been expected in view of the large and increasing number of non-nuclear states and the increasing theoretical capacity of the nuclear powers to hit them. But one is left to face the oft-repeated argument: would the USA have used atomic bombs against Japan in 1945 if the Japanese had had some themselves? However, it should be noted in passing that this argument, so often regarded as a devastating riposte to unilateralists, is also an argument against the first use of nuclear weapons against a nuclear power: in other words, against a part of current NATO strategy.

The blackmail problem, which has usually been presented in a very simplistic form, points towards a more fundamental weakness of the unilateralist position, namely the lack of clarity about what kind of defence system is to replace that which is being opposed. This lack of clarity is very understandable. Trying to work out a sensible defence policy is inherently very difficult. Moreover, the unilateralist movement in Britain includes people of many different political persuasions, and to get them all to agree on one particular approach to defence is bound to be well-nigh impossible. However, the lack of clarity about defence is also crippling. It leaves the unilateralist movement without a clearly articulated and convincing answer to the question of what defence policy, if any, it proposes. Like the pacifist movements in the 1930s, the anti-nuclear movement has been better at warning of the perils of the arms race than at suggesting what policy states can in practical terms pursue.

Unilateral disarmament is often seen as leading logically to a policy of non-alignment between the two blocs. While non-alignment is a policy adopted by very many states, it is not a substitute for a defence policy. The non-aligned states have not escaped involvement in conventional arms races, in foreign entanglements, and wars – including, for example, the war between Iraq and Iran which began in 1980. Those European states that have kept out of the two principal alliances have, in most cases, taken defence rather seriously and devoted considerable resources to it: the record of Sweden and Switzerland, in maintaining an extensive defence system and also keeping out of wars for over 165 years, indicates that keeping out of wars may necessitate a substantial defence effort. While Britain could certainly not copy these states' defence systems exactly, they do show how a non-nuclear policy does not mean a non-defence policy.

The inadequacy of discussing unilateralism in the abstract, without putting forward alternative proposals for defence, was illustrated very clearly during the US Defence Secretary's trip to Sweden and Britain in October 1981. Caspar Weinberger publicly praised the Swedish defence system, which is indeed impressive. Then, when he came to Britain, he uttered dire warnings against unilateral disarmament. Now, Sweden is, as Weinberger was presumably aware, a state that has deliberately opted not to develop its own nuclear weapons, and has also kept out of the NATO alliance system. So one might think of it as unilateralist. But Weinberger did not, because the image of unilateralism that is held by him and his like – an image that is, incidentally, very convenient for them – is of rejection of national defence as such. All too often unilateralists themselves have helped to foster such an image.

Rather than thinking of unilateral disarmament as the only alternative to present armaments, or as the only means of breaking the deadlock in disarmament negotiations, it may be useful to change the terms of reference of the debate: to concentrate, not so much on what this and other countries should abandon, but rather on what defence policy they might sensibly pursue. If the adoption and maintenance of a non-nuclear defence policy can be defended on prudential grounds, it may be far more influential in the long run, including on the conduct of potential nuclear powers, than would any single gesture of unilateral disarmament.

PUBLIC OPINION AND DEFENCE

Much evidence can be found from opinion polls to support the basic contention being made here – namely that while concern over the role of nuclear weapons is considerable, the policy options cannot and should not be presented simply as 'uni' versus 'multi'. A few examples of such evidence will have to suffice.

Public concern in the UK about nuclear policy has evidently been growing, although perhaps in intensity as much as in extent. Numerous polls over the years have reported findings that some 70 per cent say they are worried about nuclear weapons. They also show a consistent distrust of the USSR, and a rising number (to over 50 per cent) who have little or very little confidence in the ability of the USA to deal wisely with world problems. But these views do not easily convert into the familiar policy options. On multilateral disarmament, there seems to be much doubt as to whether it is attainable in view of international distrust. On unilateral disarmament, the polls have quite consistently shown that less than 35 per cent of the population supports this approach. In November 1981 some 31 per cent believed that Britain's possession of nuclear weapons increased its vulnerability to nuclear attack, while 36 per cent did not. In the summer of 1982 some 33 per cent favoured abandoning reliance on nuclear weapons, while 58 per cent did not.[7]

Subsequent polls confirmed the modest level of support for unilateral nuclear disarmament. A Marplan poll in September 1982 indicated that 31 per cent of respondents believed Britain should abandon nuclear weapons, compared with an April 1981 figure of 23 per cent. A later Marplan poll, in January 1983, showed only 21 per cent in favour of a British abandonment of nuclear weapons.[8] Although there is a lack of comparable evidence for the pre-war period, the percentage of the population advocating unilateral nuclear disarmament in recent decades does not appear to have been much higher than the percentage of the population that in the 1930s supported a line critical of national armaments.

However, there is evidence of majorities – albeit narrow ones – against particular nuclear weapons systems, including the 160 cruise missiles due to be deployed in southern England at the end of 1983. Thus the January 1983 Marplan poll showed 61 per cent who 'disapprove of the Government's decision to allow the Americans to base cruise missiles on British soil'; and 56 per cent who 'disapprove of the Government's decision to purchase at an estimated cost of £5 billion the Trident nuclear missile system'.[9]

The important question of first use of nuclear weapons has seldom if ever been raised in British public-opinion polls. But it was addressed in a survey conducted by the US International Communication Agency (ICA) in July 1981. The survey, conducted in four NATO countries (Great Britain, France, Italy and West Germany), shows clearly that only small minorities, ranging from 12 per cent in Italy to 19 per cent in Great Britain, approve the use of nuclear weapons by NATO to defend itself if a Soviet attack by conventional forces threatened to overwhelm NATO forces. Those opposed to use of nuclear weapons against a Soviet conventional attack ranged from 66 per cent in West Germany to 81 per cent in Italy, the figures for the UK being 71 per cent and for France 76 per cent. The same survey shows clearly that opposition to first use does not necessarily mean opposition to all use of nuclear weapons: the numbers agreeing to the proposition that NATO should not use nuclear weapons of any kind under any circumstances ranged from 24 per cent (Great Britain) to 44 per cent (France). What these findings overwhelmingly suggest is that NATO's strategy of possible first use of nuclear weapons is quite hopelessly out of line with public opinion; and that any concerns on this matter that we have in Britain are shared even more strongly in the three other principal Western European states.[10]

Although there is great disquiet in Western Europe about certain nuclear weapons systems, this does not seem to derive from a view that defence in general should be down-graded. Taking figures for the UK alone, the September 1982 Marplan poll showed a total of 76 per cent thinking that military spending should either be increased or held at the present level. If one recalls the finding in the same poll that 31 per cent want Britain to abandon nuclear weapons, it would appear that a significant minority wants *both* to abandon nuclear weapons *and* to keep the defence budget high: indeed, an analysis of the detailed breakdown of the poll shows that in all political parties, in all age groups, and among both sexes, there are some people who support both these things.

One should be cautious about playing the public opinion polls game in aid of any particular approach. The questions asked are often simplistic, and the policy options offered are confined to a narrow range. The difficulty of constructing actual policies on the insecure foundations of opinion polls is notorious. The polls do clearly establish that there is a substantial measure of concern about the current nuclear situation; and opposition both to particular new weapons systems, and to first use of nuclear weapons. But they do not point clearly to unilateral disarmament, whether nuclear or general, as the way forward. The responses do seem to point to the need for a wider range of options than those that are usually presented to the public.

BRITAIN'S SECURITY SITUATION

In debating British defence policy, it ought to be a rule that one should give at least some indication as to how one assesses Britain's security situation in general, which in turn must include some consideration of how one views the Soviet role in the world. Often, though by no means always, disagreements about defence are related to different assessments of potential adversaries, and one owes it to the reader to be reasonably clear on these points.

For better or for worse, the UK's defence policy is at present largely associated with the security of places outside the island of Britain. It encompasses a curious collection of historical commitments, to places ranging from Northern Ireland, within the UK, to distant colonies such as Gibraltar, Hong Kong, and various small Caribbean islands. It also involves an apparently open-ended commitment to the Central American ex-colony of Belize.[11]

The resulting burdens are diverse and, in some cases, difficult to alter. Thus the maintenance of over 50 000 troops in West Germany over 35 years after the end of the Second World War may seem anachronistic, but so far as I am aware no one in Britain has both advocated their withdrawal and explored in any detail the possible consequences of such a course on West Germany's internal politics or on its defence and foreign policy.

The 1982 Falklands War served as a reminder of the diversity of the UK's defence commitments, and of the variety of threats that may have to be faced. Even though Britain's international legal title to the Falklands Islands proper is debatable, and some of the yellow-press political rhetoric of the war was reprehensible, important international principles were involved: the non-use of force in settling territorial disputes, and respect for the wishes and interests of inhabitants of disputed territories. The fact that the British public supported so strongly the re-capturing of the Falklands from Argentina is one indication that distant commitments, however much they seem like albatrosses around our necks, are not likely to be easy to remove.

Thus the issue of whether British security policy is over-extended is central, but also difficult. To remain a major nuclear power, to exercise a substantial maritime responsibility in NATO, to be committed to maintain the British Army on the Rhine, to tackle insurgency in Northern Ireland, and to continue to protect various distant outposts and dependencies, both colonial and post-colonial, is to risk undertaking too many tasks on the basis of limited resources. The post-Falklands Defence White Paper, published in December 1982, understandably avoided hard choices between these tasks, but the question of over-extension will inevitably return to haunt us.

That the Soviet Union is Britain's most important security concern is obvious. To say that is not to imply that the Soviet Union is a uniquely aggressive or unreasonable power. It is deeply preoccupied with security against outside threats – justifiably so in the light of Russian history. It feels threatened not just by the nuclear weapons of the West, but also, in a quite different way, by Western political and economic ideas. Its concern with security does not wholly preclude, and may indeed lead to, offensive policies and attempts to extend its latter-day empire. Its foreign policy is probably not determined by any plan for world-wide revolution – an always fanciful idea which has lost most of its operational meaning in view of the intense conflicts between socialist states. It is more successful in military production and organisation than in most spheres of activity, and this is leading to a heavy degree of reliance on military hardware, methods and personnel. It is acutely aware of the fragility of many of its foreign policy achievements, as shown in the Middle East War of 1982. It is also aware of the tendency of allies to defect (Egypt), to suffer embarrassing internal troubles (Poland), or to be very expensive to maintain (Cuba and Vietnam). It nevertheless values foreign policy achievements that undermine its adversaries, especially the USA, or that seem to indicate that it is on the side of national liberation and socialist advance (Vietnam). It also values the framework of international legal agreements to which it is a party; but it has shown a disturbing tendency, at least in acute crises within its own sphere of influence, to relativise international law by putting a greater stress on the higher cause of the world socialist community. It is understandably fearful of the prospect of facing major adversaries on two fronts (the West and China); and, like so many beleaguered central powers, it may react paranoically to that prospect. In short, in many ways, though by no means in all, its foreign policy can be seen as similar to that of great powers throughout history; and it does not feel itself to be an outstandingly secure great power, nor on the crest of a historical wave.

Such a view of the Soviet Union, crudely outlined here, suggests that it is a power against which we should have some defence, just as it is entitled to some defence against the historic if for the moment improbable threat from the West. Even if the Soviet Union has no militarily aggressive designs against the West at all, it is desirable that we should have some defence system so as to discourage it from developing any such designs, and so as to reassure people in Britain and Western Europe that they are not entirely defenceless in a manifestly dangerous world. But it is also important, and it is sometimes done, to bear Soviet security concerns in mind while framing the security policies of Western states; and to explore any potentially fruitful areas of agreement.

None of this presumes that the Soviet Union is the only potential adversary to be considered when framing a security policy. The almost exclusive preoccupation with the USSR on the part of some of those involved in defence decision-making is narrow and regrettable. The 1982 British Defence White Paper suggested, rhetorically, that future Soviet leaders were more likely to be deterred by an invulnerable second-strike submarine-launched ballistic missile force than by 'two additional armoured divisions with 300 extra tanks'. This argument is in itself debatable: those two armoured divisions might help fill a much-publicised gap, and their actual use is more credible than is that of nuclear weapons. But the whole underlying assumption of the pro-position is also debatable because it may be necessary to deter other potential adversaries besides the USSR. With the wisdom of hindsight, and *pace* the Franks report, it might not even have taken two armoured divisions, but simply one submarine or gunboat, to deter General Galtieri in 1982: our ballistic missile force did not and could not stop him in his tracks.

PROPOSED DEFENCE OPTIONS

Can any defence system be envisaged that could (a) get away from relying on the threat, at once extreme and incredible, of relying on possible first use of nuclear weapons; (b) reduce the number of possible nuclear targets in Britain or its allies; (c) offer a credible deterrent or defence against potential attackers; and (d) command a greater degree of public support than do present security policies? It is a tall order, but it is worth bearing such criteria in mind in considering possible alternatives.

For the sake of simplicity, different possible defence options are often presented in the form of rather extreme paradigms. Thus it is easy enough to speak of defence by non-violent resistance, or alternatively of a militia-type defence, and one can envisage these ideas in the abstract. However, reality is likely to be much more complex and messy. Thus, in considering the options put simply and much too briefly below, one must remember that in practice they would have to be relevant to, and be implemented by, the actual population of actual countries in actual situations, with all the modifications that would inevitably flow from this.

The forms of defence that offer the most radical departures from existing policy, and that in particular mark a sharp break from the race in offensive armaments, are those that are based on the idea, not of long-distance airborne retaliation, but of making a country inherently hard to conquer. Such forms of defence are usually based on the idea of popular resistance (whether guerrilla or non-violent) to foreign attack and occupation. These are briefly considered first.

Defence by civil resistance. This is a policy of national defence against possible internal threats (for example, *coup d'état*) and external threats (for example, invasion) by advance preparations to resist such threats by civil (i.e. non-violent) resistance. The aim is to deter or defeat such attempts not simply by altering the will of the adversary, but to make such usurpations impossible through massive non-co-operation and defiance by the citizens. The technique of civil resistance has certainly been used very extensively in this century, including in many struggles against foreign occupation regimes.[12] The approach should not be dismissed without careful consideration of the historical record. Nevertheless, it undoubtedly has weaknesses. The fact that the widespread resistance at the time of the Warsaw Pact invasion of Czechoslovakia in August 1968 was followed by a creeping capitulation to the main demands of the Soviet leaders reinforced an awareness of the limits of civil resistance. There are considerable difficulties in trying to base a country's entire defence policy on this approach. Will all elements in society accept such a form of defence? How does it relate to maritime defence, or the defence of thinly inhabited areas? Does it have a capacity to deter foreign attack, or is it rather a means of reacting to a *fait accompli*? Can it completely get rid of a foreign aggressor, or simply modify the terms of occupation? There may well be answers to many of these questions, but no country has yet been sufficiently persuaded to put reliance on this approach. My own conclusion in the matter is not that this approach is irrelevant – far from it – but rather that impossible claims should not be made for it, and the idea that civil resistance should be *the* basis of a state's entire defence policy involves placing a greater weight on this technique than it is capable of bearing. As I said at the end of a study I conducted for the Swedish Defence Research Institute on the possible role of civil resistance in Swedish defence policy: 'If it is true, as it is bound to be in some countries, that civil resistance is not seen as being able to provide a complete and total alternative to military defence, it does not follow that it is a mere "complement". It may be a special option for special circumstances.'[13]

Territorial defence. This is a system of military defence in depth, aimed at deterring or defeating foreign attack by making it clear that an invader, even though he may for a time gain possession of part or all of a territory, will be harrassed and attacked from all sides. It is a form of defence strategy that is liable to involve substantial reliance on a citizen army, including, for example, local militia units. It is normally based on military structures and weapons systems of a manifestly defensive type. Certainly there are many cases in this century of protracted struggles, involving some element of guerrilla warfare, helping to rid a country of alien control, even against larger and better-armed adversaries. Moreover, many states have incorporated some element of territorial defence, and/or of a militia organisational system, into their defence planning: for example, Switzerland, Yugoslavia, Finland, Sweden, and China. They have a very good record of successfully deterring foreign attack thereby. However, there are some clear limits to this approach. It seems to be most suitable in conditions where a state already has some tradition of either guerrilla warfare or militia organisation; and its applicability in heavily urbanised areas, with their intensely vulnerable populations, is debatable. This is one reason why, although many countries place heavy reliance on territorial defence, none has a 'pure' territorial defence system. Always it is combined with some degree of reliance on regular forces, on frontal defence, on air and naval units, or even (as in the case of China) on nuclear weapons.[14]

Both the non-nuclear defence options mentioned so far share in common the characteristics that they are in large measure inherently defensive, based around the idea of making a society hard to conquer. This is relevant for a state preoccupied above all with defence of its own territory, as is the case with China or, even more, with some of the European neutrals. However, it raises particular problems for states, such as the UK, whose defence commitments are, for better or for worse, largely overseas. Since the desire in Western European countries for some kind of collective defence system can hardly be called unreasonable, and evidently remains strong, the continued involvement of the UK in Western European defence seems inevitable. For us, therefore, territorial defence could only have a limited role, unless it was the case that the societies overseas with whose defence we are concerned are themselves willing to adopt at least some elements of a territorial defence approach.

The inherently defensive character of both the options considered so far also mean that they are, in and of themselves, devoid of a major retaliatory capacity. Even if an adversary could not conquer and subdue a country, could he threaten it with nuclear blackmail? Thus the 'blackmail' objection to unilateral disarmament can also be made in relation to either of these options if they are the total basis of a defence policy. However, (a) in practice this has not proved a crippling problem for non-nuclear states with a territorial defence policy, and (b) in the event of a major crisis with a nuclear power, a state with such a defence policy might receive some support from another nuclear power. In that event, such a policy would represent, not a complete escape from reliance on nuclear weapons, but rather a down-grading of the emphasis placed on them. This is even more evident in the next defence option.

A non-nuclear role in NATO. A third defence option sometimes suggested for Britain is a non-nuclear role within NATO, comparable to the roles of Denmark and Norway, two NATO member states that do not have nuclear weapons or foreign military bases on their territory in peacetime. These states have adopted this policy partly because of the survival of certain traditions of neutrality, and partly also perhaps because of a concern to avoid provoking a direct military confrontation with the Soviet Union, especially as that might make Finland's independence harder to maintain. Clearly the idea that Britain might have a comparable non-nuclear role has certain attractions – not least that it would reduce the number of likely nuclear targets in Britain in the event of a nuclear war, and that it would enable us to put more emphasis on conventional weapons. The approach does run into the practical objection that the Alliance can tolerate and even approve this approach in small peripheral states, but it expects and needs bases of various kinds in Britain. However, now that the US has so many nuclear forces of intercontinental range, the presence of forward nuclear bases in the UK seems either to be a matter of operational convenience, or a means of maintaining a European regional nuclear balance in order to shore up NATO's present policy of possible first use. Neither of these rationales for nuclear bases is sacrosanct.

The 'non-nuclear role in NATO' approach also runs into a more absolutist rejection from moral fundamentalists both on the Left and on the Right. Those on the Left argue that if having nuclear weapons at all is undesirable on moral grounds, then getting rid of them, but remaining allied to a nuclear power through NATO, is inconsistent. Those on the Right argue that since we accept alliance to a nuclear power, the USA, we should be willing to share the risk and have its nuclear bases on our territory. Both sets of arguments are serious. However, they do illustrate the kinds of difficulties that can arise if one seeks to base a security policy on one single moral absolute. The case for a non-nuclear role in NATO is perhaps best argued on the basis that several moral criteria are involved in security questions; and that moral considerations cannot lose touch with prudential ones without losing their own validity and relevance.

SOME STEPS FORWARD

If there is, in the next few years, any practical way forward amid all these tangled arguments, it may be by looking at defence policy in a Western European as much as a purely British framework. The most urgent need, and perhaps the greatest possibility, is to get NATO strategy away from its present degree of reliance on nuclear weapons. This will not solve all the problems of British defence policy indicated here, but it may help with some.

There have been many proposals for improving NATO conventional defence capability in recent years, and they inevitably cost money. Thus a 1982 survey in *The Economist*, under the challenging heading 'Do you sincerely want to be non-nuclear?', suggested that for an addition of 1 to 1.5 per cent a year in what the NATO countries spend on defence, they could strengthen their armed forces enough to have a good chance of fighting off a Russian attack for about a month.[15] General Bernard Rogers, the Supreme Allied Commander Europe, made a similar argument in public a couple of months later. If the price of reducing reliance on nuclear weapons is a modest increase in the defence budget, it is a price worth paying.

Important as such proposals are, they do contain risks. If they were to lead to a conventional build-up that seemed to pose a real offensive threat to Eastern Europe, or if they led to a roaring conventional arms race, they would achieve little. Thus the argument should not just be about whether more money can be prised out of hard-pressed budgets to pay for increased conventional forces. It is also about the underlying philosophy of defence. Do we want to continue to rely on the extreme and incredible threat that if war comes, we will deliberately make it absolute – an idea that goes flatly counter to all traditions of restraint in warfare, to the basic underlying ideas of the laws of war, and to the interests of crowded and vulnerable societies? Could there be equal deterrent power in relying on a more modest threat, that any attack will be countered and attempted occupation resisted? Is the possibility that a local conflict in Europe might get out of hand a sufficient deterrent to military adventurism, or do we need to put all our eggs in the basket of threatening to ensure that it does? Do we want a coherent European defence concept, or to remain pathetically reliant on the threat of US escalation of a war – a reliance that creates a permanent dependence on the vagaries of US politics? The answers to such questions are not simple, and even so may prove hard to apply to difficult problems such as the defence of West Berlin. But it may be worth indicating briefly some possible directions of answers.

First of all, it needs to be clearly established that security policy is based on the idea, not of exact numerical balances with possible adversaries, but of stability. Numerical ratios have their importance, but balances when so many different states and weapons systems are involved are impossible to calculate and unattainable anyway. Pursuing the will-o'-the-wisp of balance is a recipe for arms racing. The idea of stability, whether at the conventional or nuclear level, is a better guide to policy. Stability may be quite compatible with numerical imbalances in nuclear forces; and, in the conventional field, with reliance on weapons systems and force structures very different from those of the Warsaw Treaty Organisation.

The endless problems raised by NATO's reliance on possible first use of nuclear weapons cannot be ducked any longer. There is much merit in changing to an unambiguous policy of 'no first use'. This would reduce expectations that any war in Europe must inevitably be nuclear – expectations that could create pressures for pre-emptive strikes. Such a move could provide a basis for public consensus on defence. It might even reduce the appetites of planners for theatre nuclear forces. But it would only have much meaning if a serious attempt were simultaneously made to build up a credible system for defending Europe against a massive conventional attack.

To build up a credible defence is not just a matter of having 'conventional defence' in place of 'nuclear deterrence'. It is a matter of conventional, and even unconventional, deterrence. It is likely to involve, as one aspect of a larger concept, building up a system of defence in depth to make invasion and attempted occupation very hazardous for a potential adversary. This is not just the argument of an Englishman being prepared to die to the last German. Such a cause is advocated by some in West Germany; is in keeping with the results of some West German opinion polls; and could involve much use of allied forces and logistic support, as well as of German full-time and part-time forces.[16] Since it is desirable that such a system be manifestly defensive in character, and since it would be there to meet a threat that is massive but not very likely to materialise, any defence system could well involve increased reliance on some kind of militia-type forces, which are the time-honoured means by which the more successful European neutrals have deterred attacks from larger and more powerful neighbours.[17] This might (though I am not certain that it would) involve grasping the difficult nettle of reintroducing conscription in the UK.

The development of new conventional weapons in the past two decades has reinforced the case for such an approach. The new precision-guided weapons are unlikely to bring about the total transformation of warfare that their more enthusiastic advocates claim. They cannot prevent a conventional war from being a major disaster. But they may somewhat increase the power of the defensive in modern war, they may have some deterrent capacity, and they already provide at least a partial answer to the Soviet preponderance in numbers of tanks and fighter aircraft in central Europe.

Against the background of such an approach, actual deployments of nuclear weapons could be reduced. Many nuclear systems, including the thousands of NATO front-line tactical nuclear weapons and the land-based missiles in Britain, might be withdrawn unilaterally. The main British nuclear force, presently based on Polaris submarines, might be brought into negotiations, but the basic issue is whether we want it or not. The answers to these and other questions of nuclear possession and deployment, although they will never be easy, may at least fall within some logical and coherent framework if first of all we can establish a policy on non-nuclear defence.

A shift towards greater reliance on non-nuclear defence, towards a reduction in the quantity of nuclear weaponry in Europe, and towards a doctrine of 'no first use', might also make possible some attempt to devise a coherent policy on civil defence. It is noteworthy that none of the three Western nuclear powers currently has a serious population-protection policy. If there were no suspicions that civil defence might be viewed as part of a first-strike policy, if civil defence was presented honestly and realistically, as a means of coping with nuclear accidents as much as war, if it was part of a programme for reducing both reliance on nuclear weapons and numbers of nuclear targets in this country, then there could be a serious case for it. The management of civil defence in the UK has been scandalously incompetent. There should be a commission of inquiry into the entire subject.

Such an approach as is advocated here is tediously reformist. It would not eliminate the role of nuclear weapons in NATO policy, but it would represent a move towards a view of them as weapons held in reserve, in case the adversary would be mad enough to resort to them. It could involve a shift in the division of labour within NATO, with more states (Britain included) putting more emphasis on non-nuclear forces. It might even result in a defence system comprehensible to the public as well as to possible adversaries. Even a limited change such as is proposed here would inevitably be hard to agree on in NATO, since the difficulty of getting fifteen or sixteen members to agree to anything creates very strong inertia. However, inertia is not a substitute for policy. Tediously reformist as it is, the question of alternatives to our present heavy reliance on nuclear weapons probably does begin at this point.

NOTES

1. Most of these considerations are mentioned in the short 'essay' entitled 'Nuclear weapons and preventing war' which was written by Mr Michael Quinlan and appeared in the 1981 British Defence White Paper.
2. Harold Jackson, 'US to pull back war centre to Britain', *Guardian*, London, 10 December 1982. See also the issues of 11 and 16 December 1982.
3. I have made a fuller analysis of nuclear deterrence and its shortcomings in a paper, *The Critique of Nuclear Deterrence*, presented at the annual conference of the International Institute for Strategic Studies in September 1982, and published in 1983 by the IISS in Adelphi Paper No. 183.
4. On the thinking – or lack of it – behind the MX missile, see the articles by Steve Smith in the May/June and November/December 1982 issues of *ADIU Report*, published by the Armament and Disarmament Information Unit at the University of Sussex; and by Bruce George MP in the September/October 1982 issue of the same journal.
5. For details of this 1962 paper see Sir Michael Wright, *Disarm and Verify: An Explanation of the Central Difficulties and of National Policies* (London: Chatto & Windus, 1964) pp. 80–2 and 247–51.
6. Philip Noel-Baker, *The Arms Race: A Programme for World Disarmament* (London: Stevens, 1958) p. 544.
7. The preceding information is entirely based on David Capitanchik, 'Public Opinion and Defence', MS, 1982. This is the basis for a study being published by Routledge for the Royal Institute of International Affairs in 1983. I am grateful to David Capitanchik for discussing his findings with me.
8. Detailed breakdowns of these two polls were published in the *Guardian*, London, 23 September 1982 and 24 January 1983.

9. *Guardian*, London, 24 January 1983. Other polls (for example, *The Sunday Times*, London, 23 January 1983) have come up with similar results.

10. Leo P. Crespi, *Western European Public Opinion on Defense*, unclassified report of the US International Communication Agency, where the author is a Senior Research Adviser in the Office of Research.

11. On the British commitment to Belize, against which country Guatemala has a territorial claim, see the report of the Commons Select Committee on Foreign Affairs, published on 16 December 1982.

12. On the historical record of civil resistance, see Gene Sharp, *The Politics of Non-Violent Action* (Boston: Porter Sargent, 1973); and Adam Roberts (ed.), *The Strategy of Civilian Defence: Non-Violent Resistance to Aggression* (London: Faber, 1967).

13. Roberts, *Civilmotstandets teknik* (Centralforbundet Folk och Forsvar, Stockholm, 1976) p. 103.

14. For a fuller exposition of the subject, see my *Nations in Arms: The Theory and Practice of Territorial Defence* (London: Chatto & Windus, for the International Institute for Strategic Studies, 1976).

15. *The Economist*, London, 31 July 1982.

16. For a German discussion of such ideas, see, for example, Horst Afheldt, *Verteidigung und Frieden* (Munich: Deutscher Taschenbuch Verlag, 1979).

17. For a recent examination of the relevance of the military systems of European neutrals to NATO, and particularly to the problem of raising the nuclear threshold, see John L. Clarke, 'NATO, Neutrals and National Defence', *Survival*, London, November–December 1982.

9 The Crisis of Atlanticism

DAN SMITH

British defence policy is beset by four basic problems. In turn, they are economic, technological, strategic and political. Proposals for changing defence policy, whatever their nature, ought to be judged at least partially by whether or not they address these problems and offer some resolution of them.

The economic problem is swiftly summarised: military spending and plans for it through the 1980s are too ambitious for the UK economy to bear. Allocating a relatively high proportion of Gross Domestic Product (GDP) to military preparations, as Britain has done, is directly and causally related to a relatively low allocation of resources to investment.[1] The consequence is lower growth in productivity and output than in countries where military spending consumes a smaller proportion of the GDP. The further consequence is a loss of competitiveness in internal markets and economic decline. Plans to increase the proportion of resources allocated to defence therefore offer the prospect of intensifying recession and slowing recovery. Moreover, even on relatively optimistic assumptions about British economic growth in the rest of the 1980s, these plans would effect a decisive and relatively swift reversal of the trend from the early 1950s to the late 1970s of allocating a declining proportion of GDP to the military. This trend, however, was not accidental. It was the outcome of the complex interplay of social and economic demands upon available resources across nearly three decades.[2] Despite the political pressures to increase military spending, overturning that pattern of socio-economic preferences will not be easy, even for the most determined government. Planning on the basis that the pattern will be upset is likely to lead to a series of cutbacks and readjustments in the second half of the 1980s.

The technological problems concern the spiralling cost increases and often counter-productive degree of sophistication produced by constant technological advance in weaponry. These problems exacerbate the

economic ones. They will be familiar to readers of such diverse writers as
Franklin Spinney, James Fallows and Mary Kaldor.[3] It seems they were
also familiar to Sir John Nott, formerly the British Defence Secretary:
the problems of rising costs were emphasised in the 1981 White Paper
and of over-sophistication in the 1982 statement.[4]

The strategic problems boil down to NATO's reliance on nuclear
weapons and on their early use in war. Criticisms along these lines are no
longer as heretical as they once were, as the writings of such eminences as
Lords Carver and Zuckerman show.[5] Indeed, in the critique of NATO's
strategy, though not in the conclusions drawn from it, there is a large
and perhaps surprising degree of common ground between writers such
as these and the disarmament movements of Western Europe.

The political problems arise from a fundamental discrepancy in
relations between NATO states. The role of the USA in the economic
reconstruction and political development of Western Europe in the late
1940s generated strong dependence on US capabilities and policies. This
is continued in the strategic field, with the defence policies of Western
European NATO states predicated on US nuclear capabilities and
strategy. Among the effects of this is that of binding Western Europe
into an arms race that most people seem to agree is increasingly
dangerous, to make Western European security dependent on American
policies primarily developed to conform with American interests which
may well be different from Western European ones, and to deny Western
European states the opportunity of independent initiatives to reduce
confrontation with the Warsaw Pact. Yet the economic and political
trajectory of these states has been away from their former reliance on the
USA. It is in this discrepancy between continued strategic dependence
and growing independence in other areas of policy, often quite closely
related, that the crisis of Atlanticism is to be found. For the fundamental
meaning of Atlanticism, generated in the period after the Second World
War when to many there seemed to be no real choice in the matter, is a
dependent partnership with the USA. When the dependence was
seamless, the politics of Atlanticism were less tortured than now.
Disputes over energy and economic policies, over steel and interest rates,
over the Middle East and Central America and over the Siberian gas
pipeline are notorious. The contradiction between dependence and
independence cannot be better encapsulated than in the action of Mrs
Thatcher, one of President Reagan's staunchest allies in Western
Europe, when she instructed a British company to defy US sanctions on
providing equipment for the pipeline.

Each instance of disputatiousness and independence is but a bubble on a stream that moves with a very strong current. But the current of Atlanticism is not weak. It flows from a deeply embedded political consciousness and experience in Western Europe since the Second World War. The outcome of the crisis of Atlanticism turns on which of these two currents finally proves to be stronger in Europe, or what compromise can be effected between them. How these issues are resolved or, if they are not resolved in any real sense, how they are merely coped with, will affect the possible solutions for the other basic problems of British defence policy.

TECHNOLOGY AND THE BUDGET

For economic reasons, British military spending needs to be reduced, and the resources released in that process need to be directed into an effort to rebuild the country's productive industrial base. As well as being economically desirable, this operation is technically feasible if it is adequately planned and associated with a general programme for economic recovery. The preferences of the Conservative government and of the armed forces lead in the opposite direction, and many will regard economic guidelines to the level of military spending as arbitrary. However, defence planning ought to accord with long-term availability of resources, calculated on the basis of modest assumptions about economic growth and other demands on available resources. The past thirty years of defence planning have seen a series of policy reviews and chopping and changing which have marked the failure of successive governments to plan defence in line with resource availability and which have caused unsettling and often difficult adjustments in the forces. There are, then, sound strategic reasons for accepting modest economic assumptions as firm guidelines for defence planning, despite their seeming arbitrariness.

But it is not only the government's strategic preferences that generate pressure for higher military spending. There is also a permanent technological pressure within the budget and the way it is allocated to various functions. In the 1982–3 budget, spending on equipment accounted for 46 per cent of the total. This is a very high proportion. It is only recently that it has risen to this level. In 1950, about 30 per cent of the total budget was allocated to equipment; in 1975, the proportion was 35 per cent; in the 1981–2 budget, it was 41 per cent. If this trend continues, and even if it levels out at a plateau in the 40–50 per cent range, it will place intolerable demands on resources available for military spending. Either the whole budget must increase, and probably more sharply than is now planned, or other components of the budget must suffer. This would bite into funds available for personnel, meaning cuts in either their numbers or their salaries. This kind of process was experienced under the 1974–9 Labour government and led to a major and well-publicised crisis of morale in the armed forces.[6]

Reversing the trend, however, will be difficult. There is a large degree of inertial momentum in any kind of budgeting. The room for manoeuvre for decision-making is restricted by previous decisions and the commitments they have led to. Spending on research and development implies future spending on production. Spending on the production of new equipment implies future spending on producing spares as well as on operation and maintenance. Moreover, the rolling programme with which arms procurement and military industry operate means that current spending on research and development implies future spending on those activities unless industrial capacity is cut and technological capabilities lost. This rolling programme is sustained and justified by reference to the constant need for technological advance in armaments which is directly associated with constant increases in their real costs. The consequence is an ever-growing pressure to increase the military budget unless spending on research and development is declining as a proportion of the whole. But this decline is not happening: from the 1977–8 budget to 1982–3, the research and development share was relatively steady (at 13 or 14 per cent) in a growing overall expenditure. The planned purchase of Trident missiles and submarines is a further source of pressure, which is not fully reflected in current spending on research and development, since the missiles have been developed in the USA.

Plans for the rate of increase in military spending to slacken in the late 1980s therefore necessitate reductions in equipment programmes or other sections of the budget. By a miracle of planning, British military spending is both too high and too low: too high for the economy to bear, too low for the military.

Remedies for this predicament meet several constraints. Faced by the need to reduce actual or planned military spending, successive governments have adopted the expedient of withdrawal from Empire. There is not much of this left and some of it pays its own way, so the budgetary impact of further contractions, except from the Falklands, would be minimal. It would, moreover, go against the grain for a government committed to protecting interests outside the NATO area, and that has recently won a war in the South Atlantic.

However, if attention is directed at the major NATO roles to find candidates for cutting, there are numerous obstacles. The Royal Navy provides about 70 per cent of NATO's naval assets in the Eastern Atlantic area, and reducing that would encounter serious opposition. It would also, of course, reduce and possibly remove the ability to fight a war like that in the South Atlantic in 1982. Reducing the British Army of the Rhine (BAOR) is something we are only allowed to discuss *sotto voce* because nobody across the Channel likes it very much, as the Foreign Office is always quick to remind us. Britain's air defence could scarcely be reduced since it has been so low for so long and the current emphasis is on increasing it. Cutting air power in Europe might not be terribly popular with the BAOR, and the Royal Air Force would complain to everybody if its strike role were eliminated so that Tornado could be cancelled. Cancelling Trident would not alarm any NATO ally very much if at all, and is a very likely option. But I am sceptical that this would be enough to ease the pressure on the budget in the late 1980s, since it still seems as if Trident is being spirited into future spending plans without really confronting the need to make room for it by removing other projects. It would certainly not be enough to reduce the overall budget.

If the basic strategic and political framework of NATO policy and British defence planning remains unchanged, it is extremely difficult to see where the necessary cuts could be made. It would therefore seem desirable to tackle the problems of technological pressure on the budget at source. The aim would be to fulfil the same roles as at present, but to do so at less cost by opting for less elaborate and therefore less expensive equipment. This would require an effort to change both the prevailing philosophy and the major institutions of the processes of arms production and procurement. If it worked, it would be a genuine technical fix.

STRATEGY AND TECHNOLOGY

NATO's strategy of nuclear deterrence and flexible response obviously demands technologically advanced nuclear and conventional weaponry. But it is not at all clear that it necessitates the degree of sophistication that characterises so much of Western (and, increasingly, of Soviet) arms production. There is now a well-established critique of this sophistication and of its effects on cost, performance and readiness.[7] If this critique is accepted, the adoption of less elaborate equipment would be seen to provide greater military effectiveness and therefore be desirable whatever the strategic framework.

Strategy and military technology are not, however, as disconnected as that suggests. But the connection between them does not exist at the simple level of policy. The problem of over-sophistication derives not from the strategic premises in defence policy but from the armaments culture. By this I mean not just the organisations involved in the development, production and deployment of military technology, but the attitudes that pervade those organisations and come to dominate the views of politicians and the public. The need to maintain a permanent technological capacity for advanced weapons has become a basic tenet. Maintaining this capacity requires that it be in continual operation. This in turn is justified by the assumption that each new project must be better than its successor, and the concept of 'better' has come to be translated to mean 'more complex'.

The attitudes of the armaments culture are so pervasive that they are found even in critiques of its effects. The 1982 Defence White Paper argued that perfecting a design can cost a great deal, referred to 'the often high marginal costs of the last few degrees of performance', and summarised the case by saying, 'The best is often the enemy of the good.'[8] But the fundamental critique of over-sophistication is that 'the last few degrees of performance' confer no benefits. The point is not to make do with less than the best because it is cheaper, but to understand that what is most sophisticated is neither necessarily nor probably the best. Simplicity is embraced as an aim in itself, because it means technology that is more reliable, easier to use and maintain and, at the end of the list, is cheaper. A case in point is the adoption of multi-role aircraft:

> The disadvantages of versatility in aircraft design are the same as those inherent in any sort of general purpose machine. First, while it can perform several different operations, it is generally less proficient at doing any single one than a machine designed specifically for that operation and no other would be. Second, a machine intended to perform several operations must have the performance qualities needed to satisfy the most demanding one, and when it is used where lesser performance would suffice, efficiently suffers from overdesign. As was discovered in Southeast Asia, the expensive qualities built into tactical aircraft to carry out deep penetration missions are not only unnecessary but can actually be a hindrance in performing close air support.[9]

It is 'overdesign' that is the real target of such critiques, and it is against that practice and philosophy in the modern armaments culture that remedies should be directed.

This would be a major task, carried out against the resistance of arms industries, their political allies and much of the military. It could never be a mere technical, administrative operation. The resistance to it would force it into being a political campaign. And there lies the core of the problem and the relationship between the technological and strategic problems of defence policy.

It is hard to envisage a government remaining fully committed to NATO's central strategic premises, while attacking the institutions through which those premises are translated into tactics and hardware. Underlying flexible response and nuclear deterrence is the assumption of the necessity of permanent armed confrontation with the USSR and its allies. It is in the name of confrontation that the arms industries have been mobilised. It is in its name that they are kept in continual operation, justifying their permanence by developing new and 'better' weapons. The nuclear dimension of confrontation intensifies it, simply because of the immense destruction it threatens. Steps justified on one side as purely defensive and conducive to deterrence seem fearfully threatening to the other and justify counter-measures that seem threatening to the first side. And on it goes.

Were the confrontation not nuclear, its momentum might possibly be less. The atmosphere of ambient insecurity on which the armaments culture thrives might be less persuasive. These arguments are, naturally, impossible to prove, partly because they depend on imagining what modern history might have been like without nuclear confrontation. It has been such an essential part of international politics in the northern hemisphere since the late 1940s that one feels its absence would have made a profound difference – but one cannot prove it. None the less, it seems reasonable to argue that if NATO's reliance on nuclear weapons were at least reduced, this might affect the nature of confrontation enough for it to be possible to tackle the institutions and attitudes of the armaments culture. In turn, this might not only make us all safer but also make it possible to adopt a different, less elaborate direction in crucial aspects of conventional military technology.

NUCLEAR DETERRENCE AND FLEXIBLE RESPONSE

For the purposes of this discussion, there are three key elements in

NATO's strategy of flexible response. First, it is designed to cope with all eventualities, all levels of threat. Second, it includes a range of undisclosed options, so that the aggressor cannot predict the precise nature of the response. Third, if aggression cannot be rebuffed at a relatively low level of force, it contains the option of using nuclear weapons whether or not the USSR has already done so, in the hope of terminating the conflict.

In a sense, flexible response is a catch-all strategy. If an eventuality can be envisaged, a strong argument for counter-measures can be made. If there seems to be a gap in the range of deterrence, a strong case can be made for filling it. Its deliberate vagueness means it can be used to justify an extraordinary range of options, capabilities and weaponry. It is the ideal strategy for the armaments culture. These days, however, that is not enough. As Lawrence Freedman points out:

> Current doctrine fudges so many issues and places so much weight on increasing uncertainty in the minds of potential aggressors that it cannot create certainty among the defenders and therefore does not lend itself to confident exposition.[10]

Indeed, the emphasis on creating uncertainty, especially about first use of nuclear weapons, probably derives in part from the lack of obvious sensible uses for tactical nuclear weapons. With NATO's strategy now the subject of intense controversy, its unsuitability for 'confident exposition' is a political liability.

Fudging, however, is not the only political problem for NATO strategy. One part of it has been clearly understood, and proven to be exceedingly unpopular. The commitment to nuclear escalation if necessary is accompanied by a commitment to terminate the war then if possible. Thus the concept of limited nuclear war is at the heart of flexible response. This is evident not only in logic but in the official arguments for tactical and theatre nuclear weapons, that they provide a nuclear option below the level of strategic nuclear weapons, the use of which could perhaps be avoided if the lower-level option were taken up. This intermediate option between conventional and strategic nuclear war would be pointless if it were only there to ensure that the escalation to strategic holocaust is orderly. Unless the idea is that the war might be stopped by a sufficient display of resolution, there is neither a combat nor a deterrent role for tactical or theatre nuclear weapons that makes any kind of sense. US Army doctrine holds that use of tactical nuclear weapons must not only have a decisive tactical effect, but must also be such as to encourage the enemy into negotiation.[11] I have never followed this logic. I am far from convinced that this mode of nuclear strike exists, or that commanders could identify it in the thick of battle, or that the Warsaw Pact would agree to play the game. The most prevalent view today seems to be that NATO has it all wrong and that, past a very limited use of nuclear weapons, there is no chance of nuclear war staying limited.[12] The strategic logic of this is that nuclear weapons in Europe have no role and there is no reason to keep them; in this light, arguments for keeping them and even introducing new ones are essentially political except when they are either dishonest or illogical.

Writers such as Carver, Freedman and Zuckerman are noted for criticising NATO strategy along similar lines. The orientation of their proposed strategic changes includes reducing reliance on nuclear weapons, especially on the first use, and organising a proper conventional defence of Western Europe. Effectively, they are advocating a strategy of minimal nuclear and strengthened conventional deterrence. I have little doubt that this approach would provide a sounder strategy for NATO and a safer situation for humankind. A common criticism of such suggestions is that they would prove too costly. But if a new approach to technology could be adopted which stressed the merits of simplicity and reliability and undermined the tendency for each new weapon system to be more sophisticated than its predecessor, the problem of costs would be eased. Indeed, for reasons discussed already, it is essential that such an approach is adopted. And this change might be feasible if it were accompanied by some reduction in tension, such as a move away from NATO's intense nuclear reliance might accomplish. There are, however, two reasons why these proposals for strategic change fall short of what is required.

POLITICS AND STRATEGY

Carver, Freedman and Zuckerman are all loyal Atlanticists. That is, they believe that the defence and cohesion of Western Europe is best assured through a close alliance with the USA. That this alliance must be, at least militarily, a dependent partnership is equally accepted. Their fundamental aim could be summarised as saving Atlanticism from the mistakes that have been made by NATO and by US administrations. They are Atlantic reformers.

However, to the extent that they wish to reduce reliance on nuclear weapons, the political effect of their proposals is to reduce reliance on the USA, since the vast majority of NATO's nuclear weapons are American. But the USA does not show an active wish to see Western Europe reduce reliance on it. To be sure, the Reagan administration, like Carter's before it, wants the European members to increase military spending and strengthen armed forces. But this has never been proposed as a way of challenging the basic strategic reliance upon the USA. In a report that is not much discussed now but was in many ways the forerunner to the current debate on nuclear weapons in Europe, James Schlesinger, then US Defense Secretary, commented:

> For many years the United States has strongly encouraged its allies to depend on US nuclear weapons, rather than developing and deploying their own.[13]

US policy has not changed in the meantime. Nor is it likely to of its own volition, for it is clearly in US interests to maintain this strategic dependence by Western European states.

Since nuclear weapons are at the heart of NATO strategy, relying on US nuclear weapons is a particularly keen form of dependence. The sensitivity of the issue can be grasped only in the context of current controversies between NATO members. While the Western European members have important disputes with each other, their disputes with the USA tend to unite them more. Lying behind this is the long-term erosion of the USA's economic dominance and political leadership. The USA played a fundamental and essential role in the economic reconstruction and political construction of Western Europe in the late 1940s and early 1950s. Since then, its former dependents have become its commercial competitors and political rivals, even while remaining its allies.

The strategic changes proposed by the Atlantic reformers would fit well with the Western European tendency away from reliance on the USA and give it expression in the strategic field. This is not what the reformers intend. But it would be interpreted in this way. If it gathered political momentum in Western Europe it would be supported at least partly for that reason, and it would also be opposed for that reason. The first major shortcoming of the Atlantic reformers, then, is that they have not thought through the political meaning of their strategic nostrum.

The second difficulty stems from continuing allegiance to the fundamental idea of nuclear deterrence. The objection is not to nuclear deterrence *per se*, but to the particular form it now takes. Similarly, nuclear weapons themselves are not seen as the problem, but the number and types now available are. Thus Lord Zuckerman inveighs against the nuclear technologists 'who have succeeded in creating a world with an irrational foundation, on which a new set of political realities has in turn had to be built'.[14] Meanwhile, Freedman inveighs against the way in which the hawks have subverted NATO strategy:

> For the last 10 years, the hawks have been exposing the underlying incredibility of NATO's nuclear deterrent in the belief that they could devise a technical fix to the problems of deterrence ... The hawks' quest has proved futile because of the misguided notion that there can be a nuclear strategy that uniquely favours the West.[15]

There is much to be said for both these arguments, although the criticisms are mildly unfair. The nuclear technologists are but producing something for an eager consumer, while the hawks seek merely to solve inherent problems of nuclear deterrence with concepts that are well in tune with the main lines of NATO strategy and ideas of limited nuclear war. But the nuances of blame are less important than the relationship between the two sets of people and activities at whom Freedman and Zuckerman direct their criticisms.

It is hard to conceive of nuclear deterrence except in circumstances of competitive confrontation. It is therefore bound to be connected to a competition in arms technology which will, to some extent, shape it. Similarly, as long as the competitive confrontation continues, so too will the problems of deterrence upon which the hawks focus. Their objections seem to be based on dissatisfaction with the passivity and constraints accompanying any 'mutual assured destruction' or minimal version of nuclear deterrence. These objections are cogent. Moreover, the continuing process of technological development – of bright people having bright ideas and selling them to other people who are easily dazzled – will inevitably provide seeming possibilities for evading those constraints.[16] The stability of deterrence is constantly undermined by deterrence itself and by the conditions in which it thrives and which it helps reproduce. The partnership of strategic bright boys and technological wizzards is a product of nuclear deterrence.

Two things follow. The cogency of the hawks' objections to mutual assured destruction will be matched by the cogency of their predictable objections to minimal deterrence. If nuclear weapons are consigned to the role of deterrence in the last resort, the obvious question is what happens when you reach the last resort? Do you then decide upon a course of mutual suicide? If this is the outcome of changing NATO's strategy, what was the point of all the effort? Surely it would still be true that no American President would want 'the single option of ordering the mass destruction of enemy civilians in the face of certainty that it would be followed by the mass slaughter of Americans'.[17] If the hawks' arguments have made headway in the USA over the past decade or more, then it is probable that they would make similar headway in the wake of NATO's introduction of minimal deterrence. Meanwhile, the continuation of nuclear deterrence would ensure the continuation of the research and development laboratories from which would emerge technological options seeming to fit the hawks' strategic proposals.

There is no doubt that Freedman is right to criticise the hawks' arguments, the fallacies and dangers that lie within them. They are far more crippling than the problems in other conceptions of nuclear strategy. But they have been attractive in the USA and in other NATO countries because they do address real problems. Neither Freedman nor Zuckerman acknowledges that the targets of their criticism are inevitable products of the system they seek to reform.

Essentially, the Atlantic reformers propose a 'moderate' version of nuclear deterrence as a way out of the crisis of Atlanticism. Though it is more attractive than current strategy, it is likely to be neither politically nor strategically feasible. Their current political visibility is a result of that crisis, but their proposal will be undermined by the contradictions that have produced it. As a compromise, it might be adopted, but would be inherently unstable. At most, it would be a relatively brief stopping point along the way.

ALTERNATIVES

If Atlanticism is to survive in approximately the form it has had till now, strategic change in NATO is unlikely. At best, arms control negotiations between the USA and USSR might achieve a lower level of forces in Europe, but this would not affect the fundamentals of NATO's strategy or its reliance on US nuclear weapons. This is a possible outcome of the present political and strategic controversies. But it is not a happy outcome.

On the other hand, if NATO strategy does change so as to reduce reliance on nuclear weapons, it does not seem possible for Atlanticism to escape unscathed. Unless a major change comes over US politics and strategic concepts, reversing all their premises of the past thirty-five years, it does not seem likely that the USA will easily accept greater

Western European independence in these affairs. But if Atlanticism is to survive, the USA's preferences must play the major role in determining alliance strategy. In which case, reduced nuclear reliance seems unlikely.

The strategy of reduced nuclear reliance would make more sense if its implicit politics were followed through explicitly. As a deliberate way of reducing dependence on the USA, the strategy begins to make political sense, though not the sense its proposers want it to make. However, the explicit pursuit of this logic leads to a Western European minimal deterrent. The capability for this already exists. This would effectively lead to the formation of a new nuclear bloc. It is not inconceivable that it could exist within the framework of NATO, though without an integrated command headed by a US General, in a new and more equal partnership with the USA. This development would be profoundly alarming and immensely destabilising. It would raise the spectre before the USSR of a German finger on the nuclear trigger. We might then finally find out whether Soviet fears of West German militarism are figments of propaganda or genuine. We might not like the outcome of that test. Moreover, such a development would entrench the armaments culture in Western Europe, and the minimal deterrence with which it began would all too probably be swept aside with the passage of time. If anything, this is a worse outcome than the survival of an unreformed Atlanticism.

Finally, then, it would make sense to pursue the strategic as well as the political logic of the Atlantic reformers. Although this is not the case with the French version of minimal deterrence (which, in any case, is not genuinely minimal), it seems to me that the strategic logic is a reliance on conventional defence as the main form of deterrence. Nuclear deterrence is relegated to the role of a fail-safe device, though it is not very safe. Lawrence Freedman, in particular, argues very strongly for conventional defence as a major deterrent in its own right.[18] The dangers of remaining as we are now, the worse dangers of moving to a Western European nuclear bloc, and the effectiveness of conventional deterrence combine into a very strong argument in favour of relying on conventional forces and doing away with nuclear weapons entirely.

CONVENTIONAL DETERRENCE

Two major objections to this alternative concern, first, the problem of nuclear blackmail – or, more generally, the problem of a state or alliance without nuclear weapons facing a nuclear-armed adversary – and, second, the question of cost. The orthodox wisdom has it that conventional forces are inherently more expensive than nuclear ones. But if this is true then resource constraints, at least in Britain's case, rule out the option of conventional deterrence. There are, however, various possibilities for conventional deterrence just as there are for nuclear deterrence. These two objections depend on particular and linked assumptions which need not be accepted.

The problem of a state or alliance without nuclear weapons facing a nuclear-armed adversary is a serious one which cannot be wished away. But it is not new. North Vietnam managed it against the USA and Yugoslavia against the USSR. Close parallels need not be attempted with either of these two very different cases, but there is at least some encouragement here for removing nuclear blinkers in thinking about international politics. In the Western European context, much depends on the defence policy and on the overall policy of war-avoidance within which conventional deterrence must be situated. The greatest fallacy in these debates is to assume that security is purely a matter of military preparations. These can undermine a policy of avoiding war by apparently or actually threatening other states, but they cannot substitute for it. What we should be looking for is a defence policy that is as obviously and exclusively defensive as possible within the limits of technology and general paranoia, set within a foreign policy that both sustains independence and minimises confrontation.

Such policies would reduce the risk of nuclear blackmail in the course of war by reducing the risks of war itself. And they would reduce the risk of nuclear blackmail out-of-the-blue by reducing the general degree of confrontation and therefore mutual hostility. In any case, for the USSR to threaten nuclear blackmail in time of peace would mean it would be breaking an inhibition that it recognises to be of great importance. If the issue at stake is so important, it might equally attempt to blackmail a nuclear-armed state, because the decision on how to respond would be just as agonising whether or not the victim had nuclear weapons.

The question here, then, is how to structure a defence policy based on conventional deterrence so that it fits with and strengthens a war-avoidance policy based on the reduction of confrontation and tension. Of course, reducing and finally eliminating reliance on nuclear weapons will itself help reduce confrontation. But Anders Boserup points out the potential problem of strengthening conventional forces, whether to raise the nuclear 'threshold' or to replace nuclear weapons:

While it is perfectly sensible for us to increase our defensive forces to a point where they match the offensive capability of the other side, the problem is that these defensive forces add to our offensive capability and thereby fuel a further round in the arms race.[19]

There would be precious little point in leaving the nuclear arms race behind us merely to intensify the conventional arms race. It is very likely that the result would simply be a later reintroduction of nuclear weapons, just as the likely outcome of shifting to a policy of some kind of minimal nuclear deterrence would be to foster the conditions in which its 'minimalism' would be washed away. If we are to break out of this kind of cycle, we need an approach that is fundamentally different.

Like many other writers,[20] Boserup hinges this approach around the distinction between offensive and defensive capabilities. The aim would be to strengthen the latter while deliberately minimising the former. To pre-empt the obvious criticism of this distinction, note that it is directed not at individual weapon systems, which in virtually all cases are offensive or defensive according to their mode of deployment rather than their intrinsic qualities, but at the totality of military preparations by a state or alliance. However, the policy that follows from this distinction must be reflected in actions, including weapons procurement as well as force structure and deployment, not merely in declarations. As Boserup argues:

> The distinction between offensive and defensive capability is an absolutely crucial one but it is in such disrepute today that it is almost always ignored. It is a widely held belief, for example, that peace and stability are promoted by a so-called balance of force. Yet it is patently wrong. Even if it could be defined, agreed upon and implemented – which it cannot – an equality of forces does not in the slightest degree guarantee peace and stability. These do not arise, they never have arisen and they never will arise from any kind of equality; they depend upon an *in*equality, namely the superiority of the defensive capabilities over the offensive capabilities of the countries or alliances concerned.[21]

Seen in this perspective, there are two equally important sides to the coin of strengthening defensive capabilities while minimising offensive ones. First, there is the question of the effectiveness of the defensive capabilities. There can be no objective test short of war as to whether armed forces are adequate to their allotted tasks. But within that limit, what is being discussed here is serious provision for conventional defence – not tokenism. Second, there is the question of the signals that one sides gives to the other with the forces it deploys. As we know from the way in which commentators ignore Soviet professions of purely peaceful intent and point to Soviet armed forces, the messages transmitted by choices of force structure, whether those messages are intended or not, are often more clearly received than statements and declarations. The aim of strengthening defensive while minimising offensive capabilities is not only to deter aggression but also to demonstrate a lack of aggressive intent.

There is a particular reason for opting for this policy, which I term 'defensive deterrence'. It derives from an assessment of the threat of war in Europe. That threat does not derive from conflicts within Europe itself, nor from Soviet desires to conquer Western Europe. Rather, it grows from the essential fact of military confrontation, from the fact that in Europe both sides deploy forces which threaten the other. Neither the conquest nor the incineration of Western Europe are identifiably intrinsic Soviet interests. The claim that they are rests on a demonology of the USSR together with a consistent exaggeration of its military strength. That the Soviet leadership could decide under certain circumstances to launch an offensive into Western Europe or to incinerate it is, however, all too easily conceivable. These circumstances are war or impending war. The Soviet military threat to Western Europe is contingent rather than intrinsic. In these conditions, that contingent threat can be reduced by demonstrably reducing the threat from Western Europe. It is possible to conceive of such action also inducing, over time, some reciprocation by the USSR. In the armaments culture, the USSR has been the dedicated follower of fashions set by the USA, to such an extent that it can now initiate a few fashion lines of its own. It is not entirely unreasonable to suppose that defensive deterrence could also set a fashion, especially if the Soviet leadership desired to eliminate waste (though this cannot be taken for granted). But if such reciprocation were not to ensue, defensive deterrence would remain, providing both the capability of defence and the demonstration of non-aggressiveness.

It is not difficult to translate this approach from the abstract to the concrete. Large amoured forces, the capability for long-range air strikes, seaborne invasions or large air landings, whatever the strategic rationale behind them, all look threatening and can be taken as evidence of aggressive intent whatever the declaratory policy. A policy of defensive deterrence would minimise these force components while emphasising relatively short-range defensive capabilities in the air, on land and at sea.

In part by utilising precision-guided munitions, it would be possible to design forces capable of mobile and dispersed action which would inflict enormously high costs on any aggressor but be effectively incapable themselves of mounting offensive actions over significant distances. Perhaps the most important attributes of such forces would be their capacity for operation in dispersed, relatively independent, small units. This would both strengthen the defence and deny an aggressor the kind of concentrated targets that might seem right for attacking with tactical nuclear weapons. While a nuclear-armed aggressor might still inflict defeat by adopting a campaign of nuclear terror, the result of this would be simultaneously to destroy the fruits of victory. By offering the prospect of enormous costs and either non-victory or, at most, a meaningless victory, defensive deterrence would be effective as a deterrent without accentuating the confrontation and tensions which themselves could be the occasion for war.

This strategic shift would eliminate many of the most costly components of armed forces. Combined with opting for relatively simpler and therefore cheaper technology, this invalidates the assumption that conventional deterrence would necessarily increase military spending. In these respects, as well as in its emphasis on defensive capabilities and dispersed operations, this approach differs sharply from the 'Rogers proposal' for greater spending on conventional forces and the integrated high technology of the Air Land Battle concept.

PROSPECTS

In the perspective of this discussion, unilateral nuclear disarmament is bound up in a major shift in defence policy. It could even be said to be one name for that change in policy. The current strength of the disarmament movements in Western Europe reveals the potential strength of the political constituency that could be mobilised for this change. Indeed, if anything, the potential constituency is wider than the movements. However, the change is predicated on breaking with two central assumptions of defence planning in the European NATO states – the reliance on nuclear weapons and the reliance on the USA. Both breaks are overdue, but neither is easy. Obstacles to this shift in policy are therefore to be found in the continuingly strong pull of Atlanticism and the ideology that surrounds nuclear deterrence of confrontation and competition. Old habits die hard, and these habits are central to much Western European thinking about international politics as well as about military force. Further obstacles lie in France, where no significant independent disarmament movement so far exists and in the possible capacity of the USA to apply effective influence against the new policy. But the most important obstacle is the difficulty of getting the Western European states to agree on anything – especially on a project as ambitious as the one I have outlined. In the present state of things, it may even be argued that this is the wrong time to be proposing grand schemes: the stresses and uncertainties of international crisis and recession engender caution, tending to promote short-term pragmatism and suppress long-term visions. To this it should be added that my conception of the role of defensive deterrence in the very long term is merely as a stepping-stone along the road to so reducing confrontation that further and really major cuts in arms become possible. However ambitious it may be to argue for Western Europe states to co-operate in a strategy of defensive deterrence, that is but one component of the ambition within which that strategy sits. Yet crisis is also a time, an occasion and even a mechanism for change. The changes that grow out of the current crisis may be for good or for ill: they may mean a resurgence of US leadership and reliance on US nuclear strategy; they may mean the emergence of a Western European nuclear bloc; they may mean a decisive shift in defence planning in Western Europe towards defensive deterrence; or they may mean a further alternative I have not considered here. Whatever the outcome, it will result from political choices made, as ever, within constraints. Both the choices and the constraints can and will be affected by domestic political developments within each country as well as by other factors. At present, I would not rate the prospects for a shift towards defensive deterrence very high – but I do not regard that situation as set in granite.

It is a central assumption of my argument so far that the most desirable setting for UK defence policy is within a co-operative Western European approach. My further assumption is that a British government can and should attempt to force the pace, by shifting its own defence policy in the direction of defensive deterrence. This not only means, initially, refusing the deployment of cruise missiles and cancelling the procurement of Trident. It also means scrapping all other UK nuclear weapons and forbidding nuclear weapons from British soil and waters. More than that, it means changing military planning so as to minimise offensive and strengthen defensive capabilities. While it will necessarily take time for these changes to feed through into deployed forces, a start can be made forthwith. This approach would find many important political allies in Western Europe. Forcing the pace further would entail making British participation in NATO conditional on the alliance moving towards defensive deterrence. The inadequacies and generally tattered state of NATO strategy together with the importance of the UK's contribution to NATO could mean there would be plenty of takers. The policy could be based on a phased series of conditions, moving from declarations of intent through enunciation of new strategic doctrine to changes in forces.[22]

It is not a course without risks. None of them is as bad as those that attend trying to stay on the same dismal course as now. But central among them is the evident risk that either there would be no takers for the conditions of continued British participation in NATO or, at least, not enough takers of sufficient weight. In that situation, after allowing a reasonable period for the assessment of the proposals in other countries, the basis of conditionality is that if the conditions are not met participation would cease. The result would be, at least, the withdrawal of UK forces from NATO's integrated command and from the Continent. This is not the most desirable outcome. In principle, the more states that move in the direction of sanity, the better. But remaining fully committed to NATO while objecting to its basic strategic assumptions would raise a series of contradictions within both defence and foreign policy which would ultimately be unbearable. To return to an earlier theme, I wonder if the same is not true of the Atlantic reformers who argue loyally in favour of NATO membership while arguing against core components of alliance strategy. I wonder how long that dichotomy could be maintained if the changes they seek are not made. Indeed, I suspect that over the course of time many loyally Atlanticist critics of NATO will be driven towards some form of Western European defensive deterrence.

NOTES

1. R. P. Smith, 'Military expenditure and capitalism', *Cambridge Journal of Economics*, vol. I, no. 1, 1977.
2. See D. Smith and R. Smith, 'British military expenditure in the 1980s', in E. P. Thompson and D. Smith (eds), *Protest and Survive* (Harmondsworth: Penguin, 1980).
3. F. C. Spinney, 'Defense facts of life', mimeo (US Department of Defense, 1980); J. Fallows, *National Defense* (New York: Random House, 1981); M. Kaldor, *The Baroque Arsenal* (London: Andre Deutsch, 1982).
4. *Statement on the Defence Estimates 1981*, Cmnd 8212-I, p. 45; *Statement on the Defence Estimates 1982*, Cmnd 8529-I, para. 411.

5. Lord Carver, *A Policy for Peace* (London: Faber & Faber, 1982); Lord Zuckerman, *Nuclear Illusion and Reality* (London: Collins, 1982).
6. See D. Smith, *The Defence of the Realm in the 1980s* (London: Croom Helm, 1980) pp. 144–8.
7. Spinney, 'Defense facts of life'; Fallows, *National Defense*.
8. Cmnd 8529-I, para. 411.
9. W. D. White, *U.S. Tactical Air Power* (Washington, DC: Brookings Institution, 1974) p. 56.
10. L. Freedman, 'NATO myths', *Foreign Policy*, no. 45, Winter 1981–2, pp. 49–50.
11. *Nuclear Weapons Employment Doctrine and Procedures*, FM 101-31-1 and FM 11-4 (Departments of the US Army and Navy, March 1977).
12. See D. Ball, *Can Nuclear War Be Controlled?*, Adelphi Paper 169 (London: IISS, 1981).
13. J. R. Schlesinger, 'The theater nuclear force posture in Europe: a report to the United States Congress', mimeo (US Department of Defense, 1975).
14. Zuckerman, *Nuclear Illusion and Reality*, p. 106.
15. Freedman, 'NATO myths', pp. 55–6.
16. See A. Krass and D. Smith 'Nuclear strategy and technology', in M. Kaldor and D. Smith (eds), *Disarming Europe* (London: Merlin, 1982).
17. President Richard M. Nixon, quoted in J. H. Kahan, *Security in the Nuclear Age* (Washington, DC: Brookings Institution, 1975).
18. Freedman, 'NATO myths', pp. 65–6.
19. A. Boserup, 'Nuclear disarmament: non-nuclear defence', in Kaldor and Smith, *Disarming Europe*, p. 185.
20. See the survey of the literature in B. Dankbaar, 'Alternative defence policies and modern weapon technology', in Kaldor and Smith, *Disarming Europe*.
21. Boserup, 'Nuclear disarmament: non-nuclear defence', p. 187.
22. A fuller discussion is in D. Smith, 'Fighting for peace – inside NATO', *New Socialist*, no. 3, February–March 1982.

Index

239